Anatomy Of A Life Possessed

Maria Ferrara Pema

Winner Episode Press • New York

Winner Episode Press
P.O. Box 1530
New York, NY 10021-0093

Printed in the United States of America
ISBN 0-9719221-5-2

Library of Congress: 200-21-04852

Contents

Introduction 1

Part One 3

1 My Family 5
2 The Nazi Invasion 14
3 The New Enemy: Communism 20
4 Discovering My Roots 24
5 Rasputin And My Great Uncles 32
6 Experiences In The Opera Ballet 40
7 The Dolce Vita In Italy 48
8 Spending Time With The Movie Stars 55
9 The Only Husband I Ever Had 59
10 The Beginning Of Being Possessed 67
11 The Transference Of Someone Else's Sickness To Me 75
12 Discovery Of Spiritual Sexuality 81
13 Electromagnetic Communication 88
14 Film Festival in Cannes 93
15 Complete Isolation 98
16 Terrible Betrayal 104
17 Abandoning My Husband 109
18 Friar G.'s Possession: Will It Ever End? 114
19 My Encounter With Gurumayi 120
20 The Letter to the Pope 127

Part Two 133

Introduction 135

21 The Very First Discrimination 137

22 Who Possessed Jesus? 152

23 Does The End Really Justify The Means? 164

24 The Catholic Church And Its Approach To Sexuality 177

25 The Untouchable Truth: The Story of Padre Pio 184

26 My Last Revelation For The Third Millennium 202

27 Buddha And Confucius 228

28 We Are All Children of the Stars 238

29 Penetration Between Two Entities: The Basis of Life 247

30 The Physiology of Manipulation 259

31 Destiny Does Not Exist and God Does Not Design Our Future 275

32 Is This The Meaning Of Real Love? 292

33 Why Do We Need A God? 315

Epilogue 337

Anatomy Of A Life Possessed

Introduction

You won't take this into account. If you had written it instead of me I probably wouldn't believe it. At best, I would have credited you with writing a bizarre novel. Possession, brainwash, mindset is simply not credible. It is the stuff of horror and science-fiction.

And yet everything on the following pages is the truth, as I have lived it, for many years and in numerous countries. I no longer have the strength to debate with skeptics. It has taken all the power left in me to combat the possession itself.

The torment is never ending; the Friar's presence is a constant obsession. He is with me night and day. Nights are the worst. As soon as I get into bed, I beg Friar G. to allow me a few hours' sleep. But as soon as I fall asleep I plunge into a dream about him. He comes to me as a beautiful man, and in the dream I must tell him I love him. As soon as these words leave my lips, I wake up terrified at the sound of my own voice. I am full of revulsion and hatred for him.

I need to write. It is the only means I have to understand my situation and somehow derive some meaning from my experience. He is stopping me from completing my account. I often feel as if my brain is becoming paralyzed; I am numb, I cannot think; Friar G. overwhelms me, inducing a terrible lassitude in me. I feel that at any moment I am going to faint. But then in an instant this sense of languor is transformed into such a state of sexual arousal that it is practically orgasmic. My anger towards him remains undiminished.

Since I am still here and have managed to put these words down on paper, I don't want to consider myself a hopeless victim, not anymore, at least. This book is my weapon, my answer to decades of the life I have felt siphoned out of me day by day, week by week, year by year. I have no illusions about this. Even this book comes too late for the numerous relationships, including those within a marriage, that have been sacrificed at the altar of emotional tyranny. But by the same token I have neither the time nor the capacity to marshal my remaining forces for rebutting those who believe I should have been put under professional care a long time ago. No Ophelia has ever been urged to get herself to a nunnery more often and more strenuously than I have been advised to get myself to a mental institution. I have no more time for such mechanical reactions.

The one regret I have even in putting down these words is that the sheer exotic nature of many of my experiences will make them seem completely alien to readers. Mongols, Tibetan medicine, the Russian czar, mad monks, Rasputin, Nazis, Stalinists, the ballet world and the Italian motion picture industry—these are not the usual elements in an American life. But they have been the elements in my life. And that is what I reclaim with these pages.

Part One

Chapter 1

My Family

My twin brother George and I were brought into the world far from the homelands of our parents, in the Polish capital of Warsaw. My mother, Tamara Brzozowska, was the daughter of a Russian general. My father, Prince Zasogol Badma-Buryat, was a Tibetan aristocrat. Along with his uncles, Cultim and Zamsaran, he had served as a personal physician to Czar Nicholas II. Cultim and especially Zamsaran had become so influential at the Russian court that the Czar had sought out their advice not merely on health and medical issues, but also on political strategies regarding Asia. This was not as strange as it might seem, since my father's family can be traced back to Genghis Khan and enjoyed enormous respect in Mongolia and Tibet. The House of Romanov had benefited from their prestige because of the love my great-uncles had for the Czar. No Russian ever loved his country more than its adopted sons, my great-uncles.

For all that, Zamsaran, while staying behind himself, insisted that my father, mother, and her son from a first marriage get out of the country in the wake of the Bolshevik Revolution. It was then that my parents fled to Warsaw, where my father established another medical practice. Thanks to his mastery of Tibetan healing practices, he was soon flourishing, and his patients included the President of Poland and the highest officials of the armed forces. In 1929, my older brother Peter was born, joining my half-brother Richard in the household.

My mother was a beautiful, elegant woman, with an innate sophistication. She paid a great deal of attention to her appearance. Even early in the morning, when I rushed into her bedroom to kiss her before going off to school, she seemed as coiffed as she had been the evening before. Her peignoirs were more like party dresses than nightgowns. When she leaned down to kiss me, the aroma of her perfume made me feel happy and secure.

My mother's favorite place to visit was Paris, and she went often, always returning with boxes and boxes of clothes for everybody. Shopping for her was a talent, a duty, and a passion all rolled into one. Even after World War II in bombardment-devastated Poland, the mere fact that she no longer had a car and chauffeur didn't deter her. She took taxis to her shopping destinations, expecting the drivers to wait for her while she negotiated her purchases and not giving a second thought to the steadily running meters. She never stopped organizing parties and outings; she needed to be the center of attention at all times. She had to be loved and admired but not, she made it clear, touched. As much as her beauty could overwhelm people, I have always imagined it must have also underlined her distance from them. It certainly did in my case. I was never to hug her, because that might muss her makeup or her dress. One day, when I was very small and tried to nestle against her warm chinchilla coat, she pushed me away. "What are you doing?" she rebuked me. "You are ruining my fur! Sit up!"

Hurt or not as I might have been that day, I inherited my mother's great love of beauty, of the elegant and of the polished. I particularly appreciated people who know how to act and dress elegantly, but also with that soupçon of eccentricity. My mother was also given to being swayed by her emotions. As warm, generous, and loving as she was capable of being, she essentially remained unpredictable, making it impossible to know where you stood with her from minute to minute. Smiles could melt quickly into frowns, laughter into screaming fits with the servants.

Worse for me, I seemed to be her preferred target for such outbursts, nowhere near as acceptable to her as my twin George or older brothers Richard and Peter. There was nothing extraordinary about this attitude. At that time, in that place, boys were considered the pride and honor of the family, and their upbringing had priority. Girls were regarded as inherently less intelligent. My brothers loved to make me the brunt of their jokes, most of them sharing the theme of my alleged stupidity. I don't think I would have minded so much if my mother had not encouraged them with her laughter. Together with that busy social schedule of hers that left little time for me, her behavior at such moments struck me as complete rejection As much as I loved her, as much as I felt attached to her, I began to hate her.

My father was close to 60 when George and I were born in 1933. But he still possessed the energy of a teenager and could be surprisingly playful. One summer at our home by the Baltic Sea, he watched in amusement as several of his students and their friends tried to outdo each other in pushups. Finally, he abandoned his observation perch, got down on the ground, and, laughing as he went along, did 120 pushups without stopping. The students gaped at him in astonishment, then burst into applause and carried him off the beach on their shoulders.

For the most part, my father was either engrossed in philosophical meditation or preoccupied with his patients. He was so absent-minded that my brother and I sometimes wondered whether he even remembered our names. His examinations always ran more than an hour and pointed to his Tibetan training that healing involved treating the mind as much as the body. In the Tibetan monastery where he had grown up, doctors were so highly regarded that they were thought of as lamas for their highly refined sensory skills. Intuition, dialectical thinking, meditation, contemplation, and empathy were all put at the service of the physical, the mental, and the psychological, and Tibetan doctors were expected to devote their lives to perfecting these qualities.

In dealing with his patients, my father's ability was simply that of listening, both to what the patient was saying and to what he was leaving unsaid between the lines. For Tibetan medicine, it is imperative that the physician intuit this balance between the explicit physical state of the patient and his implicit psychological condition. Specific treatment varied with the personality and needs of the patient. In his opinion, for example, it was a mistake to treat an eye problem without also testing a patient's hearing and sense of smell or touch. All the senses, he believed, were inextricably connected to the will, knowledge, and love.

As he once explained it in a book written about his practice in Poland: "Just as there is only one truth and one way to get to it, if ever this truth is lost, our psychological state becomes unbalanced and this, in turn, causes an imbalance in the body. Vice versa, depriving the limbs of blood causes a person to feel cold and powerless, almost as if he were shrinking. Unwittingly, we expose ourselves to many such upheavals and much unhappiness."

I think my father's most remarkable quality was how accepting he was; I can't recall him ever being critical. He loved sharing his deepest thoughts with people, especially when he was relaxing with guests or students. True to his philosophical origins, his idea of leisure was exchanging knowledge, trading insights. He really didn't know what hatred was except as an obstacle to creativity that could cause sickness in our entire being and rob us of a true sense of life and happiness. Love or hate, his actions even more than his words said, was a voluntary choice our choice.

Although he appreciated the comforts that the money from his practice brought, my father acted indifferent to material worries. He was one of the least practical people I have ever known, and he left daily needs up to my mother. That was hardly an ideal arrangement, of course, since my mother, in her own way, was as impractical as he was. Little surprise, then, that she was constantly reminding us how difficult her life was because she didn't have enough money for this or that bill.

It was really another time, the kind that only the oldest of Hollywood movies depicted. Every morning my mother, still in bed, summoned the servants to discuss the day's agenda. She decided everything from the day's menus to the clothes my father would wear to his studio. If there were a social engagement in the evening, she would send a servant to my father's office in the afternoon with a change of clothes. Most times, he was only vaguely aware of the evening commitment and would ask why he had to change for it. After enough practice, the servants would know to reply only: "I don't know, Professor. I'm only telling you what I was told."

Of course, my father always changed and went off with my mother to the dinner or the party. Not that he truly minded: These were just more occasions for him to share his thoughts, and rare was the evening that he didn't keep his listeners enthralled for hours with the latest ramifications that had occurred to him about his philosophy of life.

Not that my mother was ready to believe the processes of Tibetan meditation were his only train of thought. She never hesitated to accuse him of being unfaithful to her with the women who had been drawn to him initially at the social functions she herself had insisted they attend. As far as I knew, however, my father's only conspicuous forays away from his family and his medical practice were in the country weekends he regarded as a necessary return to nature.

Whenever he announced another weekend jaunt, my brothers and I ran for the nearest closet or hid behind the closest piece of furniture. We were simply too immersed in our own games to appreciate the opportunity he wanted to give us to see the sun, the sea, and the woods without the usual urban filters.

I now regret having avoided as many of those trips as I did. My mother did, too, so my father often ended up going alone. This, in turn, prompted more gossip from the well-intentioned and not-so-well-intentioned that he had spent the weekend in the company of another woman. Inevitably, this produced more scenes at home, most of them in a confusion of the Polish both my parents had adopted and the Russian he had learned as a second language. To this day, I can hear the curious singsong of my father's thick Russian-Tibetan accent, as he tried to defuse her screeching indignation that he had made her life so difficult.

After a while, these quarrels assumed their own ritual. For the most part, my father gave up attempts at reasonable replies after a few minutes, just shutting my mother out. The only exception to this tactic that I recall vividly was the evening that he became so infuriated by her nagging that he hurled a statue against a wall. My brothers and I were impressed, because it had taken three burly men to move the piece to its place of prominence. For her part, if she became exasperated enough, she would order him out of the master bedroom and exile him to a room on the other side of the house. Since we had twelve bedrooms, this was no small distance. But then, with reconciliation, she would order the servants to restore his things to the master bedroom.

My father couldn't have been more serious about, or more in need of his weekend communions with nature. As soon as he set foot in the country, he became a frolicking child, running through fields and along beaches with his arms flung out as though he wanted to embrace the entire universe. He loved scampering naked through the rain, throwing himself on the grass and rolling in it. After a rain shower he would run from tree to tree, shaking every branch he could reach onto his skin so that not a single drop of rainwater was wasted.

My brothers and I? Well, naturally, we were perplexed. There was no denying the spontaneity of his feelings, but we also told ourselves we were grown up and superior to such immature nonsense. Now that I am older, I would love to return to my childhood once again, just to enjoy the simple happiness I did not appreciate then, and even run in the rain. It took me a long time to grasp that he was trying to teach us to connect with the universe as part and parcel of achieving complete self-awareness through contemplation. He would point to the sun, reminding us of its power over Earth through its impulses of warmth and light. "You must be as constant as the sun in your love and willpower," he told us repeatedly. "With warmth and light you will learn to appreciate life and obtain wisdom. Without those impulses your life too will end."

According to my father, what was weak in us had to be kept under control by will, sometimes an extremely dangerous exercise, since willpower could become enraptured by its own strength and strike out in false directions. We had to tame our wills, lead them in the right direction. He also made us aware that life was a series of obligations. But while we devoted our days to acquitting them, we also had to savor the nights when, with our muscles relaxed, we could allow our brains to absorb different levels of thought not always immediately on call for our obligations. It was then that we had to hone our conscience for processing our actions in the right way and develop our powers of analysis for arriving at our individual sense of truth. Only in that way, he told us, would we ever achieve complete human independence.

At times, it seemed like every particular of creation existed as a prop for my father's talks. He loved flowers not only for their beauty but also for the healing powers that they possessed. He was once quoted as saying: "Why do my medicines work? Because of my herbal medicine, which comes from plants and herbs that contain elements essential to our well-being. If one bodily element is lost or depleted, the whole body feels the loss of balance. That's why we turn to things like flowers to replace that element."

Flowers were a crucial part of the field trips he would organize for his students. "You'll never understand what a flower is all about if you pay attention only to its color and scent," he would say, stopping next to some sprouting. "You need to go deeper to the bud, to the root. Only then will you start to see how flowers are connected to the earth and, by extension, to the sun and the cosmos itself. A flower is a part of nature, and since we are, too, we should recognize ourselves in it. There is nothing about life, including our own lives that you will understand if you stop at the first impression. Each day should be taken to a deeper level, toward the root of the truth. By studying the essence of plants, flowers, and trees, we will be able to understand ourselves. Whenever you feel small and unrealized, just take a deep breath and look around you. You will start to grow. You will discover a gold mine within yourself."

As beautiful as such sentiments were, they meant little to me and to my brothers. We wanted the very practical guidance that my mother seemed to possess in greater supply. It's horrible to admit it even after all this time, but since my father acted totally ignorant of our daily needs, we tended to dismiss him as something of an absent-minded professor. One incident stands out. When I was a precocious member of the opera ballet company, I looked forward to sharing my experiences as a dancer with my family at lunch. At one of these midday gatherings, my father suddenly came out of his reflections and reported that one of his patients had mentioned seeing me on the stage. What did the patient mean, he wanted to know, about me being on a stage? Even my mother couldn't help laughing.

I should add here that, as accepted as some of my father's thoughts have become over the years in the West as much as they were in the East, his beliefs in pre-World War II Poland were regarded as extraordinary. Even the Marshal Jozef Pilsudski and a parade of Polish officials to his office as patients did not spare him or the entire family, for that matter, as being labeled eccentric. As might be expected, a good part of that reputation stemmed from his nonchalance about nudity.

My father's belief in the curative powers of the sun led him to sunbathe in the nude on the beach, and he insisted my brothers and I do the same. There wasn't a trace of sexual innuendo in these sessions, but some of our neighbors could never be convinced of that. Whenever he would take to running naked on the lawn during a rainstorm, drawing even my mother's laughter, there would inevitably be a call from somebody asking—sometimes politely, sometimes not so politely, if "your husband can dress himself like a normal person?"

My mother tried to be polite with the caller, but she herself never seriously questioned my father's deepest philosophical beliefs.

The love my father radiated so spontaneously in the face of encrusted social manners makes me feel close to him even today. I came to the realization that in order to understand myself, I had to understand my parents. For all the times I felt that I grew up unloved by my mother and ignored by my father, I know now how much I have inherited from them. How can I not think of my father every time I follow my meditative tendency to research the cause of things? I always try to find an explanation as to why certain things could happen the way they do. My father's love for the truth is also something that no one can possibly take from me. How can I not think of my mother when I admit to myself how emotionally vulnerable I have always been?

There were many qualities in my parents that I might have disliked, as well as other good qualities I wasn't even aware of, and now I recognize how important they were to my maturation. Good qualities, bad qualities, strong qualities, weak qualities; it would be lovely to separate them, to retain those that are commendable and discard those that reflect badly on a person. If we are fulfilled in our lives, we will recognize the similarity to our parents, but if we are miserable, we will keep blaming them. Eventually, if we are lucky, with maturity, we will come to understand both their good and bad sides, while recognizing the same polarity in ourselves.

Chapter 2

The Nazi Invasion

The Nazi invasion of Poland in September 1939 spared none of us. Soon after the Panzers rolled into Warsaw, my step-brother Richard returned from England where he had been studying at Oxford. He was immediately arrested, brutally interrogated, accused of being an English spy, and condemned to a firing squad. My mother was ready to risk everything to rescue him. However self-absorbed and impulsive she might have been, nobody had ever accused her of lacking courage.

She also had the advantage of speaking fluent German (along with English, French, Polish, and her native Russian). It was this language skill that she was depending on as her special weapon the morning she set off to find the commandant in charge of Richard's scheduled execution.

As she related later, she unleashed a tirade on the commandant for arresting a student who had been guilty of nothing except flying home to be with his family at a moment of crisis. She didn't ask for her son's release; she demanded it. In her telling, the officer was stunned by her outburst. He wasn't accustomed to being yelled at by somebody in an occupied country, let alone somebody as attractive as my mother.

It turned out to be a half-victory. She succeeded in obtaining an assurance that Richard wouldn't be shot, but not in gaining his release. Instead, he was sent to Grossrosen prison for political subversives, where conditions were even more abominable than in the jails for common criminals. For the next five years my mother thought of nothing but securing Richard's total release.

She managed to maintain contact with him through intermediaries who were allowed to see the prisoners, even occasionally slip them food as long as bribes were paid. But even these visits were hardly comforting, since the intermediaries were united in reporting how most of the prisoners were ill-treated. Whatever these men saw when they visited the prison must have been terrible, for within two weeks time, their hair had turned white from the shock. And then there was the other gnawing doubt that none of us knew for sure whether the supplies we were sending ever actually got to Richard, bribes or not.

I suppose it shouldn't have come as much of a surprise that my mother's preoccupation with Richard left her little time for me, George, Peter, or my father. Peter accidentally disrupted this single-mindedness one day, when he asked me to crawl under a net barricade with his revolver while he passed through a police checkpoint. Since I was so small, he said, nobody would notice me and I could return the gun to him once he was safely through. He was right. But I was so proud of myself that I ran home and told my mother what we had done. She became hysterical: first, because we had risked our lives so foolishly, secondly, because there had been a gun involved, and thirdly, because she hadn't known Peter had been working with the partisans. For some reason, this, too, added up to having all her fury descend on my head.

When the Warsaw uprising against the Nazis began on August 1st, 1944, the whole city was thrown into chaos. The Polish insurrection lasted for two and one half months. It began at five in the evening, against the advice of General Anders, who was leader of the Polish troops in exile. All of the Allies were against beginning the insurrection at this time, because the Poles were without military supplies. Even so, General Bor Komoroski went ahead, and as a result most of the people were in the streets on their way home from work.

It was a portent of the disaster that played out over the next two-and-a-half months. Untold thousands, caught as much in crossfires as by Nazi gunners, never saw their homes again. And the shellings and bombings were only the first act in the battle of attrition that set in.

It didn't take long for the isolated capital to run out of food. Starving inhabitants resorted to killing cats, dogs, and horses for sustenance. And through it all, even children sought to make up for the outgunned partisans by charging Panzers with Molotov cocktails. Could it have been any worse? Yes, thanks to the Soviets. While the Germans leveled Warsaw and as many of its residents who came under their guns, the Russians sat across the Vistula obeying Stalin's orders not to intervene. For Stalin, with his own plans of conquest, the Germans were providing a valuable service in eliminating Polish patriots who might prove troublesome down the road. It was only after this obscenity that the Red Army moved into the city and declared itself our savior.

Shortly before the insurrection began, I wandered away from our house in search of my mother. With my nanny off to the barber shop with George, I was completely on my own. Suddenly, there was screaming all around me. Shots were being fired. People were running toward me in panic. I began wandering, going from place to place with no idea of where I was. At one point, an old woman clutching a boy by the hand asked me what was happening and what she should do. She was as lost as I was, and even more desperate to be seeking help from somebody as small as I was. I didn't know what to say to her, and kept going.

I was lucky; a partisan, who rescued me from the streets and kept me close to him through weeks of fighting, saved me. I do remember that he called me his "mascot" and that I called him "Mister Boots." Sometimes I have images of him bouncing me on his knee and telling me reassuring stories. I also have a sharper image of him standing on the street with me before the building under his command and suddenly dropping to the ground over me. A German sniper had gotten him, and I lay under his lifeless body for what felt like hours. Finally, when the shooting in the vicinity stopped, somebody rolled him off me. I was too small to remember what I felt at the time. I remember having missed Mister Boots for a very long time and of continuing to look for him in the rubble that had once been a city. I refused to accept that he was gone forever.

All the time I was missing, my mother kept going from treacherous block to treacherous block to find me. Some streets were under partisan control, some were commanded by the Germans. She negotiated with them day after day. Then, toward the end of the insurrection, with my mother out of the house looking for me, the Germans came to arrest my father. Fortuitously, with time to take only one possession with him, and although he didn't smoke often, he grabbed a gold cigarette holder.

Along with other prisoners picked up in the sweep, he was marched through gunfire and burning buildings to a brick wall where, he realized in shock, he was going to be executed instantly. Taking out the cigarette holder, he asked the leader of the execution squad, if he could have time for a cigarette. The German grabbed the holder and, apparently considering it a fair trade for ignoring his orders, told my father that he and the other prisoners could go free, if they managed to cross the street to a partisan stronghold without drawing fire. But if the Poles began shooting, the soldier warned, the Germans would have no compunction about cutting down the civilians in the middle. My father took out a white handkerchief and, leading his fellow prisoners, ran out into the street, imploring the partisans to hold their fire. With scores of guns trained on him from both sides of the street, he managed the crossing without a shot being fired.

My brother, Peter, had joined the partisans by lying about his age, producing false documents that said he was 18, rather than 14. It is unlikely the documents themselves persuaded anybody, but they were a convenient-enough excuse for a resistance force desperate for help. At the height of the insurrection, the building in which Peter had taken cover collapsed on him under heavy German shelling. Fortunately, his comrades were able to extricate him from the ruin; unfortunately, he never quite overcame the shock to his psyche from facing imminent suffocation.

Although he was to go on to become a physician after the war, he seemed to freeze emotionally, adopting attitudes that were extreme even for a culture and class, that regarded women as second-class citizens. When I became a ballerina in the rigorous, classical program of the Warsaw Opera House, for instance, he told me I was no better than a prostitute. He also wanted me to change my name, so as not to bring shame to my parents through my choice of a career in the performing arts.

No sooner had we all rejoined each other as a family than the Germans evicted us, as part of the mass evacuation of Warsaw. We were marched into the countryside with thousands of others, not sure of our destination. The march was the least of it. Many of the people were shoeless, almost all were famished. If anyone yielded to the temptation of plucking an odd tomato growing by the side of the road, he was shot without ceremony. Finally, we were herded into a makeshift prison camp and each given a single onion to eat. That huge juicy onion may still be the most delicious thing I have ever eaten.

From the haste and nervousness of the Nazis, we deduced that we weren't going to be kept in the camp too long. As soon as they began separating the able-bodied men from the women, the children and the elderly were destined for the gas chambers. But then, just as the cigarette holder had saved my father's life from the execution squad, we were spared by another amazing coincidence.

A camp worker approached my father, who was among the thousands of evacuees, "Are you Dr. Badmajeff?" he asked. When my father answered yes, the stranger continued, "I don't know you, but I recognize you from my sister's description. She was one of your patients. You saved her life." His gratitude turned out to be so profound that he risked his life by first hiding us in an abandoned room, then, after nightfall, sneaking us into a peasant cart filled with wicker baskets and driving us out of the camp. The next day, he led us to a farmhouse where sympathetic peasants gave us shelter. We never saw the camp worker again after that day.

We spent the next 24 hours hidden under a haystack. At one point, a German patrol came by and probed the haystack with pitch-forks. My terrified mind flashed back to the march, when I watched the Nazis beat a naked man to death because he had tried to escape. But we had buried ourselves so deeply that we escaped detection. When the peasants considered it safe, they moved us from their house and got us to Krakow. We had decided on Krakow, because our one-time baby-sitter, Aga lived there. Despite having been treated badly by my mother on more than one occasion, she had always remained devoted to us. Even after she had married and left service, she had returned to our home for visits that stretched into hours. Frankly, I think she preferred our company to her husband's.

With Aga's initial help, Krakow turned out to be our home for the next three years. The devastation was so widespread in Warsaw that barely a building was left standing, and there seemed no purpose in returning there even after the end of the war. When we finally did return, we weren't surprised to discover that our home no longer existed. Once again, my father had to rebuild his life, only this time he was much older. And ironically, instead of fleeing the Russians as he had in 1917, he had to do the rebuilding under a Stalinist regime.

Chapter 3

The New Enemy: Communism

The end of the war didn't bring an end to suffering. For some people it just meant trying to suppress the anguish they had endured. For instance, my brother, Richard, once he had been released from prison, thought he could leave the past behind by emigrating to Canada to continue his studies. The truth was, he had been so physically and psychologically maimed that when my mother died, he no longer had the courage to go on. We heard only by telegram that he had shot himself to death. I couldn't help thinking of something he had said to me before going to Canada. Whenever his imprisonment had become unbearable, he had confided to me, he had told the Germans: "You can beat me, you can torture me, but as long as I can still think, I will remember. You can't kill my memory." And in fact, not even he had been able to accomplish that except lethally.

But that was still years into the future. With Poland sucked into the Soviet sphere of interest, we had a new enemy to deal with. To the extent that they posed as our friends and saviors, the Soviets were worse than the Germans. Intimidation and brainwashing were the principal currencies. And even though Marxist-Leninist dogma became everybody's curriculum in and out of school, there was a more frightening and comprehensive ideology unleashed, the ideology of silence. God-Kremlin was so powerful that it was ill-advised to voice any opinion, even within your family. Talking about superiors, in school or in the government, was altogether out of the question.

If a student made the mistake of blurting out something about a family member, an aroused teacher might pass along his suspicions to some official and that family member might never be seen again.

There wasn't even the certainty of death, as under the Nazis. Once somebody disappeared under the puppet Communist government, there was no way of finding out what had happened to him. The police denied ever hearing of him; hospitals and morgues denied ever dealing with a body; as in Latin America in recent years, the arrested person simply became a "disappeared."

One day, I opened the door to one of Peter's friends, who was weeping hysterically. While Peter tended to a head wound the boy had received, he kept crying things like, "Do you remember how we fought to liberate Poland from the Nazis? Now look at us! We're still being beaten and killed! We've just traded one enemy for another!" It was a familiar lament. In any bar in the country, fueled by the courage of a few vodkas, even the ideology of silence cracked under the enormous national sense of having been betrayed by the Russians.

We were taught that we needn't worry about ourselves, but to think only about our "God Kremlin." Our obligation was to work for the greater glory of Communism and in return, we were assured, the Kremlin would look after us.

My own strongest response to my exposure to the relentless teachings of Marxism-Leninism was that of shame. Everyone was supposed to be equal? Then why, thanks to my father's reputation as a doctor, were we still relatively wealthy? Why did so many patients continue to seek him out specifically, when we were constantly told that any form of free enterprise was evil?

And, incidentally, how come the Communists themselves had done nothing to shut down my father's practice? How come, on the contrary, just as with the non-Communist governments 20 years before, the regime's own top officials, including the prime minister and cabinet secretaries, came to him for treatment? Why, if somebody important in the government or party didn't want the public knowing of his illness, was my father brought secretly to bedrooms and hospital beds? They couldn't even be coherent about what they wanted us all to be ashamed of.

Or, was all the ambiguity the result of the regime's own shame before evidence that my father worried about the needy more than the ideologues did? The street before our house was always crowded with the poor and the destitute: Some waited there two or three days to see the physician reputed to have such powerful cures. For me, this was still another source of embarrassment, since I could never return home without some of these would-be patients begging me to put in a special word for them.

My father did what he could. And when some particularly impoverished patient admitted not having enough even for a nominal payment, he would open his top drawer and quickly pass on a couple of bills. It was a habit that usually ended with my mother finding out about his largesse and making sure there was no more money in the drawers to be passed along. Until the next time.

My mother didn't do much for my guilt complexes, either. Communist regime or no Communist regime, she was bent on maintaining the lifestyle she had enjoyed before the war. If that meant buying black market food for parties, then she bought black market food. She had no idea of the figure she was striking doing such things, while most of the population had to stand in line for hours to get a loaf of bread, a few potatoes, or whatever else they were allowed with their coupon books. Many schoolmates ostracized me because of my family's upscale lifestyle. This inequality embarrassed me so much that I wanted with all my heart to be as poor as my friends, very few of which I could invite to my home.

Today, living in New York, I look back and realize that I wouldn't have accused my mother of snobbery or superficiality in wanting to maintain the lifestyle to which she was accustomed, but rather I would be proud and certainly not ashamed. There are two other things from that period I believe are worth mentioning. The first was my mother's constant apprehension about our family background, especially my father's. We were forbidden ever to talk about his aristocratic upbringing, lest this expose us as class enemies. In retrospect, this seems a little naive of her, since the regime was hardly going to entrust some of its leading lights to my father's care without first running an exhaustive check on his background. Back then, it was also moot advice, since I knew practically nothing of my family's origins.

The other point I would like to underline here is that we never learned too much about religion at home. A Tibetan Buddhist, my father never talked about God, while my mother, Russian Orthodox by birth, seemed to regard religion only as some kind of calling card confirming her integrity as a believer. God-Kremlin, even in rejection, was about as good as it got. We were taught that we needn't worry about ourselves, but to think only about our "God Kremlin." Our obligation was to work for the greater glory of Communism and in return, we were assured, the Kremlin would look after us.

Then one morning in 1954, I saw something on the street that shook me to my marrow. Shredded photos of Stalin lay all over the gutter and sidewalk. No sooner had he died the night before, as I learned subsequently, than he had become nothing more than an irritant for the street sweeper. Seeing this image of Stalin, to whom I was obliged to give all my reverence, treated this way left me deeply shaken. The image that we had bowed to every morning as we entered the classroom was now nothing more than a piece of trash, not even noticed by the garbage man as he swept it into the sewer. It was shocking. It wasn't the way I had expected an official idol to pass on.

Chapter 4

Discovering My Roots

I was already an adult living in the West when I encountered a Russian professor who expressed astonishment at my family name. Could I be the daughter of "the famous Doctor Badmajeff?" To my great fortune he had one of several books written about my father, and I was finally able to learn about my paternal background. To say the least, it was a series of staggering revelations. Not only hadn't I known much, I wouldn't have had a clue what questions to ask.

My paternal great-grandfather, a physician named Prince Zasogol Badma-Buryat, was a descendant of Genghis Khan's second wife. The daughter of Genghis Kahn of his second wife, Choacaj, founded the Unczin-Cagan-Zasogol dynasty.

Since Genghis Khan is known mostly for his violent and brutal conquests, almost everyone knows about his merits. I myself was surprised by discovering this little biography about him on the Internet. Accordingly, I would like to shed some more light on him.

Genghis Khan was born in 1167 in Temujin, Mongolia. In 1206 the Mongols proclaimed him Genghis Khan, which meant universal or invincible prince. It was he who actually created Mongolia by uniting all dispersed Mongolians and by developing the Mongolian language. The Empire that he established was the most vast and powerful ever to have existed, greater than those of Alexander the Great, Julius Caesar and even Hannibal.

The code of laws that he promulgated was his greatest contribution to the world and have been carried from generation to generation up to the present day. He promoted the growth of trade between

China and Europe, allowing him to gain food, weapons and other essential goods. The pony express system was also one of his contributions.

He is considered a great military strategist for the unique way he structured his army by integrating soldiers from different tribes into one powerful fighting force. Not only did he have diverse people specializing in the various aspects of warfare, but he also was able to inspire loyalty to the Mongolian army as a whole rather than to a specific group of people. He created a superior fighting force through strict discipline by inspiring a great deal of loyalty in his unique way of promotion by achievement and not by nepotism. Every soldier gave his life to Genghis Khan.

Seven generations after his second wife, Choacaj in the 17th century the Unczin-Cagan-Zasogol dynasty was founded. This dynasty continued through too Prince Zagosol Badma. Born in the late 18th century, he was a very wealthy man, who had seven sons, two of whom were my great uncles: Cultim Amchi-Lama and Zamsaran. They became highly gifted doctors who ended up in the Russian court. Cultim and Zamsaran were both trained in the Buddhist tradition at the Datsan Aga Monastery in the Lake Baikal region of Mongolia.

Once elevated to the position of lama, Cultim played a crucial role in the development of the monastery as a prominent center of Tibetan medicine. Codified in the Tibetan text known as the *Zud-Shji*, this medical tradition predated the birth of Christ by hundreds of years. But it probably didn't make much of an impact beyond Tibet's frontiers until the ninth century, when the King of Mongolia invited physicians and scholars from India, China, Nepal, Kashmir, and Persia for an international medical conference. While the medical writings of the guests were translated into Tibetan, the *Zud-Shji* was in turn given to the visitors.

No foreign power has been more significant to Tibet's development than Mongolia. During the 13th and 14th centuries, when Mongolia was extending its empire through Eurasia, it incorporated

Tibet. But it was not just another conquest. In fact, after 1235, when a Tibetan physician-Lama cured the Mongolian King of a paralysis, the Mongolians came to regard themselves as the midwives of Tibetan medicine. At the Aga Monastery in the Buryat steps where Genghis Khan was born, the monks practiced the Tibetan healing arts to the point of establishing the greatest medical center in the country.

Within the upper crust it was traditional for the Dalai Lama to accept an invitation to come and observe a newborn boy in the interests of establishing his karma and deciding what his future should be. When the 12th Dalai Lama accepted the invitation of my great uncle's family, he pronounced both Cultim and Zamsaran as future doctors. This was no small announcement.

In the mystical, tranquil setting of the monastery the monks encouraged the students to utilize all the faculties of the brain with their special techniques. The metaphysical approach to understanding the causes and effects of illness is the same approach needed to understand the causes and effects of the universe itself. Tibetan medicine is based on the premise that man is inseparable from nature and that good health is the result of maintaining this relationship in perfect balance. Just as in nature where there must be balance between the sun, air, water and earth, so in man balance must be maintained between awareness, willpower and compassion. The cells in our body reflect the universe in microcosm. The living cell absorbs energy from space. Whenever this balance is disturbed, psychological disorders will result which almost invariably express themselves as physical symptoms.

Fittingly enough, it was disease, specifically an outbreak of typhoid fever in Siberia, that brought my great-uncles their first important contact with the Russians. When the governor of St. Petersburg embarked on a fact-finding mission to the afflicted region in the mid-nineteenth century, he brought along his wife, who was stricken by a mysterious illness. The desperate governor, hearing about a Tibetan who could cure what others couldn't, sent for the physician. It was my great-uncle Cultim.

Using ancient herbal remedies that he and his brother, Zamsaran, had refined over years of study and experimentation, Cultim treated the governor's wife successfully. The official was so impressed that he asked Cultim to accompany him back to St. Petersburg to treat an intestinal ailment that had been plaguing Czar Alexander II for months. Cultim agreed, but only on the condition that he was identified as a doctor, not as some vague holy man from the East. For my father's uncle, it was the perfect opportunity to introduce the real science behind Tibetan medicine to the West.

As soon as he arrived in St. Petersburg, Cultim set up an herbal pharmacy on the outskirts of the city. He was so successful in treating the Czar that not only was he added to the imperial staff as a personal physician, but also he persuaded the monarch to take up the study of Tibetan culture.

Given that he was also curing one desperate case after another, it didn't take long for Cultim to become one of the most whispered names in St. Petersburg society. In 1864 Czar Alexander II baptized Cultim Badma with the name Alexander Badmaev (or, in Russian, Badmajeff or the Polish transliteration, Badmajew, depending on the speaker and the language used), and his religion was changed from Buddhism to Russian Orthodox.

When his younger brother, Zamsaran, graduated as a doctor from the Aga Monastery in 1871, he joined Alexander Badmajeff in the Russian capital. Upon his arrival, Zamsaran was baptized with the name Piotr (Peter) Badmajeff, and also became Russian Orthodox. Peter was later to become a Professor of Mongolian language and in 1877, he began his practice of Tibetan medicine at the Medical Surgical Academy where his brother, Alexander, had already established himself. Eventually, Peter was invited to join the Asian Department of Foreign Affairs of Russia as an officer. The whole time, he and Alexander continued to serve as personal physicians to the Czar and his family.

Possessed of enormous energy, the brothers were indefatigable workers. There were some striking differences between the brothers. Alexander was an introvert, and preferred devoting his time to his medical and herbal studies. The more worldly Peter was known as a gregarious personality who embraced life at court. But for all that, Peter never neglected his origins. Precisely at four o'clock every morning, before the daily whirl began, he would ride alone on horseback out to the countryside, re-establishing his link with nature.

I must also confess to seeing the origins of some of both my father's eccentricities and virtues in my Great Uncle Peter. On the rather odd side, there was his habit of walking the streets with an open umbrella, no matter what the weather was! When passersby laughed at him, he just laughed along with them; not a thought in his head about closing or abandoning the umbrella.

Conversely he had a prodigious memory, able to recall faces and verbatim conversations dating back decades. In court he gained the sobriquet "The Encyclopedia of Russia" for his vast knowledge of his adopted land.

He never lost sight of his primary profession, however, and treated the poor as often as the rich. Even when it meant venturing into the worst slums of St Petersburg he never shied away from house calls, and had a reputation for lending money to his needy patients. Because of his exceptional memory he was able to recall the names and stories of patients even if he hadn't seen them in years.

But what was most extraordinary was that these were the poorest people in the land to whom practically no one, certainly no one of his social stature, had paid attention. It apparently never occurred to him that he was that rare member of his social status who acknowledged the poor, and treated them, usually *gratis*.

As Peter's fame grew, he became more of a routine within the Czar's inner circle, and he breakfasted regularly with the monarch. When the Czar began soliciting his advice on Russian policies in Asia, he proved the most fertile of grounds since he had been harboring his own vision of a Russian Empire that extended all the way to Mongolia, Tibet, and China.

Was he capable of such far-seeking aims? His contemporaries, in both admiration and suspicion, would have said yes. Of more immediate importance, he got the Czar's ear with warnings that only an extended railway system through such an expanded empire could prevent the British from using their foothold in India to pursue their own aims of conquest in Asia.

As fascinated as the Czar might have been with Peter's strategies, however, a growing number of representatives in the powerful Russian Parliament (the Duma) viewed his strategies as dangerous meddling in state affairs. Peter didn't help his situation by ignoring the storm signals coming from the Duma. Instead of lobbying with his own allies, he concentrated on making a reality out of his empire vision.

When friends suggested he was being too casual about the enemies he was making in The Duma, he fell back on his philosophical attitude that anything worth achieving had obstacles. In his opinion, if there are no obstacles to overcome, then the result can only be stagnation. The cycles of the "Wheel of Life," he believed, inevitably produced pain, but it was equivalent to the pain of a woman in labor, a necessary part of the struggle that brings forth a loving birth.

Neither Peter nor Alexander regarded their conversion to the Russian Orthodox faith as an abandonment of Buddhism. Buddhism honors the holy in every religion and they regarded Christ as an incarnation of truth and love. Such answers did not persuade the parliamentarians who viewed Peter as a political mercenary with his own agenda.

Czar Alexander III adopted Peter and Alexander, thereby conferring upon them the rights of Russian citizens. But by taking this step the Czar only succeeded in antagonizing the members of the Duma further. They continued to be seen as a threat to powerful interests who wanted the Czar's favor for their own schemes. They also were looked upon with distrust because they were not Russian by birth.

And, it must be confessed, that their great ambition didn't make them many friends in the government. The pair was nicknamed birds with large wings. His enemies in the Duma called Peter himself a diabolical magician. His plan to bring China, Mongolia, and Tibet under Russian dominion aroused more suspicion than enthusiasm.

Efforts continued unabated to bring him down; he was accused of stealing five million rubles, though in fact the money had been given him by Czar Nicholas II to develop a railroad system that would extend to the far-flung reaches of the empire. In any case, it is hard to believe that he was driven by greed: he was independently wealthy, a famous physician who was well-rewarded by the Czar and who numbered many Russian aristocrats among his private patients. Nor is there any evidence that his experiences in Russia had done anything to cause him to abandon the strong moral code he'd lived by all his life; first as a lama, then as a doctor.

In 1895 the Czar found a way of removing Peter from the hothouse atmosphere by appointing him as his personal emissary on a secret mission to China. The aim of the trip was consultations with the Chinese factions bent on toppling the despised Manchu dynasty. As a Buryat Mongol himself, Peter was warmly received by the rebels.

But successful as his mission on behalf of the Czar was, Peter returned to St. Petersburg to find himself accused of seeking to overthrow the Manchus so he could install a regime of his own in China. This time his Duma enemies went beyond rhetoric and rumor to demands that my great-uncle be arrested.

When the Czar showed little inclination to follow up on these calls, the parliamentarians used various pretexts to dispatch policemen after Peter on their own. Time and again, though, he succeeded in evading capture by the authorities; each time the poor of the city who loved and respected him would rally around him and protect him.

While Peter and Alexander were finding out the hard way that not every Russian was ready to welcome them as fellow citizens, they received news from home that they had become uncles. On December 10,

1884, their younger brother, Buddah, had become the father of a boy named Zamjan. Like his uncles before him, Zamjan was identified by the Dalai Lama as a future physician and sent at the age of four to study medicine at the Aga Monastery. Once he had completed his work there, he was sent to the Military Medical Academy in St. Petersburg to continue his work in Tibetan medicine directly under Peter. Czar Nicholas II, eventually converted Zamjan to the Russian Orthodox faith, baptizing him as Vladimir Badmajeff. Years later I would call him father.

Chapter 5

Rasputin And My Great Uncles

When Peter was finally eased out of the court, it wasn't because of the enemies he had made in the Duma, but because of the Czarina Alexandra's infatuation with a monk who had convinced her that only he could restore her hemophiliac son, Alexis, to health. The monk, of course, was Rasputin, and his ascendancy had a profound impact not only on Peter's position but also, by extension, on my father's.

It was also a time of St.Petersburg's decadence, in which aristocracy indulged in reckless orgies of dancing and alcoholism. During the war of 1915, when millions of soldiers were losing their lives, a favorite amusement of the aristocracy was spreading rumors of intrigue against the throne in order to inflame the proletariat against the state.

The rumor about the Empress was that she was keeping the Emperor constantly drunk and under the superstitious beliefs of fortune tellers and prophets, the master of whom was Rasputin. There was even an attempt to kill the Empress when an image of her kissing Rasputin was spread all over Russia. Any rumors or intrigue were used to degrade the Empire no matter how inconsequential they could be. Moreover, the Russian people hated the Empress, since she was German-born and not Russian.

The Polish journalist Puriszkiewicz, a man of questionable reputation, was even considered by the Duma to search for more incriminating evidence against the Czar. Puriskiewicz allegedly claimed that the Czar was being manipulated and possessed by Peter and Rasputin, as Peter supplied Rasputin with his medicines. Therefore, the medicines supposedly allowed Rasputin to manipulate the will of the Czar's family. The Bolsheviks, without any substantiation, used this accusation to further fuel their revolution.

As this was towards the end of the Russian Empire, the tumultuous time did not allow for a true revision of the facts, and up to this day the reputations of Doctors Peter and Alexander Badmajeff have yet to be cleared. Some misguided historians such as Edvard Radzinsky, the author of *The Last Tsar: The Life And Death Of Nicholas II* are still tracking false trails of information without taking up other leads.

They fail to take into consideration that in 1857, Alexander Badmajeff left the Aga monastery and established the first Tibetan herbal pharmacy in 1864 in St. Petersburg. This was long before Rasputin was introduced to the Russian Empress in 1905. His influence over government did not start until 1911, and was killed only five years later, in 1916.

The Bolsheviks took advantage of the decadence of St.Petersburg by taking complete power away from the monarchy. They confiscated all the politician's documentation, along with that of the aristocracy, including the Badmajeffs. Those documents were then given to editor W.T.Siemienkiewicz, who was officially at the service of the Soviet party he wrote *Za kulisami Cara Behind the Stage of the Czar* and, not unexpectedly, his evaluation about the Badmajeff doctors concluded they were just adventurous "birds with large wings."

In 1925 he published, in Leningrad, all the correspondence between the Badmajeff family and Czar Alexander III, and with Czar Nicholas II, and with Count Witte. It was preceded by the article, *The Tibetan Doctor and the Russian Monarch.* Some of the accusations were truly absurd. One of the worst was that Peter was responsible for Rasputin's evil.

I think that at this point it is important to introduce the story of Rasputin, not only because history always has connected him with Badmajeff, but because my future Pentecostal experience has reminded me of him. The book *The Life and Times of Grigorii Rasputin* by Alexander De Jonge was very helpful to me.

Born Grigory Yefimovich Novykh, he earned the nickname Rasputin from the word "raspustvo"—a turbulent person. The man who would one day become known as Russia's greatest love machine was born in 1865 in the western Siberia village of Pokrovskoe, 1600 miles away from St Petersburg. The desolate terrain around his birthplace had been attractive for some time to the pioneers, fugitives and rabid religious sects that wanted nothing to do with the reforms that the state religion was trying to institute in the nineteenth century. There were many people who chose self-immolation rather than to make the sign of the cross with three fingers rather than two.

Rasputin's own father was thought to be an alcoholic horse thief, who, more than once, was whipped to within an inch of his life after being caught. All three qualities, the drinking, the attraction to horses, and flagellation, were to appear prominently in his son's life as well, if in different circumstances.

Even as a youth, Rasputin was credited with the kind of psychic magnetism that allowed him to control animals, find lost objects, and assess the personality strengths and weaknesses of people as soon as he met them. He was called an evil genius and had a reputation for hard drinking, sexual precocity, and a lack of personal hygiene, suggesting more than one reading of the claims of many women that sleeping with him once was enough.

In what was to be one of several turning points in his life, he was accused of horse thievery at the age of 15 and, like his father, he was whipped mercilessly. For the next three months, he clung to refuge in a monastery, and when he returned home, he acted so drastically different that fellow villagers thought the whipping had affected his brain. His speech was reduced to incomprehensible phrases and sentence fragments, his hands never stopped twitching. No less noticeable, he went out of his way to avert his gaze from anybody who sought to talk to him.

The change in his personality, though, had nothing to do with his beating. Instead, it is believed that it came about as a result of the influence of the hermit Maccari, a monk who lived outside the religious community and held beliefs unrecognized by Christians. His cult was known as the starets. Maccari had an extraordinary power over his disciples, whose will he absorbed into his own. When Rasputin became his disciple, it was Maccari who was responsible for transforming him and giving him power.

Rasputin was forever marked by the ritualistic practices promulgated by the starets and a group of peasant, pre-revolutionary Russian Christians called Old Believers noted for its fanatic and punitive imitations of Jesus Christ. They would nail themselves to the cross, and commit dire self-mortification, like castration and flagellation. With these acts, they believed that they were taking on the sins of the world; after these acts they believed that they, too, were now God. And because a God can do no wrong, whatever they did was right. The faithful believed that only through sin could one expiate sin and attain true salvation "to use sin to drive out sin." So sins were necessary, since they represented the first step towards salvation.

This doctrine was exemplified in Rasputin's own behavior. He would dance himself into a feverish pitch, accompanied by gypsy guitars and violins and rhythmic clapping. The dance was characterized by a repetitive motion that had the effect of putting him and the women who were watching into a trance. Finally, the music would build to a crescendo that culminated in a sexual explosion.

It didn't matter who the woman was or what class she belonged to, he would convince them all that he would take on their sins. Many of these women sincerely believed that when he was kissing them and fondling them, he was actually purging them of sin. In many of the private homes he visited, Rasputin was permitted to kiss young girls or women or share their bed, all so that he could assist them in their struggle against sin. To protect them from temptation, he would kiss them until they grew disgusted with kissing. He claimed that he was tempering them against passion. He was also given to sitting for hours in a bath with his female admirers who he insisted were all spiritual sisters.

Such was the extent of devotion that women would even venerate his nail clippings and submit to unusual forms of trial by sexual ordeal. He exerted a sexual domination of such magnitude that women were hypnotized; just looking into his eyes could bring about ecstatic joy, of an intensity scarcely experienced by most mortals. They believed that they now belonged to him body and soul. It was a religious experience similar to the divine ecstasy. One woman admitted that when he made love to her, her orgasm was so intense that she fainted.

Prince Felix Yussoupov, who would later assassinate Rasputin, believed that Rasputin had such stamina and control over his penis due to a capacity for constant penal stimulation, which allowed him to make love for hours on end. Rasputin believed, as did his lovers, that by performing these sexual acts he was in fact assuming their guilt, as well as consuming their sins.

In his view, the only way to achieve redemption was through ecstasy. He believed himself to be a God and wished to be recognized as such. There is no doubt that he sacrificed many years of his life in order to develop his spirituality and acquire the capacity to hypnotize and use his power to dominate people and to compel their fascination.

It didn't matter that he spoke with an incomprehensible Siberian accent, making his conversation hard to follow. He would cite spiritual adages and quote from Scriptures, speaking in tongues, the way members of Pentecostal groups do. Though no one could figure out precisely what he was saying, they still felt the incredible possessive power he held over them.

It didn't take long before people began to consider him a holy man. And it was as a holy man that he set out on the road, getting as far as Greece and Jerusalem. He reappeared in St. Petersburg in 1905 and soon insinuated himself into the royal family. During World War I, with Czar Nicholas at the front, the way was open for Rasputin to become the most powerful figure at court. He appointed church officials and cabinet ministers and even intervened in military matters.

Even after Rasputin had replaced him with the royal family, Peter was not immune to attacks. They accused him of currying favor with Rasputin so that he could insinuate himself back into the embrace of the royal family. Some people said that without Rasputin's help, Peter would still be an obscure Tibetan doctor, though nothing could have been further from the truth, since Peter had been active in court long before Rasputin came on the scene.

But for all of Rasputin's excesses, his intelligence couldn't be denied and he was certainly aware of the limitations of his power. He realized that he could hold Alexei under hypnosis for days, long enough to keep his hemophilia at bay, for he was anxious not to disappoint the Czarina.

In Peter, he recognized a man of very high spirituality and knowledge and may have realized that Peter's power was possibly stronger that his own. The monk respected Peter not only as a man but also as a doctor. Moreover, Rasputin relied on Peter to supply him with the famous Tibetan medicinal herbs, which he continued administering to Prince Alexei. He wanted to maintain contact with Peter so that he could have the benefit of his advice.

Peter's difficulties with the Duma continued unabated. Members of the Russian parliament continued to accuse Peter of accumulating political power at their expense. For the Czar still trusted Peter and listened carefully to his advice and now he had developed a friendship with Rasputin.

Though he was no longer held in the same favor at court, Peter remained steadfastly loyal to the Czar whom he venerated. In spite of his great erudition and sophistication, he had a simple soul and a childlike personality, which probably led him to give such unconditional love to both Alexander and Nicholas. It was almost as if he saw the Czar as his father. In a letter to Countess Anna Wyborova, the closest confidante of the Czarina, he wrote, "Whatever I have, I have received from the Czar."

He remained concerned about the well-being of the royal family, especially Alexei. And like so many others, he also was worried about Rasputin's growing influence at court. Already his relationship with the Czarina had become a scandal that had penetrated into every class of Russian society. The disdain in which Rasputin was held could be seen in any number of ambiguous paintings which depicted the Czarina and Rasputin together in suggestive poses.

Peter felt it was better to affect a friendship with him, and better to understand his intentions, which is why he never refused to meet with Rasputin; yet Peter distrusted him. Whether he appreciated the irony of his situation is hard to know because while he was worrying about what Rasputin wanted for Russia, the Duma was worrying about the influence of both Rasputin and Peter himself on the royal family.

Even while Peter maintained his association with Rasputin, he was also on good terms with one of Rasputin's arch-enemies, Bishop Heljodor. By the time the Russian Revolution broke out in 1917, Alexander Badmajeff had been dead for several years, so he was spared the indignity of his younger brother Peter's fate. The Bolsheviks ordered Peter expelled from Russia, ostensibly sending him into exile together with the Czarina's confidante, Countess Wyborova. The two were put on board the ship Gwiazda Polarna, but the ship did not lift anchor nor was it supposed to.

Putting the two aboard the ship was all done for show. The Bolsheviks actually planned to sink the ship before it could put out to sea. As soon as Peter got on board, however, he discovered that the crew was ridden with typhoid fever and syphilis. Over the next two weeks, while they remained at anchor, Peter dedicated himself to treating the sickened sailors. When the order came through to sink the ship with the passengers on board, the crew refused to obey. Instead out of gratitude for his services, they freed Peter as well as the Countess Wyborova. The local governor immediately denounced him as a traitor and accused him of trying to escape Russia illegally.

But Peter stayed put, continuing to avow his loyalty to the now-imprisoned Czar, in spite of numerous threats to put him in custody.

But there was no reason for his nephew, Vladimir, or his new bride to stay. My parents had first met when my mother, then divorced with a young child, sought out my father to attend to her ailing mother. After treating the mother, my father found the occasion to see her daughter again. The two soon fell in love. Because his new wife had relatives in Poland, arrangements were made for the couple to join them there.

Peter continued on in St. Petersburg even though the Bolsheviks constantly persecuted him. His library was ransacked medical research was taken, and they confiscated his personal correspondence with the Czar. They rewritten history to portray him as an ambitious—and devious—political manipulator, the same allegations that the Duma had leveled against him twenty years before.

He was continually being arrested, interrogated and then unexpectedly released, only to be taken into custody again. Weakened by his trials, he died of an infection at home in 1919 at the age of 112. It seems that in death, the Russians were finally able to give my uncle the honor that their jealousies would not allow them to respect during his lifetime. In St. Petersburg, they have placed the epitaph: "To the Founder of Tibetan Medicine in Russia."

Belatedly, the Communists acknowledged Peter's contribution to medicine. Professor Pogozhev of the USSR Academy of Medical Science confirmed that Peter's own research, much of it represented in *Zud-Shji,* could prove of great value to modern physicians.

In 1978, the Mongolian Academy of Science also cited Peter Badmajeff as the first scientist to introduce Tibetan medicine to Russia. Now 150 years old, the Buryat Buddhologist School would never have attained the status that it has without the contribution of lamas like my uncle Peter who spread its doctrines throughout the world. The current Dalai Lama has visited Buryatia and blessed the land near Lake Baikal and all the people living there.

Chapter 6

Experiences In The Opera Ballet

My early adolescent years were difficult. For one thing, I wasn't allowed to indulge myself too much as my mother would have considered this narcissistic. It seems that this attitude of self-denial was prevalent, at least in the Europe of my generation, following the Second World War. We had grown up with too many rules, trying to teach good manners, not to mention the prohibitions imposed by the Communist government in Poland. As a matter of fact, I ended up with so many inferiority complexes, to the point of worrying about breathing someone else's air.

Also, it didn't help much growing up with two brothers, who poked fun endlessly at my grades and teased me constantly by calling me dumb. I became so self-conscious that I was afraid to express myself. "Stupid" was their favorite epithet for me. It didn't help, of course, that I was the only girl. During this time, boys were considered more important than girls in any family. They didn't believe that I could do anything right. If I should pick up a vase, my brothers, and my mother, too, would stare at me. "Just you wait," Peter would say, "she's sure to drop the vase!" And, of course, I was so nervous that the vase would slip through my hands and shatter on the floor, much to the great amusement of my brothers. What bothered me more was that my mother would join in their laughter. I had unwittingly become the family clown.

My salvation was to be music.

Thanks to my mother's insistence, George and I supplemented our regular schoolwork with the study of the piano and violin. I was also sent to the Warsaw Opera House to take ballet. It was love at first sight. The moment I saw those beautiful pirouettes on the stage, I knew I had to become a dancer. The music made my soul fly. When I was finally accepted as a member of the ballet corps, it was literally the realization of dreams I'd had for months. The sweet smell of sawdust, the hammers of the stagehands mounting sets, the costume pageantry, were intoxicating. They allowed me to conquer trepidations stronger than those I experienced daily at home in my maladroit attempts not to be dominated by my brothers and mother.

Waiting in the wings for the curtain to rise, I would be assailed by the most ferocious stage fright; I was sure I was about to make a fool of myself in public. But then, as soon as I saw my cue, my panic evaporated. Instantly, I forgot myself and became the character I was dancing for the evening. With the help of Tchaikovsky, Borodin, Prokofiev, and Debussy, I became so sensitized to the nuances of my own movements that I felt they were flowing in and out of me, as I was doing the same with them. My brothers liked to mock that dancers have all their brains in their legs. On stage, that seemed like anything but an insult.

Of course, the music always ended after a performance. Even within the company itself, I wasn't able to keep up too many illusions. Both the house choreographer and the supervisory party committee never let me forget my suspiciously wealthy background. To humiliate me, they made sure I was placed in the back line; because I was small, this made it difficult for the audience to see me. Complaining about this would have only made matters worse.

Solidarity wasn't exactly in evidence at home either, since my vain mother saw me as competition. I began to intuit that she maybe unconsciously, started to be jealous of me, since I was growing up and becoming prettier and prettier. My mother would never receive any flirtation from a man, although she loved to be admired for her beauty, her elegance and her innate class.

My brother, Peter, considered ballerinas little better than prostitutes.

He was sniping at my mother for allowing me to show my legs in public. "You should be a doctor, not a ballerina!" he snapped at me once. "This is a family of doctors. You bring shame to our father."

"Not only am I not going to be a doctor," I told him, "I'm not even going to marry one!" From that moment to the rest of his life Peter and I could count our conversations on the fingers of one hand.

My twin, George was indifferent to what I was doing. While bright and extremely charming, he considered life an easy conquest. He had no interest in the arts; his friends were the prematurely aging dregs of former aristocratic and bourgeois families. All he truly cared about were women and alcohol, and by the time he was 15, he was already hanging out at nightclubs.

Fortunately, I had friends who helped me get through the most difficult patches. Above all, there was Barbara Bittner, the company's First Ballerina. I first saw her when she made a guest appearance at the Opera in the Prokofiev *Romeo and Juliet.* I couldn't take my eyes off her beauty, her extraordinary technique, or her profound feeling for the character she was dancing—all of which seemed indistinct from one another. When she invited me to her morning training exercises, I considered it a great honor, and was determined to prove myself to her. We really didn't talk all that much. Our communication was through our dancing. I don't think it would be an exaggeration to say that I learned more by studying her movements and timing, than I did in my dance classes proper.

Then there was a choreographer, who prided himself on sleeping with all the dancers. But once he decided that I was too young even for him, he turned against me. He enjoyed giving a loud thwack with his baton, ordering the class to halt, and then berating me for holding up everybody. "Badma, you aren't doing the steps I taught you and you're not keeping time with the music," he would shout. "Let's get something straight. I am the choreographer here!" It was humiliating, feeling thirty pairs of eyes on me.

But not even these scenes could spoil my love for the theater.

The fact was, I was happier when I was working with the dance company than I was at home. And when we weren't out on the floor, we were in the dressing room or in the wings or in the orchestra, just talking. Plays, sex, art, philosophy—every subject under the sun, except politics was grist for the mill. And because many company members had to share apartments, there was never a shortage of love affairs to be whispered or joked about. For these conversations, I admit, I sat content to listen, afraid of saying something that would embarrass me.

The main thing, though, was that I felt myself completely at ease with the first creative people I'd ever known. They weren't to be the last. I've always found artists to have superior senses of humor and to be more open to life, perhaps because their art allows them to live many lives. They have to develop their emotions to the maximum to penetrate the feelings and passions of their characters, and this alone furnishes journeys of experience they can draw on subsequently. Often, they are sensitive to the point of paranoia, afraid that other people will drain them of their energy.

In some ways, they don't seem that far removed from mystics in their responsiveness to even the slightest shift in emotions. It's ironic to think that what made my mother such a difficult and temperamental person is the fuel that fires the creativity of artists and actors.

Unlike my twin brother, I was hungry for knowledge. That's why I was always surrounding myself with creative and intelligent people of all kinds: writers, poets, composers, all much older than me. Usually the most creative ones were Jewish, some of whom were among my closest friends; they were the elixir of my life. Of course, my mother didn't care for them, because they didn't come from proper backgrounds like my twin brother's friends. Never mind that they were corrupting him!

My mother's attitude towards my friends deeply offended me. Here were people whom I genuinely admired and she, who could be so superficial and unjust in the way she approached life, was dismissing them as if they were nonentities. Her unwillingness to accept my friends or my way of life caused me to become more distant from her. After spending all day rehearsing at the Opera, I would dash across the street to a club reserved for artists, where my friends would gather for another evening of talk. Those became my two homes: the opera and the club.

It was Barbara, who was responsible for my first trip abroad, in the early 1950s. A major international competition was scheduled to be held in the Italian town of Vercelli, west of Milan, and the government agreed to permit Polish artists to perform outside the Iron Curtain for the first time in years. The Polish contingent was drawn from the winners of several national operatic and ballet competitions.

Barbara took personal charge of my training, helping me to prepare a repertoire of Debussy's *Clair de Lune,* Rimsky-Korsakov's *Scheherazade,* and Ravel's *Bolero.* It was really extraordinary; she looked after me as though I were her daughter. She even cleaned my ballet shoes and brought an order to my life that my sloppiness usually didn't allow. Her generosity knew no bounds.

When I was chosen for the competition, I didn't tell my classmates for fear of arousing their jealousy, so we continued rehearsing in secret. Between the rehearsals and my regular classes I worked every day for months from eight in the morning until and one the following morning. I was never so happy.

Finally, we boarded the train for the West. After a brief stop in Vienna, we crossed the border into Italy. Our first stop was in beautiful Verona, where Romeo and Juliet had fallen in love and paid for it dearly. Was it an omen that I had first seen Barbara perform in that ballet? I didn't dwell on it one way or the other. When we got to Vercelli, we discovered that the competition was going to be held on an ancient raked stage that was sloped to give the audience a better view. A steep incline was a nightmare for dancers, and I suppose I must have looked very glum, because Barbara and her partner, Vitold Gruca, felt the need to reassure me that it would make no difference.

They were right. The competition proved to be an enormous success for us. Among the many prizes the Poles won were a first for Barbara and a second for me in ballet.

When we returned home, we discovered we had become celebrities. Reporters followed us everywhere. I received numerous invitations to perform around the country. When I wasn't on one of these trips with Barbara and Vitold, I was pursuing my opera studies in Warsaw, eventually working my way up to the principal solo dancer at the Opera House. At this point, even my mother was able to overcome her snobbery and act happy to have me as a daughter.

But at home, tensions between us never really abated. What particularly incensed me was her attitude of benign neglect where George was concerned. It didn't seem to matter to her at all that George was not only well on the road toward alcoholism, but had also begun to steal to support his idling ways. When I found my perfumes missing, I knew he had swiped them for his latest girl friend. On the other hand, when my mother found some piece of jewelry missing, she was quick to invent the most ridiculous explanation. He squandered money like some caricature of a roué, sometimes even treating his cronies to a plane trip so they could have a coffee in a novel setting.

It got so bad that finally Peter decided something had to be done, even if that meant breaking our usual silence. With me in tow, he went around to the military authorities and made a case that only army duty would help George. He even signed the necessary authorization papers. The next morning, an officer appeared at our door with a document authorizing the drafting of George into military service.

Predictably, my mother went wild. "How can you do that to your own brother?" she screamed at Peter and me. Of course, it was only a rhetorical question. Rather than have the reasons spelled out again for her, she channeled her energies, the same energies that had once saved my step-brother, Richard, from a firing squad, into persuading the officer that a serious mistake had been made. George was never inducted.

I suppose that was the last straw. I knew I had to get out of the house. Moreover, despite the celebrity and success that had come to me after the Vercelli competitions, I knew I also had to get out of Poland. I was tired of the petty party bureaucrats always breathing down my neck, weary of having to jump through hoops at home to elicit the smallest of acknowledgements from my mother. Yes, I would miss Barbara and the other friends I had made in music circles, but they were creative people. Wouldn't they have been the first ones to understand that, at bottom, we weren't Polish so much as artists? And what else had my father's Tibetan heritage given me if not the need to have a sense of inner, rather than merely geographical place?

My initial ambition was to move to the United States, but the visa problem was all but insurmountable. Visas were easier to get for Italy, where there was a strong Communist party. Besides, I had already been there, and that gave me confidence. From what I had seen, the people were relaxed and relatively happy, with a freedom I had never seen in Poland. Italy represented sun, while Poland had come to mean the gray, cold stone of her buildings and the sad, worried people, who always seemed fearful of their own shadows.

I had another important reason for setting my sights on Italy. While I was performing at the Opera, I began receiving flowers every evening from an Italian admirer named Norino. He was an international businessman, residing in Paris whose affairs brought him frequently to Warsaw. I know it was often because he never failed to call on me at home when he was in the city. I can still remember vividly the first time he came calling, how astonished he was to see how lavishly my family lived in the middle of a Communist regime. Naturally, that became part of the easy, laughing cheerfulness of his personality. It was a kind of happiness I wasn't used to. My father's, for instance, was a different kind of intellectual, philosophical joy. Norino's was more carefree.

Unlike my mother, Norino was immediately sympathetic when I confided in him about my artistic dreams, the situation with George, and the stresses from my mother. With him I didn't feel like the melodramatic queen I undoubtedly impressed others as being. And because he had important connections not only with the Poles, but also with the Russians, I knew that when he promised to pull strings for me to get to the West, they would be pulled.

Two years after the competitions at Vercelli, I obtained a visa to Italy through Paris. The combination of Norino's pressures, my father's prominent position as a physician, and my own nascent celebrity had persuaded the bureaucrats that I might prove to be more trouble than I was worth to deny me a trip. Norino was waiting for me at Orly airport, and whisked me off to the Grand Hotel. Maybe I should have been more impressed with so much sumptuousness, but I hadn't exactly grown up in a sty. I was far more taken with the Opera House, the Lido, Montmartre, and all the other beautiful Paris sights Norino couldn't wait to show me. Where else should one be in love?

Then one day we had a visitor at the hotel—Norino's wife! In my confusion, I tried to think of it as my first western shock. What I finally, belatedly learned was that Norino had set up quarters in Paris because of vague political problems (I always suspected they had to do with taxes) and that this had only worsened an already shaky marriage. But the woman was still his wife and here she was, visiting from Italy.

My reaction? Maybe I was just too young to put in any claims for my own needs, but, truthfully, I didn't feel the least bit threatened by her. I thought she was attractive, calm, and sweet. We became such good friends that Norino ended up the odd man out. Arrogant as I was, I even set about trying to get them back together. It didn't take completely, but both of them were at the airport when I left Paris for Rome. All three of us were crying.

Chapter 7

The Dolce Vita In Italy

I was totally unprepared for life in the West. Tackling everyday practical problems had not been a high priority in either my over-protective family environment or under a government regime that discouraged initiative. Without Norino's wife I don't know how long I would have survived in Rome. But no sooner had she returned from Paris than she brought me around to the Academy of Dance, an institution funded by the government and run by the great Russian dancer, Lia Ruskaya. It was not only an artistic privilege to be admitted, but I was able to earn some money as both a dancer and a teacher. I had crossed borders on an airplane, but I crossed from communism into capitalism on my feet.

Truth be told, though, the Academy didn't give me the creative freedom I was seeking. Ruskaya was a manual of rules and restrictions, and her interminable rehearsals often called for us to repeat the same small movement a hundred times in an afternoon. One day I finally had enough, sat down to take off my ballet shoes, and announced, "Enough! I'm not going to do this anymore!"

Ruskaya was shocked, and so were the other members of the class who would have never thought of opposing her formidable presence. But as much as I admired her, I knew I had to find a better way. A few weeks later I thought I had found it when I was invited to join a company touring Italy. It seemed like the most romantic and artistic of ways to see the country. We were always low on money, had to sleep in the car sometimes. So what? It was all for art's sake, right?

I don't think it was until that tour that I fully realized how ready

I was to meet the world on other than plush terms. Yes, the war years aside, I had grown up comfortably. Poverty might have been around me at home, but it had never walked in the front door. And yet even my mother in her grand way had been on guard against our growing up spoiled and greedy. For instance, she often made us give away our favorite toys to poor children behind giving a little lesson on not growing too attached to material things. As a result, there were many times when the three of us would come home from school with scarcely any clothes on our backs, because we'd given them to whoever had complimented us on them.

Actually, I found myself often worrying more about my friends' welfare than about my own. I felt that no matter what happened I would always find some way to survive. So I shared any money I had with them, even though it meant going hungry at times, which my pride wouldn't have permitted to admitted. Maybe the one person who saw through all this was my landlady in Rome, who insisted on giving me fresh eggs for breakfast every morning. And, mind you, she kept doing it even when I was frightfully behind on the rent.

Unfortunately for me, classical ballet was not one of the pillars of Italy's artistic life. In that most culturally sophisticated of European countries, ballerinas were thought to be little more than chorus girls. I became aware of this ignorance the hard way with more than one man. I was also able to attest to the thriving of the Whore-or-Madonna syndrome among Italian males, which was not altogether contradictory, at least in my case, accordingly to my brother, Peter's views of ballerinas. Between my scarce funds and the lack of appealing men, I spent most evenings alone in my apartment above the Fontana delle Tartarughe in one of the oldest districts of Rome. Sometimes I felt like Mimi in *La Bohème.*

If I had to put my finger on one failing during those first months, it was my inability to promote myself. Back in Poland, any untoward moves toward a person in authority could have resulted in a party committee hearing and the end of a career; you were what you had theoretically earned. This doesn't take you too far in a country like Italy. Fortunately for me, Norino and his wife understood that I was still a fish out of the capitalist water. They couldn't do much for me in Italy's limited dance world, but they did put me into contact with a film producer, who was looking to cast an actress with my specifications. I was so shy I spent the entire interview looking at the floor or the man's desk. I couldn't believe it when he said I had the part.

That was the beginning of my career in Italian movies. Only a few days later, I got another job as a dancer on a weekly television variety show with the Italian cabaret star, Renato Rascel. The show lasted six months, giving me enough money not only to pay my rent (and back rent) but also to afford some frilly extras.

There was no better time for working in the Italian film industry. It was the era of *La Dolce Vita*—the film of that name made by Federico Fellini and the wild night life along the Via Veneto that had inspired it. On any given night, the Veneto lived up to its reputation as "Hollywood on the Tiber," with the likes of Marlon Brando, Elizabeth Taylor, Richard Burton, Peter O'Toole, and Anita Ekberg sprawled out at the Café de Paris and other sidewalk bars. I was fortunate enough to work for the best directors in the country, including Fellini, Vittorio DeSica, and Marco Ferreri. I also appeared in several "Spaghetti Westerns"—the films made international stars out of Clint Eastwood, and gave new life to the careers of Americans, like Charles Bronson, Lee Van Cleef, and Eli Wallach. I suppose my two favorite films were *Valeria dentro fu*ori (Valeria, Inside and Out), in which I played a sadistic nun, and De Sica's *The Vacation*. While making *Vacation*, I took my first serious risk as an actress.

The picture was an endless dirge about women recuperating from tuberculosis in a sanitarium, and I played one of the nurses. My big scene called for me to introduce the heroine (Florinda Bolkan) to her quarters, and show her where things were. The length of the monologue was topped only by its banality. To wake myself up as much as anything else, I began reading the part comically. When I had finished, there was total silence from DeSica and the technicians on the set. I was sure I had earned my walking papers. But then he suddenly erupted in laughter, and everybody else followed his lead. It was one of my most exquisite moments as an actress.

Fellini called me his "witch with the diabolical eyes." I made two films with him: *Città De Roma* and *Satyricon*. But while I adored him personally as a charming, creative man with a great sense of humor, I can't say working for him was always pleasant. He liked to manipulate actors like puppets, and thought nothing of keeping us on a set for hours without letting us know when we would be needed. Worse, he rarely worked with a script, so we had no way of knowing our dialogue in advance.

Like a painter before a canvas, he had to see every detail in his head before he committed himself to the actual painting. This meant usually acting out every role of an imminent scene, including the parts of the extras. His energy was so robust that he could spend entire days rolling around on the floor, jumping up and down, and contorting his face in the weirdest shapes as instructions for what he wanted his actors to do. And, of course, even after we had gotten down what he wanted, he might decide in the editing room that it was all so much disposable celluloid. As an actor, you just had to accept those working conditions with him.

And the other thing about him was that he was more than a little superstitious; he always seemed surrounded by fortunetellers and astrologers. You sometimes had the feeling that if you didn't do things his way, you were tampering with his fate.

But all that said, I really never took advantage of the professional opportunities that working with the DeSicas and Fellinis had given me. Why think of tomorrow when tonight was still young? Why bother with next week when the paparazzi were running up and down the Veneto seeing if maybe I would sit next to somebody famous so they could sell another shot? Why worry about sleep when getting home at five in the morning usually meant another exciting night had been spent?

There are two Americans in particular I will always associate with that period in my life. One was Charlie Fawcett, who managed the neat trick of living lavishly while seldom having a lira to his name. Charlie knew the wealthiest, most important people in Rome and, through a favor here, some sleight-of-hand there, was able to organize the most sumptuous dinners without spending any money of his own.

His talent was bringing people together, whether that meant getting the Shah of Iran to a specific dinner table or some newly arrived Hollywood producer to an actor who was wanted for a role back in California. No one dared to have a party without Charlie, and he always used the occasion to organize the next evening's festivities. When I knew him, he was about 50 (50 years of charm), and he latched on to me as his favorite date. Our relationship was purely platonic, but amid the glitter and the gloss, neither of us felt that we were missing out on something. It was enough that Charlie's wreck of a car, which was always stalling, got us to where we were going.

My other guide through the Dolce Vita years was a striking black actress named Vanessa, whom I had met on a film. As elegantly as she carried herself, Vanessa projected an innocence that made me feel immediately protective toward her. Since she didn't have a place to stay, I invited her to live with me. It didn't take long for me to discover that she wasn't quite as innocent as she looked.

For one thing, she wasted no time in turning my small apartment into a hotel, moving members of her own family in and out of the yard or two of space left. On one occasion, she wanted to have a barbecue on the patio, and broke up some of my furniture to get a fire going. Or she would break something accidentally? Well, then I got the lecture along the lines of "What are you worried about? It's a cheap little thing you can always replace." Of course, that philosophy was never valid if I happened to touch something of hers.

As you may have guessed by now, Vanessa didn't lose too much time worrying about scruples in her life. If she liked something or somebody, it was to be taken, period. Married men, the lovers of her friends, they were all hers if she wanted them because, God knew, they weren't going to resist her. Credit cards were even less of a problem. If she wanted to buy something, what difference did it make if she didn't have the money for it? That was why they invented plastic, right?

Were we friends? Maybe not in the way I was with Charlie Fawcett. Most of all, Vanessa was an educational experience. I would have never dreamed of doing half the things she did. I had always been concerned with the impression I made on others, so had walked gingerly. Vanessa just plowed forward. It didn't hurt our relationship, either, that she was always whisking me off to chi-chi parties where hashish was served as openly as hors d'oeuvres.

We would stretch out on cushions placed around a floor, don headsets to listen to the music we preferred, and just drift. Conversation was unnecessary, and all but impossible in any case. After a couple of hours of this, we would pile into somebody's Rolls Royce and proceed to some fashionable restaurant. By the time an evening like that was over, I wasn't all that angry about some piece of furniture that had been sacrificed as firewood.

Getting high on drugs wasn't the only fashionable thing in those days; there were also the cults and sects that held out the promise of getting high on the Highest. Indian gurus were a particular rage. On one occasion, my friend, Giliola, invited me to go with her to London to meet Maharjii Yoga, then reaping a great deal of publicity for his relationship with the Beatles. Giliola, whose family had made a fortune in the fashion business, wasn't the most stable person I'd ever known. She had been a nun for a short while, but then had given up that vocation to hang out with the hippies on the Spanish Steps. Her flights of fancy led some people to think she was touched, but I always found her intriguing, and so I went with her to London.

It was a big letdown. I had been told the Maharjii believed he was Jesus Christ and his mother the Madonna, but since I wasn't all that familiar with Christianity, I wasn't exactly sure how outrageous that claim was. As far as I could tell, he was merely exploiting the naïveté of his young followers, an aim enormously abetted by the publicity around his ties to the Beatles. Like other cult leaders, he succeeded in tearing families apart by virtually kidnapping their children and robbing them of their money in the name of attaining purity through the surrender of worldly goods.

With that on the record, I must confess that when I returned to Rome I came across a sect that did enthrall me for a short time. Whenever they showed themselves in public, they created quite a stir, and for good reason, since they routinely paraded through the streets wearing long black coats and pulling along huge, wolf-like dogs. There were about twenty of them, men and women, twenty-year-olds and sixty-year-olds, Italians and foreigners. From what I was to learn, they believed the animals had a third eye that enabled them to view a non- earthly world. That was enough for me to accept an invitation to their place.

As it turned out, they were surprisingly sophisticated people—educated, very much aware of the world around them. They also happened to put all their belief in the primacy of the flesh. Because the body was God's most beautiful gift, they maintained, we should have no reservations about touching, caressing, and holding one another without inhibition. To help new converts like me grasp this truth, they passed out hashish. All my complexes seemed to subside.

After that first time, I went back to a couple of other gatherings. But then one morning they were suddenly gone. No one in their neighborhood had even seen them go. To this day, I don't know what happened to them. That's the way a lot of things ended back in that period.

Chapter 8

Spending Time With The Movie Stars

Then there was Tony.

One day a friend of mine knocked at my door in desperate straits. He couldn't keep Tony in his apartment, so could I help him out and take him? Tony was a monkey, and he made it clear immediately that he had no objections to moving in with me. How could I say no? From that day on, wherever you saw me, you were sure to see Tony. And I wasn't the only one taken with him. Around the same time, I struck up a friendship with a sweet elderly Russian couple, George and Zina. Like me, they were captivated by Tony and frequently asked whether they couldn't "monkey-sit" at their suite at the Resident Palace Hotel. From what I could tell, Tony had nothing against boarding for a few days every once in awhile in an exclusive Rome hotel. Tony also provided a vivid example of how little I was thinking of my professional future in those days.

One evening, I was introduced to an important Hollywood studio executive who had seen me at a party during his previous trip to Rome and had been determined to meet me. We ended up dancing until four in the morning, when he suddenly announced he had to catch a plane back to America at eight o'clock. Exhausted as I was from solid partying for several days, I invited him back to my place, fully intent on making love to him until he had to leave for the airport. But no sooner did I hit the bed than I passed out.

Then Tony moved in. Not at all used to having men around, the monkey jumped on the executive's face, first kissing him, then starting to masturbate. The poor man couldn't get away, because Tony was holding on to his hair. I woke up to screams of, "Get him off me! Get him off me!" After I had freed my important "date" for the night, I couldn't help laughing. The man laughed as much as I did. And we kept it up all the way out to the airport. "I come all the way to Rome to see you with these expectations of a great love affair!" he kept roaring. "And what I end up with is a monkey jerking off in my face!" So much for that "in" to Hollywood. But we'd had some laughs, right?

Dealing with Tony was in fact a full-time job. One of his favorite games was squatting down on the steering wheel of my car, a habit that never failed to get a rise out of other drivers. Once, when I was caught in a traffic jam, he jumped out the window and disappeared under another car. Naturally, I immediately made a show of myself by leaping out from behind the wheel and, totally oblivious to the traffic lights and the honking cars, started yelling "Tony! Tony! Where are you!" like some mother desperate to find a misbehaving child. That day I was lucky, and Tony came out from his hiding place and hopped up into my arms. It didn't always work out that way.

One morning, I wanted Tony to come with me on an interview, but I was running late and had little patience for his usual meandering around the apartment before he decided to do what I wanted him to do. When he responded to my final plea by flashing me his ass, I told myself he would be all right alone, and left. One of his favorite features about my apartment was that the balcony looked over an adjoining rooftop, allowing him to clamber down and explore more than the apartment itself. But that morning, he apparently slipped and ended up tumbling into the arms of a neighbor on the roof. The man was so stunned to have a monkey fall in his arms that he instinctively threw it off him, pitching Tony down several floors into an abandoned basement.

When I got home with no sign of Tony, I went crazy. After dashing from door to door in the hopes that somebody had seen him, I called the Fire Department. Because my neighborhood consisted of extremely narrow streets, the arrival of fire trucks backed up traffic everywhere. Like it or not, the whole quarter became involved in the search. Finally, the firemen found Tony. He had apparently hit his head fatally. Worse, the basement where he landed was home to ferocious rats. The firemen wouldn't let me see what remained of Tony, but one of them admitted that only his head was left. I was so distraught by what had happened that I called my mother and got a line through to her for the first time since I had left Poland for Italy. "Tony is gone!" I sobbed to her, "I've lost my poor Tony!"

My mother's sympathy lasted until she found out that Tony had been a monkey. Then she scolded me for crying over a monkey when thousands of people were dying around the world every hour. It was a line I had heard from her before. And I hadn't missed it.

But why have only a couple of reasons to be depressed when, with a little effort, you can find more? Around the time that Tony died, my Russian friend, George. was working on a script with Rudy Maté, the Polish-born filmmaker who had made his mark initially as a cameraman for such internationally prestigious directors, as Carl Dreyer, Fritz Lang, and René Clair and who had then gone to Hollywood to work as both a photographer and a director in *The Dark Past,* and *The Violent Men,* among others. According to George and Zina, we would have made a great match, both personally and professionally.

But as much as Rudy and I were attracted to each other, I was in love at the time with an even more noted Hollywood director, and, true to form, I couldn't see anything else. I was so in love with the director that I ignored the most telltale signs of a married man, who really had no intention of leaving his wife for me. Try this for blindness: I was so involved with the director, I even rebuffed the advances of the handsome Max Schell, then working with my paramour on a film. When, inevitably, the director returned to the States, making it very clear that our affair was over, I sank as low as I ever had up to that point. In retrospect, I realize that if I had followed the advice of George and Zina about Rudy, I might at the very least have gotten out of Italy, soon to be the scene of an unhappiness that made even my disillusionment over the director seem trivial.

The finish of my love affair was in keeping with a general sense of endings around me. Tony was gone. The dolce vita atmosphere had expired. The nights no longer seemed exciting. And worse, the practical problems that I had somehow managed to keep at arm's length for so long rushed in at me demanding more serious attention. To supplement my on-and-off income as an actress, I had to take a job as an assistant for an American production company.

There was one consolation: That was how I met my future husband.

Chapter 9

The Only Husband I Ever Had

The man I came to know as Max was a prominent lawyer in the motion picture industry. I was having coffee with a couple of producers at the Hotel Excelsior bar, when he joined us. He had startlingly pale skin, accentuated all the more by the black suit he was wearing in mourning for his recently deceased wife. To me, he looked like a dead man walking. When he first opened his mouth, he spoke in such a low, feeble voice I could hardly hear him. But this first impression was deceptive, because in answer to something else said at the table, he began telling funny stories that had me roaring. It was as though Woody Allen had become a funeral director. I was intrigued at once.

Max, I soon learned, had one of the most astute legal minds in Italy. Though he served officially as a legal counsel only for Rome-based production companies, virtually every significant executive in the international film industry held him in high esteem. He had first earned their respect as the head of Scalera film company which had pioneered the Italian neo-realist film era, marked by such monumental films as Fellini's *La Strada,* Rosellini's *Open City* and De Sica's *The Bicycle Thief.*

But even producing wasn't enough for him. When he wasn't working through the night on screenplays, he was acquiring his law degree, eventually gaining a professorship in international copyright law at Rome University. If he had his preference, I think, he would have continued to concentrate on producing and writing, but when his wife complained that he wasn't spending enough time with her and their children, he gave up the open-ended life of making movies in favor of the more regulated schedule of an entertainment lawyer. Not even that stopped some of the biggest names in the business from calling on him for help in projects that he was not directly involved in.

One of his more venerable clients was Orson Welles, who had been infamous for his ego, even before *Citizen Kane*. By the postwar years, Welles had become so imperious that few could communicate with him, and not too many of those felt they were being treated as equals. Again and again, Max would receive calls from producers or directors asking him to step in and deal with Welles, because Orson respected him. This was borne home after the death of Max's wife. Welles suddenly called from California and said he needed Max to hop on the next plane to help him out on a legal matter. When Max protested this was impossible, that he was in mourning and alone with his four sons, Welles didn't hesitate to tell him bring them along. Of course, it was a way of distracting him and the children from the pain of their loss. Such understanding friends are a lucky thing in times of deep distress. Max never forgot that gesture of Orson to whisk him and his sons away from the scene of their bereavement, if only for a couple of weeks.

It wasn't easy for me to get to know him. Aside from his shock over his wife's death and the need to raise his sons alone, he was a very shy man. But I persisted, finally using the excuse of wanting to talk business with him to get him to agree to meet me for dinner. I wore the miniest of miniskirts; it never occurred to me that my appearance would embarrass him. But his attempts to avoid admitting his embarrassment only endeared him to me more. As we talked, I felt a marvelous sense of freedom, simultaneously spontaneous and protected, and I didn't wait too long to tell him. He seemed astonished to hear such an unaccustomed mixture of naïveté and sincerity.

But while we got along famously, the thought of a romance never occurred to him. Among other things, he was 30 years older than I was. He was also a deeply religious man, approaching religion in the same way that he did the law, strict adherence to all the rules. I used to tease him about it, telling him he lived in fear of God pointing a finger at him the way Michelangelo had depicted God touching Adam in his Sistine Chapel fresco. Because Max was so reserved, it was hard to know what he was thinking at such moments. Yet, as little as he spoke, he was a wonderful listener, and this reminded me a great deal of my father.

The first time Max invited me to his beautiful home on the Via Appia, I was overwhelmed. The house reflected its owner: impeccable decor, furnished in a spare Imperial Roman style. The courtesy and discretion of the servants left me with no little doubt that the household was well-managed. The atmosphere reminded me a great deal of my parents' home in Warsaw. While I don't necessarily believe in Kismet, I really do think the two of us were brought together by an extraordinary magnetic energy.

Max's sons were 12, 15, 19, and 21. He was the kind of father who, if one of the boys did something to displease him, would never make a scene, but instead project the certainty that they were aware of what they had done and would do something to correct it in the future. He truly preferred complimenting people to criticizing them. He seemed to live according to a motto of "forget the bad and remember the good." He adopted the same attitude toward me. If I unwittingly offended some mutual acquaintance, he would just say, "Don't worry, Maria. Your little Max will always be close to you; I will never abandon you." What a great man!

Although he was short and frail looking, Max made up for it in strength of character. He didn't need to push anyone around to get his way; he used politeness and firmness, as a diplomat would have. You could never forget that he was a Neapolitan, either. Shrewdness, comic ability, and superstitiousness came in the same package. At times he would take advantage of his fragile physique to the point of winning an argument by feigning a heart attack, right down to a farcical pratfall. This was always a last recourse, however, since he also shared that Neapolitan trait of never wanting to tempt fate in case it decided you were mocking it.

But strength of character could only go so far. The fact of the matter was, Max wasn't faking all his frailties. For one thing, he suffered from Parkinson's disease, causing his hands to shake. He had also suffered physically as well as mentally from his wife's long ordeal with cancer, a five-year tribulation of losing an eye and a breast, before finally succumbing. Max had been on the verge of a nervous breakdown through this gruesome experience. He perspired so excessively that he rarely left the house without extra shirts in the car, and even they didn't always prevent him from arriving home again drenched to the skin.

One of his foibles was an inability to make up his mind, especially when it came to social engagements. If he had five given invitations on an evening, he would make sure that he would go to all of them, however briefly, rather than have to choose to drop one from consideration. The result, of course, was an incredibly hectic schedule that required all his mental agility and still left time for him to be with his family. Even as well off as he was, he worried about money, particularly after having to give some family members. "If it keeps going on like this, I'll be broke!" he exclaimed to me more than once. "Why do I always have to be the one doing everything? I work like a dog and I never get help from anybody!" Of course this venting was usually its own reward. Whenever I or anybody else would respond by offering to help with a specific problem, the answer would be a rebuff along the lines of "By the time I got through explaining what has to be done I can get it done myself."

Through this period of seeing Max I still lived alone in my apartment with my tiny black dachshund Golia (for Goliath). Golia was my constant companion, as Tony had been. Fortunately for me, he and Max got along famously. Between the two of them, in fact, I felt wonderfully protected. Max never imposed restrictions on our relationship, and I always felt free to tell him about what was happening in my life without fear of criticism. There were many moments when I believed I was as happy as I could be and that this happiness would last forever.

But then one night, returning home from an especially rowdy party, I passed out on my bed, only to come to a few hours later to find myself sitting in the lotus position near my front door and meditating. I hadn't been in the habit of meditating and couldn't think of any reason except that I had drunk too much and hadn't known what I was doing. But then suddenly I felt this tremendous rush in my head, as though a raging storm had been released within my brain.

It was an incredible sensation, and in retrospect I can only conclude that I was open to it because my overindulgence in alcohol had relaxed my nerves, muscles, and every other part of my body. I remember thinking right away that what was really stirring were my Tibetan origins, which had remained practically locked away within me. How else explain this sudden, profound desire for the stillness and calm that can be reached only through knowledge and truth?

From that evening on, I felt a powerfully hungry desire for knowledge. I became convinced that my limited schooling imposed by the Communist system left me full of hang-ups. This reminds me of my father's teaching that when our inner self is dissatisfied, our body and soul would shrink rather than grow. I resolved to change that, immediately.

No surprise, I turned first to Buddhist philosophy. I had never really learned anything about Buddhism from my father, so scouring the shelves of the public library for any and all books on the subject always brought a revelation. I began to fantasize about meeting a Lama at whose feet I would learn to attain Nirvana.

There was little abstract about my meditating. Once, I vividly recalled for the first time in many years a terrible woman with whom my mother had formed an unhealthy relationship. Despite many layers of makeup, this woman couldn't hide the fact that she didn't like washing her face, or any other part of her body, for that matter. She claimed to be a powerful medium, able to contact spirits who communicated with her in various languages. My mother had begun consulting this wretch during the turbulence of the Nazi occupation, and had continued doing so after the war, much to the displeasure of my brothers and me.

Through my meditation, I began to understand that my mother had fallen within this woman's negative magnetism, much the way the Czarina had fallen under the spell of Rasputin. And because this so-called medium was actually an envious woman frustrated in some greater ambition, she wanted nothing so much as to see her most dire predictions come true. Wasn't it Rasputin who, at the end of his life, pronounced a malediction on Russia?

As I reflected on the malignant forces that had been operating within my own family, I thought I understood my brothers better. Why Richard had embarked on the tormented path that would lead to his suicide. Why George was drinking himself to death. Why Peter had inherited my mother's dictatorial temperment and made him intolerant of others, who didn't believe and live as he did. Was it pure accident that we had all these family problems with that devious medium of my mother's around?

For sure, Max would have never abided such a woman in his household. He was frightened of fortune tellers, and didn't mind admitting he was. And to the extent that I believe they are people who can trigger a negative chain of magnetism, I think Max was right because you never know when it will stop. These people can turn your life into hell, they can take from you the clearness of your thoughts and your strong will which you need to guide your life.

And I was soon to meet the man who would do the same to me.

One day in the summer of 1972, I was meditating in my living room when Giovanni, the young florist on my corner, arrived. As he began potting flowers on my balcony, he noticed me sitting in the lotus position and laughed. I told him of my goal to study one day with a lama so I could attain Nirvana.

"What are you going to do, travel all the way to India or Nepal?" he asked. "If you want to meet a holy man, you don't have to go that far. I can take you to someone right now who's far more powerful than any Lama."

Trusting and naïve as I was, I agreed to go with him to meet this special person. I'll admit I had some when I got up behind him on his motorbike and had to hold on for dear life, while he zigzagged at breathtaking speeds for what turned out to be a fifty-mile run to the small town of San Vittorino. The most prominent structure in the town was a large, unfinished church latticed with scaffolding. Pending the completion of construction, parishioners were using an older, smaller church next to it. Nearby was a long, narrow shack largely built out of cartons, and behind that a large building, housing a convent and a seminary.

Still knowing little about Catholicism, I felt no impulse to enter the church. But what struck me immediately was the tranquility and silence of my surroundings. The air felt so charged with electricity that it seemed heavy without being onerous. It reminded me of the air before a summer thunderstorm.

I sat down on a bench under a tree, content to absorb the positive energy around me. Following Buddhist practice, I tried to create a void within me by controlling my breathing, hoping that would help me assimilate the energy, perhaps reach that higher state of awareness the Buddhists call the "opening of the kundalini "

Suddenly, Giovanni said to me, "Look over there! See that priest? That's the man I told you about! That's Friar G. !"

I lifted my eyes to take in a huge heavyset man of about 40 in a long black robe. His face was red and round, his nose was large, his mouth small and stingy, his teeth misshapen and yellow. I couldn't see his eyes—they were hidden behind dark sunglasses that accentuated his skin, a sickly, anemic white that was in sharp contrast to his robust size, for he was tall and ungainly, well over six foot, well over 250 pounds. Both of his hands were covered in bandages.

Trailing in his wake was a procession of believers, all of them emerging from the church and heading for the cardboard shack. Many in the crowd were peasants and townspeople, but others looked to be a little higher on the social scale. At the shack, Friar G. waited until everyone had gathered before him, then held out his bandaged right hand to be kissed, imparting his blessing to each congregant.

I got up from the bench and moved closer. There was a scent of perfume around Friar G. but it certainly didn't come from his mouth. I was shocked to hear the way he was addressing his supplicants—brusque to the point of rudeness.

"Look at her," he would say in a tone I immediately associated with a lowborn peasant. "What does she want from me? Take a look at that face. That's the face of somebody who belongs in an insane asylum!" Then he would turn on somebody else. "What are you staring at, you idiot? Think you're any better than she is? You don't belong here. Go home, if you know what's good for you."

At first, I excused his rudeness by recalling that Giovanni had told me he was from Tuscany. Although Tuscans speak the most classical Italian, they are also known for their casual bitterness and blaspheming. Whatever the reason, Friar G.'s behavior didn't appear to alienate the people he was denouncing as imbeciles and idiots. As I overheard one say: "What are you complaining about? He's a good man suffering for us. We should be grateful to him."

Those words were to come back to me more than once over the following years.

Chapter 10

The Beginning Of Being Possessed

My curiosity whetted, I began going back to San Vittorino without Giovanni. I never ventured into the church, but was content to absorb the atmosphere that radiated from the site. The silence intrigued me; it was truly transcendent. Imagine standing by the ocean in the middle of the night, taking in the full force of the water's energy through the sound of the crashing waves, but with the sound itself submerged by an engulfing quiet. The quiet of infinity. That was the kind of palpable energy I felt at San Vittorino. I was certain it had the power to open my kundalini and satisfy my craving for knowledge.

One day, I overheard a conversation that told me a little more about Friar G., who, it was said, had been a sacristan of another church where he had fallen under the sway of Padre Pio. As I was to come to understand, there was no way of understanding Friar G. without first understanding Padre Pio.

Padre Pio, who had died only a short time before my first visit to San Vittorino, had, by the age of five, the popular story goes, already offered his faith to Francis of Assisi and, suffering from poor health, spent many hours in church praying to the saint. He entered a Franciscan convent where, in 1918, his fellow monks found him on the floor, bleeding and unconscious, at the foot of a crucifix. His hands and feet were perforated as if by nails, duplicating Christ's wounds on the cross.

From that day on Padre Pio was frequently in a state of ecstasy when he celebrated Mass. When his parishioners began comparing him to Christ, he not only didn't dispute them, but also claimed he had a special mission to relive Christ's martyrdom. Among other things, this meant submitting to the same physical, psychological, and moral experiences that Christ had endured. In time, of course, Padre Pio became an international attraction, drawing believers (or those who wanted to believe) from around the world. Friar G. it was said, had inherited Padre Pio's stigmata, accounting for the bandages on his hands and the reverential way his followers kissed them.

Rarely did Friar G. appear without several henchmen, seminarians who had the task of supervising the people drawn to him. If a parishioner missed Mass, they would accost him and pressure him to go to confession and atone for such a sin. But none of them ever approached me or tried to get me to take an active part in their rituals. In retrospect, I have attributed this to Friar G.'s perspicacity. He must have understood at once that I was something of a wild little animal, and canny hunter that he was, knew that if he tried to force me into something, I would flee and never come back.

On my third visit to San Vittorino, I witnessed a bizarre event. A paralyzed Belgian had come to the church in the belief that its energy could heal him. I was told he had remained inside for 72 hours, marking every sunset by taking out a flute and playing until dawn. On the third day he suddenly rose from his wheelchair, exciting a great cry of "Miracle! Miracle!" from those present. I didn't know much about miracles except that I didn't really believe in them. Looking back on it, I believe that his powerful will with his own energy, as well as the present energy in the church, had triggered off such strong emotions in him that he was able to heal himself.

Months passed, and I continued going to San Vittorino and taking my place under the old tree. More and more people showed up, many undoubtedly drawn by the well-publicized story of the Belgian flutist. They were united in their fervor showing their incredible devotion by prostrating in prayer, kissing the statues of Christ and the saints, and blessing themselves with holy water. On the first day of every month Friar G. held a special ceremony for pilgrims not only from Italy, but from around the world. Sometimes there were more than a thousand people at these ceremonies.

Because of my experiences at San Vittorino, I became more curious about Catholicism, and I enrolled at the Gregorian University in Rome, one of the most important Jesuit institutions in the world. I wanted to know more about Jesus Christ, more about stigmata. Max was very proud when I told him that I had enrolled in the university's philosophy and theology classes. As far as he had been concerned, my major deficiency had been a lack of religious conviction, and he saw my matriculation at the university as a way to correcting that. His servants and some of his friends were more skeptical. All they saw was a gold-digger stooping to another tactic to gain power within the family and the household.

We ignored the skeptics as best we could, and spent a lot of time together over the next two years. We never really thought of marriage, until one day Max blurted out, "Better you should get my pension than the government." And with that deliberately unromantic pronouncement (though I never doubted he truly loved me), he proposed marriage. But because of the vast gap in our ages, he really didn't want to make a big fuss of a wedding, so we held a very private church ceremony to which only a handful of friends were invited.

We continued to maintain separate residences for awhile. After Max's middle son got married and moved his wife into the villa on the Via Appia, Max began spending more time at my apartment, commuting back and forth, as he thought the situation warranted. The fact of the matter was, he was very possessive of his sons and didn't want to share them with me. I didn't press the point, because I didn't want it to be a source of conflict between us, but it was one of several pressures on our marriage.

Another drawback was this: Through Max I met many noted producers (Carlo Ponti, Dino DeLaurentiis) and directors (Franco Zeffirelli, Michelangelo Antonioni), but they couldn't have been more paternalistic in their refusal to hire me. Whenever I read an exciting part and asked for an audition, I received the same answer: "And who would take care of poor Max while you're working?" Since I still regarded myself as a professional actress, I was deeply offended by these rebuffs. Because of Max's great popularity in the industry, the gold ring on my finger had reduced me to his caretaker in other people's eyes.

At least I got to go to a lot of places. Max was always being invited to film festivals and production locations, usually to arbitrate some quarrel. That was how we got to Tunisia to see Roman Polanski and Yugoslavia to calm down Kirk Douglas. Anthony Quinn was another who counted heavily on Max, and has told people Max had a great deal to do with his getting the title role in *Zorba The Greek*. It was also Max who persuaded Luchino Visconti that Burt Lancaster would be right for his screen adaptation of *The Leopard*.

Through all this, my strongest desire remained that of attaining the deep silence I knew was somewhere within me and that was the well of all happiness. In my search for this tranquility, I believed I was following in my father's footsteps, for he had always been meditating and reflecting on the meaning of life. I regretted not having understood this about him, when he had been alive. (He had died in 1961.)

How many things he could have taught me! I hadn't even understood how philosophical he had been in referring to the cycles of death and rebirth, the cause of one of my most embarrassing moments. One day, I had been in attendance at a lecture my father had given to a distinguished group that included university professors. When I heard him talking about death, I assumed he was talking about his own death, and began crying and screaming. He had been mortified, and the others in the audience had been no less uncomfortable. Of course, he had only been referring to the process of how a rebirth was possible only after death and that in this sense, death didn't mean the end of existence, but only the end of a certain phase of life.

Despite the obviousness of my debt to my father for my craving for knowledge, I was far from understanding the nature of the seeds he had planted. Subliminally, I began to give more credit to God than to my father. It was God and Jesus who deserved my love and gratitude. Where did that feeling come from? I didn't know, but it got stronger every day. I was so in love with God, I was astonished that a human being had the capacity to love so much.

My breath couldn't hold all this love; my heart was exploding from joy. I was profoundly grateful to God for opening new horizons to me, for introducing me to a life full of wisdom, love, curiosity and happiness. I felt reborn, and yet not with the arrogance of assuming I was unique. I truly believed that my euphoria could be anybody's with a commitment to approaching and understanding God. I couldn't have been the only one who had gone through life with melancholic longings that had actually been a desire to discover my true essence and live in full awareness of it.

Yes, I sometimes had doubts whether the sensations that gripped me were real. But my passion for God and Jesus was so intense and spontaneous that even priests and nuns were mystified. I felt privileged. What could rituals offer that I didn't already have?

But then I decided I was doing neither myself nor Max any good by always going up to San Vittorino and just camping down on my bench under the tree. So I overcame my qualms and finally entered Friar G.'s church. I began praying there for Max, who was becoming sicker by the day. His Parkinson's had degenerated to the point that he shook uncontrollably whenever he lifted a glass. How could I not avert my eyes sometimes when his face would abruptly turn to a ghostly white or his irises would seem to vanish, leaving only the whites of his eyes visible? And so on down the list: He was losing weight, he could barely sleep, his blood pressure was abnormally high, he even had a thyroid imbalance that was playing havoc with his hormones. This man, I thought to myself, was finished. And it was clear from the anxiety in the voices of his friends that, whatever reassurances they might have given him, they thought so, too.

I was worried that his sons could not sustain another death. I was so concerned for Max and his sons that I would have gladly given my own life, if in so doing, I could have assured their happiness.

Within a few months of entering Friar G.'s church, I began going to Confession and taking Communion. I also decided to go on a Lenten retreat. It lasted ten days and was conducted by the Jesuit who had married Max and me and who had taught my stepsons. When he began talking about the mystery of God's revelation to humanity, I was so moved I sobbed openly. The Jesuit later phoned Max to tell him that he had never witnessed a more sincere conversion than mine, that God must have touched me with a special grace. I was constantly crying on my knees in gratitude for the love God gave me. I was talking to birds and asking them to fly higher so that they could convey my love to God directly.

I had a fixed routine. Every morning, I attended a six o'clock Mass. From there I went to the university. Then, promptly at one o'clock, I was back in church. Whenever I was in church, I recited a rosary to the Madonna. Never did I have a moment of doubt. The truth I believed I possessed didn't leave any room for doubts. I felt as innocent as my father had been, completely trustful.

Breaks in the routine were occasions when I thought I could show my devotion even more visibly. For example, I once volunteered for a pilgrimage to Lourdes, the noted sanctuary in France. Every day there, I went to the spot set aside for devotion to the Crucifixion. Here I watched thousands of pilgrims every day say their rosaries, a tactile reminder of Jesus's Via Crucis. They fell to their knees, they wept openly. For so many of them, it was the last hope of a cure from some physical ailment or of a solution to another kind of problem. They were ready to part with their last dollar if it meant a miracle that would transform their lives.

Sometimes, the attendants drenched the pilgrims with freezing water. The shock to the system, I was told, was supposed to make a miracle more likely. A nun warned me not to submit to such treatment, saying that some elderly people in particular had been known to die from either the shock or from a flu contracted from the water, but I didn't pay much attention to her. I was too euphoric for such practical considerations.

I, too, began to identify myself intensely with Jesus and with his suffering on the cross. I'd stop at each station, tears pouring from my eyes. In the end, though, I was weeping more and more. I was gripped by such a visceral need to release my emotions that it was as if I no longer had any control over myself. The suffering I was experiencing was hysterical and irrational. I was in a frenzy of desire as I tried to identify myself with the image of Jesus, using all my senses so I could partake of his suffering, though without understanding why I wanted to do such a thing.

It was so satisfying, and so emotionally exhilarating, and my senses were heightened to a point of extreme sexual gratification. Only in this case, the sexuality was being sublimated into spirituality. I would return from my visits to the shrine with a sense of utter fulfillment. I finally understood the attraction of these shrines for pilgrims, why they went through such difficulties to get to them, and why they longed to go back again and again.

My husband was always in my thoughts, and I kept praying for my dear Max. Yet I have to admit I was still so self-absorbed and so delighted to discover more about God's love for me and my immense love for Him that it dominated my body and spirit, leaving little room for anything else.

I was introduced to some Pentecostal groups, who were just as passionate in their convictions as I was in mine. I couldn't help being drawn to them because they, like myself, were in search of energy. It was a complete obsession. They were even wary of shaking hands, because it might mean a loss of energy. And they believed in miracles, which were manifested in the laying on of hands and speaking in tongues. They were completely convinced that they could cure those who were sick or incapacitated through the power of prayer. After half an hour of fervent devotion, during which they would clap their hands and babble in tongues, one member of the group would stand up and announce that the sick person in their midst had been saved. One such episode still sticks in my mind.

"Stand up," the leader shouted out jubilantly, addressing a man for whom the group had been praying. "You are cured through the power of Jesus!"

"I'm sorry," the man mumbled, "but I can't stand. I'm too sick to stand."

"What do you mean, you can't stand?" the leader demanded. "You have been saved by Jesus, you can stand."

But the man remained obstinately in his seat.

"If you can't stand, it can only mean that you are not a believer in Jesus! If you were a believer you would be healed."

That was how it was: Those for whom miraculous cures failed to have any effect were cut off from the congregation; their faith was simply not strong enough.

But over time, I realized that the Pentecostals were as powerful an addiction as any drug for me. I'd grown so morbidly attached to them that I didn't want to abandon them. Yet even so, I became suspicious that perhaps they might represent a coercive force. It was painful trying to extricate myself from their pull on me, and now that I reflect, I realize that I couldn't have done it on my own. My suspicion was correct; I was being helped by Friar G. He was responsible for causing me to doubt them and to finally end my association with them out of his fear of losing me. My destiny lay elsewhere, in St. Vittorino.

Chapter 11

The Transference Of Someone Else's Sickness To Me

I became a regular at the rites at St. Vittorino. As soon as I had finished my university classes for the day, I would make the fifty-mile trip from Rome. Among the other regular visitors was a 20-year-old I came to know as Paolo. He was blond, skinny, and with a paralysis that he was clearly counting on combating through the intercession of Friar G. I sensed a deep psychic connection between the young man and the monk. How could I not, when each time the two of them were together, Friar G, began shaking his head vigorously, somewhat like a chicken pecking for grain? My first thought was that this bizarre movement was meant to release the excess energy, positive or negative, that Friar G. had absorbed from everyone around him, particularly from Paolo, whom he was trying to heal. In the event, I was half-right.

Friar G.'s benediction consisted of blessings with holy water and the kissing of his bandaged stigmata. His followers used the occasion to ask him for his special prayers for them and their loved ones, and their rapt expressions while they conferred with him stunned me. Suppose he did help them, I wondered? Why not also me and Max?

Finally, during one benediction, I summoned the courage to approach him. The stigmata seemed to give off a scent of gardenias. When his penetrating eyes settled on me, my expectations leaped into my throat. "Please," I asked, "pray for Max." His only response was a slight nod, but then and there, that felt like enough. Since I believed that Jesus Christ lived through Friar G.'s stigmata, how could

I feel anything but invigorated? I came away convinced that Max would shortly be restored to health.

My excitement became such that one Sunday I got Max to agree to come with me to St. Vittorino. Not only didn't he object, he acted proud of me for trying to find my way toward the truth of things. As he himself had a habit of saying, "The ways of God are many. You never know which one is the right one." When it came his turn to kiss Friar G.'s hand, he simply said: "Please, Friar G., would you be so kind as to pray for my sons?"

One day not long afterward, I found myself in church moving my head back and forth. It took me a moment to realize I was emulating the movements Friar G. had made with Paolo and at other blessings. At that moment I couldn't explain why; perhaps I was in an hypnotized state. I accepted everything that went on at the "sanctuary," no matter how bizarre, without question. I just took it for granted that I would experience unaccustomed sensations. For some reason, I felt that the movement of my head was connected to the healing process necessary for Max's recovery. Friar G. was transferring my husband's sickness to my body!

I wasn't worried. As a physician's daughter, I had become accustomed to making light of health concerns, and believed I had a strong constitution. (Max himself never tired of teasing me about my attitude. "We better be careful with her around," he liked to say. "She's a descendant of Genghis Khan.") Nevertheless, I began to feel a vague soreness. My limbs suddenly felt inflamed, as though from some mild attack of arthritis. And then my hands began to shake, just like my husband's.

The reassuring part of this was that the shaking confirmed in my mind that Max's illness was being transferred into my body. The worrying part was that the pain and the shaking got worse. My will was abandoning me, I became short of breath. My lungs had to make the greatest effort for every intake of air. My mind became muddled. The simplest thoughts seemed to evaporate before I could seize them fully. I began to function like a robot, concerned only with moving through the least sources of pain. As weeks stretched into months, the pain only intensified. What got me through it, even with a sense of satisfaction, was that it was all happening so Max could regain his own health.

And Friar G.? Even in my anguish (because of my anguish?) I was captivated, a slave without protest. Wasn't he actually bestowing his grace on me? Wasn't he, through this act of transference, trying to strip me of my worldly nature and join me to a greater spiritual reality? I was gradually falling under the power of Friar G. without realizing that his transference filled my head with his words and I repeated them over and over again; I couldn't stop. I felt like a puppet on a string, bobbing my head up and down while I mumbled, "Jesus, Jesus, Friar G., Friar G., have pity, have pity, mea culpa, mea culpa, I love you, I love you."

And then there were the tears. The only logical explanation I had for my sudden habit of crying whenever and wherever was to recall that psychotherapeutic process in which a profoundly repressed feeling is brought to the surface. Friar G.'s transference, I told myself, was designed to cleanse my ego, to free it of unnecessary desires, thoughts, and impulses, and no human action reflected that process better, both literally and symbolically, than crying.

Of course, this wasn't always a pleasant experience, far from it. Among other things, my tears unleashed an old resentment over the way my mother had treated me. I believed that the love I was receiving from Jesus was filling a void that she had left in me. It reminded me that I was still, emotionally at least, an infant lying in an incubator desperately in need of the most basic parental warmth. Every teardrop was regret for what I had been denied and gratitude for what I had finally been given.

These energy surges overcame me everywhere: at St. Vittorino, in Rome, on the road. I believed I abetted the experience by never being without my rosary, fingering the beads as a constant prod to my devotion. And little by little I also became convinced that the energy given to me was not for me alone, that I had to share it. It was in this state of mind that I began doing something that, only a short time before I would have been mortified even to contemplate doing, accosting strangers on the street. "Please listen to me," I would say. "There is a great spiritual leader you must go and see. He has stigmata. What clearer sign can there be that Jesus lives through him?"

Of course, some people fled. But not that many less than I might have expected. There seemed to be genuine curiosity about what I told them. I didn't really understand why until one day in the center of Rome, a man asked with a smile whether I didn't have anything better to do with my time. I realized with a shock that we were connected, me and this perfect stranger, through an intense sexual energy. Moreover, there was nothing I could do about it; it was happening against my will.

The penny dropped. It was this sexual energy that Friar G. was using to draw people to him through me. They were attracted to me sexually, so they were vulnerable and followed me to St. Vittorino where he could enlarge his following. I understood that the most powerful possessions happen through sexuality. It struck me that all my spiritual experience, my love for God, even my constant need to cry was the manifestation of sexual energy.

Despite this realization, which made me feel used, I continued going to St. Vittorino. I became so obsessively attached to Max that suddenly all life revolved around his salvation. Meantime, the same monotonous words dictated by Friar G. poured from my lips: "Jesus, Jesus, Friar G., Friar G., have pity, have pity, mea culpa, mea culpa, I love you, I love you." Somebody was taking over my life. It became impossible to pursue my studies, my head began to feel emptier and emptier and I couldn't find a point of reference in my brain.

I couldn't take the exams and I felt ashamed when I had to withdraw. I had so much wanted to live up to the expectations my teachers had of me. In many ways my time at the university had been the most beautiful period of my life; it had broadened my intellectual horizons thrillingly. I missed my studies very much but there was no way I could have gone on, not with my constant physical pains and a growing mental fog that seemed to leave only Friar G. and his priorities visible.

With the loss of my self-control, I became increasingly disoriented. To leave my apartment became an agony. Like a small child, I became fearful about crossing a street. And then I realized something else about my persistent pains and increasing difficulties just to get around: I was worse off than Max. It couldn't have been pains that I had adopted through Friar G.'s agency! Max was nowhere near as paralytic as I was becoming.

Then I remembered the 20-year-old blond man, Paolo. He had been paralyzed. I had been there the day he had gone to Friar G. for help. They had both seen me. Was it possible that Friar G. had detected in me a healing ability that I had never been aware of? Was it possible that in fact I had actually inherited such an ability from my father without knowing it? That seemed to be only one answer. And it infuriated me. Friar G. was using Max as a facade behind which he hid the paralyzed Paolo. Once he developed in me a morbid and terrible attachment to Max by intensifying my love and affection, like a thief in the night, he stole them and deployed them for his own purposes. No wonder I couldn't walk and instead of getting better I was getting sicker and sicker. The transference had not been only from Max to me, but also from Paolo to me.

What about this beautiful God and this beautiful Jesus that Friar G. was showing me? Where was He really? How could I have suspected that He would turn out to be a hallucination? What kind of God would allow Friar G. to use such deceit as exploiting the stigmata in order to achieve his own false and woefully human ends by cheating and stealing?

I began to go from one church to another. Always I would do the same: walk in, fall down on my knees, and beseech Jesus, the Madonna, the Holy Spirit, God the Father to set me free. I continued to pray for months, but there was never an answer to my prayers, only a terrible silence.

I grew sicker. The monotone rhythms of my life reduced my days and nights to a virtual fog; one flowed into another until the passage of time was lost to me. I began to intuit that I was possessed without knowing anything about these matters. I was void, my body merely a container. I dared not tell anyone, even Max, what was consuming me. I was afraid they would think I was insane. In fact, I felt lifeless, as though I were buried alive and was powerless to resist.

I spent untold hours in bed, constantly jerking my head back and forth. As I moved my head, I tried to focus on the response of the muscles and nerves around my vertebrae. I was becoming aware that by doing so I was provoking a neural reactivation, transmitting at least a residual elasticity to the muscles and tendons. Was this not the ultimate practice, and desperation, of the paralytic? And who, after all, could possibly be more of a paralytic than I was by this point? My complete domination by Friar G. was giving him access, I supposed, to the synapses of the neurons in my brain through which he was able to transmit his message, commanding me to assume his burden. I'd undergone a complete change; my nerves were raw, I'd become oversensitive and strung out. Friar G. was manipulating my emotions, magnifying them to keep me frightened and guilty.

One day I was seized by a panic attack at the kitchen table. It began as a stirring, then engulfed me completely. I was shaking in terror. I don't know where this fear came from. I looked over at the window. It seemed to beckon to me. I felt an overwhelming urge to go through it, five floors down to the street. I was so terrified by the impulse that I clutched at the table with all my strength. It became my life preserver. As long as I held on to that table, I told myself, I would not lose consciousness, would not make one surrender too many.

Chapter 12

Discovery Of Spiritual Sexuality

I don't remember how long I sat there gripping the edge of the table. But finally the attack passed, and I calmed down. I was certain Friar G. had been responsible. But what conceivable reason could he have had for putting me through such a terrifying experience? I could imagine only that he had wanted to free me from my innate sense of fear. I thought of Max. Following his wife's death he had been one great pocket of fear, and only his strong will had allowed him to maintain self-control.

I came to the conclusion that all humanity has this sense of fear buried deep inside them. I instinctively connected my experience with that of primordial humans. The fear that afflicted our ancestors must have originated as a response to calamitous natural phenomena that they were unable to explain. On the other hand, by repressing the fear, we don't recognize the truth that is inside us and so we hold back our emotional freedom.

Once I brought a young woman to Friar G's church. She was very sweet, about twenty years old. Having accomplished my mission and gotten her to the church, I lost contact with her. But one day by chance I happened to meet her mother, who let me know that her daughter had committed suicide by jumping out of a window. Apparently, she'd suffered a sudden attack of panic and fear. Immediately my thoughts turned to Friar G. I knew the terror that he could arouse in his parishioners, and that he'd aroused in me. The same fear that had prompted the poor girl to leap out the window had nearly caused me to do the same. I couldn't sleep all night thinking about her. I remembered her sweetness, and how embarrassed she was about herself because she was so undecided about her life and so lost.

I began to think that like Jesus, Friar G. has always used violent techniques to "cleanse" us by ridding us of such stagnating feelings as resentment, hate, and so on. But is this the way to liberate us from our fear, provoking complete psychological instability, and traumatizing us to the point of committing suicide? Instead of increasing our fears, why don't these powerful people change feelings into knowledge and help us to understand the reasons for our fears?

Friar G. might have freed me from a more primordial fear but that didn't mean that he freed me from the fear that he himself induced. I continued to be a virtual prisoner in my own home. Worse, I had begun to lose connection with this world. My perception of space was completely distorted, and my disorientation made me feel like an outside observer of my own life. My sense of time completely disappeared. It was up to me to combat it with my will. This, I told myself, had been Friar G.'s intention.

But for all that I was also fascinated by what might happen to me next. Might it all be just the prelude to penetrating the mysteries of the universe? One part of me said I was being liberated from my ego, but at what price? What good did it serve to surrender my ego if I was robbed of my life at the same time? I was truly afraid of shriveling up to nothing, of leaving no physical trace of myself behind. But it was useless to scream in protest against the violence being done to me. That only brought telepathic threats from Friar G: "If you refuse the grace that Jesus grants you, Max will die." All I could do was mindlessly repeat the words: "Jesus, Jesus, Friar G., Friar G., I love you, I love you. Have pity, have pity." My brain had become like a radio transmitter tuned to a single station.

The torture went on day and night without respite. Through his mind control Friar G. sadistically magnified every negative thought suggested to me. He instilled a guilt and a sense of humiliation that caused me so much unbearable pain that I would throw myself on the floor and begin rolling around. It was as if some one was reaching into my stomach and ripping out my entrails. Then, finally, one day, I felt as if he had reached all the way inside to pull out my inner self. I could feel the disappearance of my ego physically. I felt depleted of my will. I wept for the person I had been, the dancer, the wife, the daughter. Everything was lost, my life, my senses, my essence. He had left me with nothing. The pain was excruciating. I screamed.

My first impulse was to escape from my apartment. I ran out toward my car, also fearing that my screaming might alarm my neighbors. I continued yelling as I drove. "Why are you doing this to me, God?" I cried. "It isn't fair after all the love I've given you!" Of course the other drivers on the road heard me, and stared at me. I was afraid that they would stop me and I yelled at them about a person having the right to scream but, embarrassed, I drove home.

Back in the apartment I curled up on the floor in a fetal position. I don't know how long I lay there crying. Then a strange, new feeling overcame me. At the same time that I experienced an incredibly powerful love for Jesus, I was overcome by a convulsing spasm of sexual arousal. I had never had such sexual pleasure. "This is Jesus's way of showing you how much he loves you," Friar G. insinuated to me, and I could only yell out, "Jesus, Jesus, this is truly ecstasy!"

But when I opened my eyes, there was no one there. Still under the grip of this strange spell, I believed that Jesus was advising me to touch myself. But was it really Jesus? It could just as well have been Friar G: after all, he had Jesus' stigmata on his hands. Whatever the nature of the entity that I was dealing with, it continued to plant insinuations in my head. I was being told that this was exactly the way Jesus had shown his love for Mary Magdalen, that in this way he had transferred other people's sicknesses onto her. Now I was re-enacting her role.

Of course, I was astounded by the revelation, and yet in a curious way, it helped explain Jesus' deep connection with Mary Magdalen. It followed that if Friar G. claimed that he was reliving Jesus' life, therefore, he decided that he would need to use a woman to act as Mary Magdalen and I had become that woman. It was also suggested that Mary Magdalen, too, must have masturbated, not for pleasure, but for a far higher purpose. I believed that he must have received that intuition from someone like Padre Pio, who would have revealed this healing process to him. Friar G. being a simple man growing up as an altar boy without any personal history, how could he possibly have such an idea by himself?

Intuitively, or as transmitted to me by Friar G. I understood that at the moment of orgasm, if energy is released it will dissipate. But if healing is to occur, the energy must be controlled and redirected to the spinal cord so that it can be used inside the body to stimulate electrical impulses. This practice of redirecting sexual energy just before orgasm occurs by breathing up from the genitals the unexpelled energy and drawing it to the spinal cord which will then go to the brain. Consequently, the excited neuron can transmit stimulation to another neuron, even awakening dormant nerves caused by paralysis. If done correctly, this would stimulate our brains and heal us, giving rise to the illusion of miracles.

Such miracles, it seemed to me, must have been carefully orchestrated by Jesus, with the beneficiary chosen in advance Mary Magdalen she must have acted as Jesus' secret partner. Much later I have heard that this redirection of the sexual energy is nothing new in the Orient, particularly in India. Whoever was searching for enlightenment was attracted to the concept of Kundalini, which is the essence of redirecting sexual energy to stimulate our brains beyond reason to a superconscious level of knowledge and to awaken our dormant power.

Therefore I presume that Jesus who is reported to have been in India was well informed about Kundalini and even, presumably, practicing it himself. In order to make full use of the Kundalini power, it is necessary to keep it in an excited state that could be sustained by concentrating on the thyroid gland, which when, excited, enriches the pituitary gland, the king of all glands, consequently arousing our sexuality. Kundalini is located in the coccyx of the sacral nerves, the tail of the spinal cord and it needs to be in constant contact with our sexuality excited by imagination.

After Friar G's revelation about his methodology used for healing, he didn't leave me in peace. From that moment he forced me desperately to proceed with his technique more and more intensely. To achieve that energized state and to awaken the nerves around my vertebrae much faster, I started to use a vibrator. During these states of heightened arousal I kept moving my head and neck back and forth concentrating as strongly I could on my spinal cord and its muscles and tendons by pulling them by the constant movement of my head and neck, always hoping to succeed in healing as sooner as possible and make ease the ever-present pain in my vertebrae.

Not that I could get too distracted. If even for a single moment I lost interest in sex, Friar G. would fill my head with such lurid, titillating images and drive me crazy sexually that I had to get back to it. I had grown up with little interest in sex, had probably sublimated all those impulses into dancing, so that these urges were absolutely revolutionary to me. My fantasies began change as time went on. Ever more lascivious scenarios played out in my mind. Friar G. was particularly perplexed by my lesbian fantasies and seemed to exert special efforts to steer me back toward conventional, heterosexual inspirations. His manipulations left very little pleasure for me as it was hard work with very little sexual gratification.

As usual, I tried to puzzle out a cause for my latest distress. I was still convinced that I could find an explanation for my plight through the process of deduction. In nature, I concluded, nothing is wasted: On the contrary everything is used, only then it comes back in a different form. Even the energy generated by an orgasm can be tapped for the purpose of healing. There is so much for us to learn about the energy that emit from our body and her potentialities.

Throughout this period I screwed up my courage on more than one occasion to ask for an appointment with Friar G. It was the equivalent of asking for a trial by fire. After being forced to wait for hours on the appointment day, you would get only a couple of minutes with him, barely time enough for him to promise that he would pray for you and to remind you that everything was in the hands of Jesus. He was also given to telling most of his supplicants that they needed psychiatric help. That's why I didn't go through with my appointment requests. In my case, I was sure, he would tell me to skip the psychiatrist and go directly to an insane asylum. So, I thought, why bother trying to talk to him? If I dare complain about his abuse, he'll simply insult me. It was bad enough that he was already threatening me telepathically, telling me Max would fall ill if I tried to defy him.

Sometimes I'd be out for a walk, the simplest thing. Suddenly I would lose my footing and go flying through the air. On the ground in a daze I couldn't believe how easily I had been knocked off my feet. But as people came over to help me, I realized how it had happened: he had made it happen. By then I understood that Friar G. had made it clear he would not tolerate rivals. If I kissed or paid too much attention to my husband, the threats increased. I'd had been warned: To show Max any affection meant that he would come to grief.

One day in 1986 I had special reason to regret having ignored the warnings. A telephone call announced: "Your husband has been in an automobile accident. Come to the hospital at once."

When I arrived at the hospital in a panic, I learned that Max's car had been hit from behind by a woman, causing him to bang his head on the dashboard. Fortunately, he suffered only a deep cut, but as a warning it proved effective. Fearful of inflicting any further harm on Max, I began behaving increasingly insensitive and cool toward him. He might have been the only person in the world I loved more than myself, but with Friar G. hovering as he was, there was nothing else I could do. Though the humiliations my poor husband had to endure were deeply disturbing to me.

I was too frightened to tell Max what was going on. He would come home day after day to find me still in bed. Never once, though, did he ask me why. We scarcely spoke. Our lack of sex was never questioned. Max must have known that Friar G. was responsible for the change in our lives, but I believe he was too brainwashed and consequently afraid. Maybe he also sensed some benefit from my forced, unnatural activity and preferred not to interrupt the mysterious silent atmosphere that we shared. After all, Max was always saying the ways of God are infinite.

It occurred to me that perhaps I would have been better off enjoying a short and peaceful life rather than suffering a life filled with bitterness and rancor provoked by Friar G. The situation became intolerable. How could I not realize that I had allowed Friar G. to destroy not only my life, but Max's as well?

Max and I were happy together for all those years we were unmarried, and simply living together, and thankfully, without knowing Friar G. We had scarcely been married one year when I began being possessed by Friar G. This was to change the course of both of our lives. We were so open and generous in our own natures that we were completely unsuspecting that one could enter a little church outside of Rome and soon find themselves possessed.

Max was traveling a lot without me because of my condition, I felt guilty about having him travel alone. On one occasion I asked my husband's secretary to attend the Spanish film festival in San Sebastian, because I just wasn't up to it. Her name, believe it or not, was Maria Ferrara. She was thrilled to have such an opportunity, she must of thought I was out of my mind to invite a young woman to go on a trip with my husband. It was 1988, the same year Max was called to go to Africa for Franco Zeffirelli's *Jesus of Nazareth.* He took all of his sons. Of course I was very upset, because I wanted to be with Max on an exotic set instead of at home, sick and desperate.

Chapter 13

Electromagnetic Communication

Although Friar G. was never physically present, I continued to hold thought communication with him. The phenomena seemed to take the form of electromagnetic impulses transmitted by the priest that were then deciphered by my brain.

In an effort to thwart Friar G.'s power over me, I began to read whatever I could on the subject of possession. I was struck in particular by what the theosophist-scientist E. Lester Smith said about telepathy in his book, *Inner Adventures*. Smith noted the conjecture about telepathy involving electromagnetic radiation at some wavelength beyond the normally mapped out spectrum of brain waves. He also speculated that distance doesn't seem to impede telepathy that the inverse square law for the propagation of electromagnetic radiation doesn't apply in this case.

Many international scientists have confirmed the existence of psychic energy manifesting itself through the psycho-magnetic field. They have shown that telepathic clairvoyance is based in part on the capacity to receive electronic impulses sent by electromagnetic mental waves. Telepathy actually relies on magnetic energy, being established by the rapport between the transmitter and the subject, using the power of suggestion at a distance, thought transference and the use of hypnosis.

It would seem that the electric current and the electrochemical energy transmitted by the brain through cerebral waves, together with psychic waves, can modify the subject's reaction both electrochemically and physically. The magnetic energy sent from one person to another can be so strong as to cause the deformation of the personality as well as produce psychological changes.

I had no doubt of it since I went through many deformations, biological as well as psychological. I was also convinced that I could communicate with Friar G. as much as vice versa. "Why are you using me as a conduit to cure this paralyzed boy, Paolo?" I asked him on one occasion.

"You are mistaken," he replied immediately, as though the two of us were sitting at a table together. "What you are feeling is the illness that's been transferred to you from your husband. You should be ashamed of yourself for questioning your condition because you are receiving the grace of Jesus Christ."

Naturally, before this standard tactic of his, in which he overwhelmed me with hypersensitivity, making me feel as if I were opposing Divine Will, I ended up collapsing on the floor and weeping. My tears were born of the blackest despair. "Jesus, please forgive me," I begged, "please have pity on me!"

All this time I was living in a semi-stupor, so drowsy I felt that I would pass out at any moment. I was very lonely, but afraid to reach out to my husband, for fear of Friar G. who was creating more and more distance between us. My only consolation was my little dog Golia, who accompanied me even to Friar G.'s church. Forcibly shut off from the rest of the world, and depressed by the accumulation of emotion and love that had been building up inside of me, I had placed all of my affection in Golia—what a burden for such a tiny little one! One day, it was too much and all this pent-up energy simply exploded in me. I reached down, scooped up the animal, and embraced him so passionately that I terrified him. He bit me on the nose and leaped away. My need for an embrace ended in a pool of blood.

Looking around for some therapy that might succeed, I became obsessed with the idea that a regimen of sauna baths might speed up my healing process. I bought an electric portable sauna, installed it in my bathroom, and indeed found it quite liberating. It seemed to reduce the tingling and numbness in my body. The right part of my brain at times felt more paralyzed, which brought me to the conclusion that the boy's left side had been most damaged by the paralysis.

I would linger in the sauna for hours, moving my head and neck in an attempt to stretch my nerves and tendons. The sensation of gallons of water constantly pouring from my head seemed to relieve my pain.

Then one day the sauna caught fire from overuse. That left me with my bathtub. Bemoaning the loss of my sauna, I sat in the tub adding more and more hot water. I got so carried away I nearly scalded myself. But the water felt so hot as to give a sensation of freezing cold. I recalled the theory originally proposed by Aristotle that life is the same in all its forms, that the only thing that really changes is the nature of its state or the degree of its intensity. Without even being aware of it, he contended, we can pass from one state to another, just as a solid can turn into liquid and a liquid into gas. In the same way we can transcend our natural state, using our rational minds to do so. But rationality by itself will never be enough if what we are looking for is a sublime state of pure intellect. We have to move beyond rationality to a higher state, where knowledge and the love of knowledge resides. Only through the dialectic of logic can we attain wisdom, which is real happiness.

My thoughts about Aristotle temporarily distracted me from concentrating on my body. Suddenly, I became incredibly nervous; I felt an urgent need not to waste any more time. It was Friar G. reminding me that, I had forgotten my mission? always to remain in a submissive animal-like state. People, he suggested, would only divert me from my objective. So I was made so nervous and impatient that I ended up alienating them intentionally; this way I would no longer have to deal with them.

One day my friend Paola came by. A former model of Picasso's, she was always trying to lure people into projects, promising them the world in exchange for a small investment of money or time she had no intention of ever paying back. So why should I have expected that, on that day, she had come to return the money I had loaned her? She was barely through the door when I began screaming at her. "You're a phony and a user! You haven't had a single scruple since the day I've known you!" When she tried to get a word in, I shut her up. Worse, I began lambasting her with obscenities. Paola couldn't believe what she was hearing. She was almost in shock as she bolted through the door, taking with her the thousand-dollar debt she had with me. Naturally, I never saw her again.

Sometimes I had no idea what I was saying. The words seemed to have been put in my mouth against my will. The obscenities became commonplace. Son-of-a-bitch, piece-of-shit...they began tripping off my tongue as though I had been using them all my life. Even Max, the most forbearing of men, had to remind me one day that he didn't like "turpiloquio," the Italian word for "vulgar language." My response? "Turpiloquio? What the fuck is that?"

Inevitably people began avoiding me. I became even more isolated, just as the Friar wanted. He had no competition now—I was all his. I'd undergone a complete change. Whereas previously I had always tried to please people and help them, now I only seemed to want to embarrass them. Would it have helped to tell my victims that the one responsible was Friar G. that he was humiliating me to reduce me to his level? I doubt it.

Within my family not even the coolness that had settled over my marriage satisfied the monk. He next instigated a break between me and one of my stepson's wives. Friar G. persuaded me that this woman was trying to get her hands on the family money and was manipulating everyone to that end. I respected Max so much that, in my more rational moments, I told myself that I had no business meddling in his son's business and that, in any case, the whole thing was petty.

Yet I couldn't help myself. Just to create more distance between my husband and myself, Friar G. made me obsessed with this woman.

I was constantly arguing with Max about her. Max was understandably upset. The last thing he wanted was for me to interfere in his sons' lives, and here I was trying to get him to go against his own nature. It seemed the few times that Max and I did talk turned into arguments over his daughter-in-law. I screamed at him, berating him for his weakness, forcing him to take sides. The whole thing was so repetitive. It was so difficult for him to constantly have to face my tirades against this woman again and again. The situation was ridiculous.

All I could think was that I was becoming a bored narrow-minded housewife the kind of person I'd always loathed, a woman so bored that she can think of nothing else but to fill her life with frustration and resentment. Not surprisingly, my horrible temper tantrums did nothing to help my husband's health. A good case could be made that I was making things worse for him. In the midst of one of our more heated fights, he became so agitated that he suddenly slipped and tumbled to the floor, momentarily losing consciousness It wasn't a heart attack, and that was the first thing I had been able to feel grateful for in a long time

Chapter 14

Film Festival in Cannes

In spite of our tensions Max continued to ask me to accompany him to the various film festivals where he would meet with the producers and directors he represented. For reasons of his own using me as a disciple to spread his message? Friar G. didn't object to these trips. Still, with all sense of shame expunged from me, I would sit in the airport constantly moving my head back and forth, totally unconcerned about the impression I made on others. As soon as I was introduced to someone, be it an important actor, producer, or director, I would immediately launch into a speech about Friar G., urging him or her to convert. It didn't make any difference if my victim of the moment was Christian, Jewish, or Muslim. It didn't matter, either, if they all thought I was being ridiculous. And mind you, many of these people were actors and directors I'd dreamed of meeting my whole life!

Of course, where Friar G. was concerned, one humiliation merely led to an even more debasing one. One day, while walking along the Crouesset in Cannes, I suddenly lost control of my bladder and began peeing in the street. Who should be walking along behind me but a famous director! I was so mortified that I could only think to tell him that I was carrying a flask of whiskey in my pocket and that somehow it had opened. I'll never know if he believed me. But after that incident I knew I had to stop going with Max to such public events.

When I returned home from Cannes, worse was waiting for me. One morning in my apartment I was seized by the feeling of a great ball of air squeezing my heart harder and harder. I was in a panic to vomit, but my mouth was so full of saliva that I couldn't bring up anything. Then my lungs began to wither under an excruciating pain. I was sure I was about to suffocate, and couldn't, didn't dare, move from the floor. I was bathed in a cold sweat. If anything pulled me through that attack, it was the thought that what I was experiencing was the kind of heart seizures that had afflicted Max. If that were the case, I told myself, it was really his illnesses that I had been asked to assume as a burden.

Not a day passed that I didn't feel compelled to take the 50-mile trip from Rome to San Vittorino. Once I persuaded the director Franco Zeffirelli to come with me. He had been in a car accident with Gina Lollobrigida and had damaged his sinuses, and I had convinced him that Friar G. might help relieve his suffering. But once we arrived at the sanctuary Zeffirelli showed far more interest in one of the altar boys than in Friar G. I was afraid that the monk would unleash his brutal temper and condemn Franco to hell. He didn't, though. All he kept talking about was how much he had liked Zeffirelli's *Jesus of Nazareth*.

They finally finished the new church in San Vittorino. It was enormous, and drew huge crowds. It actually resembled a circular arena more than the traditional rectangle. The floors were laid with marble, stained-glass windows ringed the circumference, and a modern tabernacle centered devotions. But for all the money that had clearly been spent, the overall effect was very spare. There were no statues of saints, only a freestanding Madonna of Fatima and crucifix. The crucifix was so big and grotesque; it dominated everything else, and not so prettily either. But what struck me as much as its size and vulgarity was that the crucified Christ bore an eerie resemblance to Friar G.!

Certainly, it is one of the tallest churches in Italy; it can be seen from miles away and pilots of low-flying aircraft have to be careful not to hit its steeple. So imposing is the structure, in fact, that I thought of the Pharaohs and their timeless pyramids. I imagine Friar G. sees his church as his future "pyramid." Maybe he too wants to achieve personal immortality just as the pharaohs. Padre Pio also built a grand church. It is difficult for me to understand why Friar G. felt it necessary to build another , since he received his stigmata from Padre Pio and as I was told Padre Pio even lives in him, couldn't he continue his sainthood in Padre Pio's church? Perhaps every saint needs their own monument, their own "pyramid." But what about eternal life?

The church irritated me. I had no doubt that it had been financed on the money and jewelry of the parishioners. Why couldn't that money have been collected for the poor in the Third World? As if Italy, of all places, had needed another church! Was there any question that Friar G. had extorted the building funds, preying on the fears of his followers? Far from being impressed by this new structure, I saw its every stone as a testament to injustice.

Of course, none of this would have fazed Friar G. He had been listening to objections of that kind for years, and always had a ready answer: "You don't need to accumulate money for yourselves in this world. I am giving you eternal life." Ignore that warning and you would almost certainly be punished.

This was brought home to me one time at Cannes, when Max and I were having breakfast in a hotel dining room. A woman known to Max was sitting at the next table with three men. Suddenly she jumped up from her chair yelling, "My bag! My bag is gone!" A quick search turned up nothing; indeed, her bag had been stolen. But then, as she sat resigned to her loss, she said something that chilled my heart. "Friar G. did this," she sighed, "because I didn't give him any money."

Needless to say, I was speechless. I had never spoken to the woman about the monk, had had no idea she was acquainted with him. But what I could not accept as pure coincidence was that this woman, immediately after spurning a charity request from San Vittorino, broke with her practice and put all her most expensive jewels into a bag for the trip to Cannes. A similar loss happened to me as Friar G. is able not only to disturb thoughts but also affect the eyesight.

I knew my disdain for his new church was going to cause trouble for me with Friar G. There was no way he was going to ignore such a contrary attitude. My first act of obeisance was his telepathic suggestion that I should feel profound gratitude toward his family, accept that they were as spiritually elevated as he was. He introduced his mother as a second Madonna, his sister as a virgin saint, and his father as a "just" man. In fact, when these people weren't busy being the Holy Family, they were plucking and killing chickens to make a living.

On one occasion he even bewitched my husband to kiss the hand of his father. It was terrible to see how the Friar went about humiliating such a dignified man. Other times, while I was praying in the new church, I couldn't help noticing what a big ass Friar G.'s mother had, and I could only conclude that he was directing my gaze there deliberately, reminding me that I wasn't even worthy of her posterior. Who was I to question the value and splendor of his new church?

Like a slave, I continued going to the church, staring at Friar G. and repeating the words "I love you! I love you! How beautiful you are!" I watched him so intently that people began to murmur about my odd behavior. How could they know what a nightmare my life had become?

For all that and for all my physical suffering, I thought I retained a degree of control over his manipulation. But then the daily burden became too much, and I found myself overwhelmed by self-pity. I had never thought of myself in that light before, and could only conclude that Friar G. had changed his tactics, unable to annihilate unhappiness and depression from my brain, he provoked me to weep instead.

He wanted me to cry for myself until my heart was empty and my inside was completely void, no longer approachable not only by other people, as well as by my own emotions and feelings. I was to be left an empty container. It's practically impossible to describe what an agonizing sensation it is to have somebody reach inside you and manipulate your emotions, ripping away the very fabric of your being. I realized that emotional memory is what keeps our rational memory alive and can be erased only through the emotional state.

I would never have suspected that loving Jesus and God would involve being subjected to intimidation and blackmail. Nor would I have imagined that I would spend so much of my life rolling on the floor like a mad woman, sobbing and begging.

Then Max came to me one day and said, "I've been to see Friar G. I was worried about you and because I know you spend so much time at his church, I thought he might be able to advise me."

I was astonished; Max had never before gone to San Vittorino on his own. "What did he say?"

"He said I should send you to a doctor."

I was incensed, but not surprised. Friar G. was telling people to go to mental institutions all the time, after he had been the one to make them sick! "What else?"

"I asked him if it wouldn't help for you to resume your studies at the university since you were happy there, but he said only devils graduated from Gregorian University."

"That was it?"

"Well," Max admitted, "I gave him a thousand-dollar donation for his church.

Friar G.'s tyrannical attitude was getting worse and worse. I identified with the prophets who were possessed in the same way as I. The Lord spoke with them day and night. He was so severe with them that in the book of "Lamentations" Jeremiah cries out, "O lord, I am an object of laughter, everyone mocks me. Whenever I speak, I must cry out, violence and outrage is my message . . . Cursed be the day on which I was born!" "How long O Lord? I cry to help but you do not listen." "I have forgotten what happiness is; I tell myself my future is lost."

Like the prophets, I felt despair, felt my tears were in vain, and that I was completely in his power.

Chapter 15

Complete Isolation

My torment went on and on, and no matter how hard I prayed for help, I received only silence for an answer. Finally, one time, with Max off on a trip, I couldn't stand it anymore. Sitting alone in my bedroom I went through two liters of wine, then decided that wasn't enough, so went into the medicine cabinet in the bathroom for the vial of sleeping pills I knew was there. When I went back to bed, I felt calm and relaxed, no regrets for what I was about to do. Then another pill, another sip until I had taken them all. Now, I thought as I drifted off, it's over, I will be where Friar G. can't touch me.

The next thing I heard was a pounding at my door. I stumbled over to open it. Max and one of his sons, a sledgehammer in his hand, were standing there. In fact, they had already made a pretty good start in breaking down the door.

"Are you all right?" Max , his face a fright of worry, asked.

"Of course." And it was true, I realized: I wasn't dead. "I've been trying to get you for two days."

"Two days! What's today?"

"Wednesday."

I couldn't comprehend what he was saying. Wednesday meant that I had slept three days straight. I scrambled to reassure Max that there had been nothing to worry about, but it wasn't the greatest of performances. For one thing, not even I could come up with a coherent explanation of how someone had been able to ignore a ruckus at the door for so long. Then there were the suspicious looks from Max's son: His father might have been eager to accept any reason that approached plausibility, his expression said, but not him. And of course through it all there was my wonder that I was talking to the two of them in the first place. I hadn't counted on ever seeing them again.

Finally, I managed to get rid of them. I think it was only after they had gone that it dawned on me how odd it was that I should be feeling as well as I did. Despite all that wine and all those pills I didn't feel the least bit groggy or disoriented. I was absolutely alert. Was it possible that, fearful of losing me as his receptacle, Friar G. had taken over my body's functions and even started breathing for me?

My suicide attempt did nothing for my relations with Max's sons. Max, however, never pressed me for explanations. I didn't know whether it was because he was also very much under the influence of Friar G, but I was relieved not to have to go into too many specifics. In the meantime I was back to uttering my ritualistic adulation of Friar G. at Mass every morning, "I love you, I love. How beautiful you are!"

To give myself the benefit of the doubt about this incantation, I think I was trying to convince myself that, as ugly as he was physically and as ruthless as he was toward others, that Friar G. could still have a beautiful inside. Perhaps like Jesus, I argued to myself, he was ready to use any means to awaken us from our inertia. In his particular case that meant constant snarling. I came to the conclusion that Friar G. must have the ability to penetrate the minds of others and also be capable of stimulating or magnifying their anger, hatred, and nervousness. The strongest reaction he provoked was the feeling of hate. By pulling out all these negative feelings from people, he was actually giving them freedom. Foreseeing that he would provoke violent reactions against himself in some of his followers, Friar G. therefore required my constant support in the form of those repetitive and empty words: "How beautiful you are."

I could go only so far with that comparison. While Jesus might have stirred others from their inertia, Friar G. appeared bent on reducing me to complete stagnation. The cycle was interminable: I would feel emptied of all love and he would suggest to me telepathically that this was the necessary prelude to enjoying God's love. I would think that such divine love wasn't all it was cracked up to be, and he would make me feel guilty for having entertained such blasphemy.

As I have already suggested, this kind of vicious circle left me little time for other people. Those who ventured to visit me received a lot of proselytizing for Friar G. for their pains. On one occasion I persuaded an elegant woman we'll call the Contessa to accompany me to San Vittorino. The Contessa was a lesbian, a particular source of vituperation where Friar G. was concerned. And in fact, as soon as he saw her, he even forgot about me to lash into her.

"Go to hell!" he thundered, striking the woman dumb.

That visit made me wonder whether I had brought the Contessa to see the monk for some other reason. Being an aristocrat, she was bound to have irritated him with his peasant background. And a lesbian on top of that? Maybe, I thought, I was getting to the point where I had to try anything, even using other people, to divert Friar G.'s attention from me.

"Why is he so rude?"

"This is the way Jesus wants it" I heard the Friar reply.

Not even my brother Peter was safe from my compulsions about the monk. I hadn't seen him for more than 20 years, since he had left Poland to practice medicine in the United States. But one Christmas holiday he decided to have a family reunion in Rome with me and his two children, both adults carrying on the family tradition by studying medicine in Poland. Despite the fact that I hadn't seen him for so long and hadn't met his son and daughter at all, the first words out of my mouth were that they all had to go with me to San Vittorino. They were all exhausted from their flights to Rome and clearly needed a rest, but I wouldn't hear their objections. How could I explain to him that I was too frightened to forego my daily ritual? "You must come with me right now," I insisted. "It won't wait."

Peter was astonished by my adamancy, and talked his children into going along. Naturally, none of them had the slightest interest in the proceedings and seemed baffled by my eagerness to get in line with the other parishioners in order to kiss Friar G.'s stigmata. At one point during the ceremony, I saw Peter motion for his daughter to accompany him outside. When I finally walked out of the church, they were still deep in conversation, and what I heard him saying shook me.

"You want to have relations with men, fine," he said, sounding like a father who had waited a long time to get something off his chest. "But make sure you never masturbate." Not for moral reasons, he lectured her in his usual pompous fashion, but because masturbating would have given her such a distorted view of sex that she would never be able to have pleasure with a man.

I proceeded to make matters worse. Peter's wife, Tosia, had only recently passed away, so I interrupted. "Couldn't you do this another time? Wouldn't it be more appropriate if you thought about your dead wife and the children thought of their dead mother than talking about sex so close to church?"

It was the beginning of another end. Peter blew up at me for questioning his authority with his own children, and one heated word led to another, some of them extending back to our childhoods in Warsaw. Finally, he stormed off with his son and daughter in tow. It was the last time I saw any of them.

In spite of the fact that Max had given him a thousand-dollar donation, Friar G. resented my husband, regarded him as an obstacle to his domination of me. He still needed my body to serve as a container for himself. Often as we were returning to Rome by car from San Vittorino, Friar G. would suddenly start screaming at Max through my voice, offensive words toward my husband that were injected into my mouth. "You're a psychic vampire! You sucked the life out of your first wife and now you're trying to do the same to me! Why do you keep complaining you're ill when you know that God has already healed you!" Through all of these things I was saying to him, I would be driving so fast that poor Max looked like he didn't know whether he was going to die of a stroke trying to calm me down or simply end up in a fatal car accident.

No surprise, the rift between us grew only deeper. Our sexual relations had become history. At the same time Friar G. continued to sexualize me and force me to keep the pet technique of his healing. I didn't think I was alone, either. One Sunday morning the priest celebrating the Mass began to act oddly. As he delivered his sermon, his face reddened, his eyes bulged. I couldn't help but think that he, too, had been possessed. And then he suddenly burst out from the pulpit: "My dear faithful, masturbate, but keep going! Don't stop! Go forward!"

I couldn't believe my ears. But when I looked around, it was as though only I had heard those words: Nobody else showed anything. I decided that the priest's outburst, or at least what I had heard as an outburst, was Friar G.'s encouragement to me to continue with his "healing" process .

I was so desperate for help from any source that I tried to communicate with my dead father, figuring that his philosophical insights might provide me with a clue for escaping my nightmare. But Friar G. would have none of it. He was afraid that if I actually communicated with my father and anything good came from it, my father would loom in my eyes as the more powerful of the two. So instead he had me dwell on the most unflattering things about my father that occurred to me, and that discouraged me from trying to communicate with him.

So what was left for me? My generous husband had been turned into a vampire, my mystical father was reduced to the status of moral reprobate. Here I was, harshly judging my poor family, while at the same time Friar G. was busy arousing me with his own brand of strange, titillating fantasies.

One thing that continued to infuriate me was the idea that I should also act reverential toward Friar G.'s family. During one of my visits to San Vittorino I was told that I needed to beg Friar G.'s mother to intercede with her son for my husband. Since Max was on a business trip in America, I felt safe in voicing my indignation, saying wasn't I doing enough? I had no intention of begging the old chicken-plucker for anything.

The next day I received a phone call from the airline Max always used. "Your husband has had a serious gall bladder attack," the caller said. "He's been put on a flight back to Rome." I don't know if the attempts to heal him has provoked this reaction and if it was for his good or not but the coincidence makes me suspect vindictiveness on the part of Friar G. because, maybe, of the long history of his always threatening me.

When I picked him up at the airport, I was horrified to see him in a wheelchair. He looked so bloodless and frail that, as we rushed to a hospital, I begged Friar G. to pardon my defiance. In the end, they had to remove the gall bladder. Even though he pulled through, he was still incapacitated. But rather than staying by his bedside holding his hand, I was forced by Friar G. to keep in the usual way, even in the hospital bathroom, generating sexual energy which is supposed to heal him. Even though I still remained convinced I was healing him this way, I felt also terrible because I wasn't staying close to him tending to his needs. But the truth is that his fast recovery surprised even his doctor.

And when Max was released from the hospital, rather than take him home, I insisted on driving up to San Vittorino. It was a bitterly cold day and Max was freezing in the car. No matter. The important thing was for me to run into the church, fall down on my knees, and keep repeating, "I love you, Friar G. You are beautiful. Please forgive me."

It may sound cruel, but I truly believed that if I didn't obey Friar G.'s injunctions, my husband would die. My husband was always left to his own devices. There was nothing I could do about it in spite of the pain that tore at my heart. But I couldn't change it. I was so scared.

Chapter 16

Terrible Betrayal

As low as I usually was, I still had moments when my situation was clear to me. Rather than allow these glimmerings to escape, I would set my thoughts down on paper. I was also rational enough to feel a tremendous loss at the sight of normal, healthy people walking along the street or doing the other things those not in the grip of possession did every day. How much I had missed out on! How many opportunities, as a dancer, actress, wife, I had squandered!

And for what? I had been sidetracked from my destiny by somebody apparently hell bent on becoming a saint at my expense. Friar G. had ruined my life acting for the glory of God but at the end, it was for his own glorification.

It came as quite as a surprise to me that God needs our miracles to prove his existence. Of course he claimed that the miracles ascribed to him had been performed through Christ, but who would remember my sacrifice and me? Who really makes miracles? We humans do. If only we continued accessing the hidden powers of our minds, we would be able to create our own.

But as clear as these thoughts were to me, they remained brief interludes in my daily routine back and forth between Rome and San Vittorino. When the disruption came, it wasn't because I had finally found the strength to oppose Friar G. but because my bizarre behavior had become an increasing source of gossip and indignation among the other parishioners.

Evidently afraid of what I was doing to his reputation, Friar G. waited until he was leading us all out of church after Mass one morning, then suddenly whirled around, and in front of hundreds of people, began shouting at me, "What is this woman doing here? Instead of praying, she stares at me all the time! Look at her! Get out of here, you! You belong in a mental institution! Never come back here again!"

I was in shock. I fled to my car as fast as I could. Behind the wheel I let out a shriek like a wounded animal. I implored God for justice. I asked my mind to wipe out the memory of what had just happened. Naturally, God was silent and my memory remained vivid. I have no recollection of the drive back to Rome that day. All I know is that all at once I found myself standing before my house.

As a result of that experience I told myself that I understood poor Judas, I could identified with him, I even felt sorry for him. No one can understand his personal tragedy more than I. He was manipulated by Jesus Christ in a horrible way. This may have been the worst and most dishonest possession of all.

Judas was pushed to denounce Jesus. In John 13, we read: "Jesus dipped the morsel and handed it to Judas." After he took the morsel, Jesus said to him, "What you are going to do, do quickly." When Judas had left, Jesus said, "Now is the Son of Man glorified, and God is glorified in him." Jesus filled Judas with love for him, making him one of his followers. Then the same love which had once burned in Judas' heart for Jesus was turned into hate by Jesus. After that Judas' spirit and heart became filled with guilt for denouncing Jesus, even though it was beyond his control.

How betrayed Judas must have felt; how desperate and guilt-ridden! Judas didn't just hang himself because of his act in betraying Jesus, but because of the unjust way in which he'd been used by Jesus, with no consideration. Jesus had needed Judas, for all the steps leading up to his crucifixion, as a confirming argument that he was the Son of God. Without his crucifixion, who would remember Jesus? To this day people think of Jesus in these divine terms while regarding Judas merely as the traitor of traitors. And me? How many people will think of me as some poor schizophrenic while Friar G. goes on to whatever glories the Catholic Church has in mind for him? Oh yes. I found it very easy to identify with the hapless Judas.

This episode not only connected me to Judas' pain but it also surprisingly saddened me to think that Jesus was also practicing the possession of others in his time. I began to see the similarities between Jesus and Friar G. in their brainwashing as well as heart-washing techniques.

Similarly Jesus stripped away the apostles' egos, reducing them to unthinking beings moving them like marionettes, and using them in the same way as Friar G. did with me. Jesus conquered them just as Friar G. conquered me. Apostles being human beings, were unreliable in their love though they couldn't unconditionally love him. Jesus planted love in their hearts until they burned with adulation for him that bound them to him forever.

Equally Friar G. in the beginning had instilled in me a supposed love for God, which was actually meant for himself by forcing me to repeat the empty words, "I love you, I love you, how beautiful you are." Like Judas, I was deeply humiliated. I began to think that the motto of the Roman Catholic Church may as well be "the end justifies the means". It doesn't matter whether human beings are turned into disposable objects so long as they serve the Church's purposes.

Being banished from Friar G.'s church in San Vittorino did not mean that I was free of him. He merely changed his tactics to attaching himself to me in a strictly spiritual way. This way he could have me in two ways; protecting his moral standing among his parishioners and by continuing to advance his intentions in secret. Who was I to stop him?

The next phase of my degeneration was drinking. I began to buy ever larger quantities of wine. Because it was delivered to my door, I'm sure my neighbors had the impression I was throwing parties every night. But, no matter how much I drank, I couldn't get drunk. Since wine is supposed to activate blood circulation, I wondered whose blood I was actually activating. It was as though I was not just drinking for myself, but also for Max and the paralyzed boy Paolo. All three of us were putting it away every night using my blood stream.

I found this very stressful, and somehow managed to become even more aggressive toward Max and my acquaintances than I ever had been during my possession. But whenever I pleaded with Friar G. to help me overcome this new addiction or simply free me of my unwanted physical responsibility for Paolo, the answer was always the same: "Be patient. It will all be over in a couple of more months."

By then, those months had added up to more than 20 years, and I saw no reason to think they couldn't go on for another 20. Why didn't I go insane? I like to think it was my instinct for survival asserting itself.

Having seen by now that praying in churches all over Rome had been useless, I decided I had nothing to lose by seeing an exorcist approved by the Church. Exorcism is actually a rite carried out very rarely by the Church, and most supplicants are instead put through a series of blessings and prayers meant to relieve at least the symptoms of their possession. That subtle difference meant little to me the day I sought out the exorcising priest at the Basilica of St. John Lateran in Rome.

Unlike Friar G. the exorcising priest was a well-educated man with a gentle manner. While I waited to speak with him, I watched him at work with other people. One was a teenage girl who screamed and cursed as her parents sought to restrain her. Inevitably she reminded me of the Linda Blair character in the movie *The Exorcist.*

Was she a victim of possession or simply hysterical? I opted immediately for the latter, then realized that people who had been watching me for some years might have come to the same conclusion about my ailment.

When my turn came to see the exorcising priest, I risked defeating the entire purpose of my visit by neglecting to share with him my belief that I was possessed by his colleague. He did not ask why I had come to him and I did not tell him. I was afraid he would throw me right out of the cathedral. In any case, he placed his hands above my head and went into meditative prayer. After a few moments he opened his eyes again and said, yes, he thought I was "possessed by some strong spirit." But that was all. He didn't specify what kind of spirit, even whether it was positive or negative. I didn't push him.

It seemed enough that I had finally found someone who, even along the most general of lines, agreed with my own diagnosis of my problem. He sent me off with two things: a bottle of Holy Water that I was to sip from every night before going to sleep and a warning that our single session would not be sufficient, that I had to keep coming back until I had overcome my problem.

For three months I did so, arriving at the Cathedral, climbing on my knees the thirty-two steps, meant to simulate Christ's walk to Cavalry. I prayed for my release from my possession on every step, eventually going over to the exorcising priest for another round of prayers and blessings. But then Friar G. came back on the air in my head and warned me that my search for a remedy with the exorcist could have terrible consequences for Max. Therefore I stopped going to St. John Lateran.

The presence of Friar G. reduced my marriage to tatters. I could see the end of our time together. I was sure Friar G. would not be completely satisfied with me until the marriage was over. The monk would switch gears, and promise that as soon as I had helped him achieve his miracle with the paralyzed Paolo, Max and I would be reconciled. And as my reward for having endured so much, Friar G. would suggest to me that I would enjoy a creative rebirth. My head would fill with fantasies of Max and I developing movie scripts together. We would become a true artistic partnership. Maybe we could even move to the United States to renew our film careers. Well, there was movement, all right. Movement that drove Max and I further apart.

Chapter 17

Abandoning My Husband

In 1993 I decided to leave Italy for America. It was the only way I could think to escape my abysmal situation. My attachment to Max had become morbid: On the one hand, I was afraid I wouldn't be able to survive without him, on the other hand, I never wasted an opportunity to treat him shabbily. It was the same when I told him I was going. He was trembling, practically shrinking under my gaze, as he watched me pack, but my only words of comfort were along the lines of "I'm going and I don't care how you feel about it."

Friar G. had turned my heart into ice; it could be that he wanted me to go out of fear that I might hurt Max in one of my uncontrollable fits of rage. I left with what I thought were no regrets. I was even able to persuade myself for a day or so that I had rediscovered my energy and that the Atlantic Ocean would be impervious to Friar G.'s spell. But no sooner had I arrived in New York than my pains returned violently. I began crying day and night that Max would never be able to survive without my protection. Ironically, my main rationalization that he would be all right was that Friar G. wouldn't dare let him die in shock over my departure because that would impede the monk's efforts to cure Paolo.

Max wasn't my only immediate cause of regret in New York. The fact was, after leaving all practical problems up to him for the better part of three decades, I was at a loss for the simplest things. I had never been particularly practical, had known next to nothing about mathematics, and now tax forms, mortgages, and the like took my breath away. Maybe it was only the day I went to an accountant a friend of Max's, tears running down my cheeks as I implored him to help me, that it sank in how hard starting my life over again was going to be.

To my chagrin, New York didn't help at first. As much as I loved the city, I realized too late that it was also a fountain of painful memories. Every store and restaurant I passed in Manhattan seemed to remind me of this day or that evening in Max's company. A few months of this, and I was only too glad to move to Los Angeles with some vague idea of making a film about my father's background in Tibet.

In Los Angeles for just a few hours a week I kept up the regimen of sauna baths, and I tried to give up my habit of rocking my head back and forth. For all that, I wanted to believe I was making progress, that I had more important things to do than to worry about helping Max back to health. But when I joined a group called Women in Film, I had to admit that my ability to think clearly remained impaired. I simply couldn't memorize names or remember faces. Learning a new skill was all but out of the question. When a friend who was trying to teach me the basic operations of a computer threw up his arms in frustration, calling me retarded, I didn't take it as an insult. That's how I felt about myself, too!

There wasn't too much else about Los Angeles that worked for me, either. My fragile mental and physical condition made it impossible to go ahead with the screenplay about Tibet. I was also hopeless behind the wheel in a city that has made a religion out of automobiles; once I got on the freeways, I was lost. With the added incentive that enough time had passed for me no longer to be traumatized by memories of my time with Max in New York, I got back on a plane and returned east, telling myself that was where I really belonged. When I quickly found a comfortable apartment on Manhattan's Upper East in a building equipped with a health club, including a sauna, I was sure of it.

Of course, I was only deluding myself that I was finally free of Friar G. One day in the sauna, my knees buckled and locked for so long that I feared I was paralyzed and would never walk again. Oh, was I furious at Friar G. for this painful reminder of Paolo! "Enough, enough!" I cried when I was able to get to my feet again. "I refuse to go on contributing to my own downfall! I don't even care if Max gets better."

And there it was, I thought later. It hadn't been enough for Friar G. to break up my marriage after 25 years or even to inspire me to leave a fragile 87-year-old man to his own devices on the other side of the Atlantic. Now he was getting me to wish for Max's death, too. Just how many sins was this man prepared to commit in the name of loving Jesus and attaining his own sainthood? Basta!

As a first step toward taking charge of my life again, I gave up my routine of languishing in bed and the sauna every day. My second step was more literal: a friend who taught ballroom dancing reawakened a long-dormant enthusiasm for the mambo, the hustle, and all kinds of other dances. I turned passionately to social dancing. How could Friar G. thwart me here?

It didn't take long to find out. After indulging my new enthusiasm a short while, my feet began to get overheated with throbbing so strong that I could neither dance nor walk. Since I had the symptom almost every night for a long period, I made the mistake of trying to ignore the throbbing, but this time one of my toes developed a deformity, necessitating surgery for the removal of a piece of bone. My brief happiness thus come to an end.

I began to think of myself as Friar G.'s personal trash container for disposing of all his old curses. Day and night every part of my body seemed to erupt like a cesspool. The only break in my physical tragedy was physical farce. Responding to my constant urge to throw up one morning, for instance, I lost my dental bridge in the toilet and then unwittingly flushed it. When a plumber retrieved it for me, he handed me a bridge beyond repair.

This led me to a dentist who had developed what he called "a painlessly inserted implant." Before he got down to what I had visited him for, however, he discovered a huge cavity which had left my sinuses exposed. Naturally, the dentist had to do extra work before my sinuses were infected. As he worked, I couldn't help reflecting that Friar G. seemed a lot less worried about healing sinuses than paralysis. Was there some kind of pecking order of physical problems requiring the intervention of a miracle?

The farce didn't stop there. Hardly had I returned home with the specialist's "painless" implant then I began writhing in anguish. Friar G. took advantage of this painless procedure by concentrating his healing on Paolo's cervical spine. The dentist was mortified, but counseled patience. Mine lasted for about two weeks without any easing of the pain, upon which he finally agreed to remove his work. Not only hadn't I had my teeth fixed, but I had paid not to have them fixed!

When my nausea got particularly bad, I went to see a doctor whom I had consulted previously about a feeling of numbness in my head. This time he referred me to a neurologist for E.E.G. tests and a C.A.T. scan. Neither showed any trace of abnormality. After reporting this to me, the doctor made it obvious he regarded me as a hypochondriac. Another doctor told me that my nausea was undoubtedly connected to some problem with my large intestine, but there, too, tests showed nothing and he too looked at me suspiciously. What was I supposed to tell these people, that I was possessed, that somebody was using my body without my authorization?

In short, I was no safer from Friar G.'s influence in New York than I had been in Rome. The Atlantic might as well have not existed for this man's demon obsession to use Paolo through me to gain sainthood. And one of the incredible things, it occurred to me one day in a spasm of pain, was that I didn't even know the person for whose recovery I had effectively sacrificed my life.

I had occasionally seen him at San Vittorino, of course, but I had never spoken to him. Someone there told me that he made his living selling black market American cigarettes. Can you imagine? Maybe I could have even found some solace for my suffering if I'd known I was making the sacrifice for a scientist or a poet or a philosopher who would improve the lot of humanity. But just so Italians would have a steady supply of cheaper Marlboros? How could I be so humiliated? To what end? To confirm the existence of God, Friar G. responded.

Chapter 18

Friar G.'s Possession: Will It Ever End?

That ripped it, as far as I was concerned. Confirm the existence of God? If God was omniscient and omnipresent, the way Friar G.'s church claimed, why did He have to have his existence confirmed by snatching away my life through pain, pretenses, and lies? And why did He need to beg for our love? Wasn't love supposed to be a freely reciprocated feeling? How could anyone ever distinguish claims of having been loved by God from an illusion caused by a ferocious will to love? We were taught that God, by sacrificing the life of Jesus for our sins, gave us a testimony of his love.

Could this cruel act be called love? And what sins were these, which we humans were so strongly accused? Socrates' definition of sins was very simple: he said that bad actions are born of ignorance. I couldn't imagine how it was possible to absolve ignorance when the only way to open someone to new visions and horizons would be through knowledge.

Friar G. under the name of a loving God introduced me, alas, only to slander, calumny, lying, intrigues, vindications, threatening. Should I assume this action to be the result of a deep lack of knowledge and not of sins? Yes, I think his vulgarity was the consequence of his crass ignorance that disabled him from respecting humanity.

While ruminating on these questions, I happened to come across some old notes I had made about a conversation I overheard between Paolo and a woman in San Vittorino. The black marketer was about 25 when the incident took place. "Ow, Paolo," the woman had said to him without preamble, "when are you going to start standing up and walking straight?" Embarrassed, he had begun stuttering, "Friar G. tells me the miracle is failing because . . ."

"Because why?" she had pressed.

"Because I masturbate," he had declared, near panic. "What can I do? My lust is so strong. I can't help myself. Surely, it is the devil at work."

It suddenly occurred to me that Paolo had been punished all these years for doing exactly what I had been forced to do, and all for the purpose of helping Friar G.'s repugnant miracle to succeed. It had never dawned on the poor boy that the sin for which he believed the miracle had been postponed had been stimulated in him by Friar G. himself as well as a sense of guilt! Could an act like masturbation be delaying a miracle? He was too ignorant to have figured it out that it was a pretext for Friar G.'s rationalizing the miracle's delay.

Was this an example of a truth confirming God's existence and our sins?

Did I mention that I'd had enough? Of Paolo, of Friar G., of his phony miracles, of my pains? I made up in what was left of my mind that the only way of saving myself was to take my body away from the monk altogether. I certainly had nothing to lose. Yes, I had tried to commit suicide before, but once on impulse and another time in drunkenness. This time was different. I was methodical to the point of figuring out where I should leave my money and consulting my attorney about a will. I was also determined to go out with dignity.

For example, I contemplated going to India where, because cremation is a common practice, I would have no problem having my ashes scattered to the four winds. I had absolutely no desire to come back as another person or another life form. I wanted to cut myself off from the world, the world of Friar G., God and the people who said they believed in God.

Naturally, my attitude depressed Friar G. and as usual he passed his depression on to me magnified a dozen times over. I was physically exhausted from the moment I opened my eyes in the morning.

People would ask me why I was crying, and I would be stunned by the question because my pain, psychological and physiological, somewhere in my body, was so severe I hadn't realized I had been weeping. I wasn't anymore expelling the sickness from my body. It was accumulating, it seems, all over. My breasts were always sore; I was so habitually out of breath I came to regard walking up a flight of stairs as an ordeal. And all through it the words, Jesus loves you, kept beating in my head. What they actually meant, of course, was that Jesus was giving me "grace" to suffer more sickness. He would keep on dissecting me, torturing me, without ever letting me die."

It was during this terrible period of time that one day a friend invited me to a birthday party. I was grateful for the invitation. It had been so long since I'd gotten out. I knew most of the people in attendance would be connected to New York's independent film world where I used to work as a volunteer. The party was so packed that you could barely move with the lights so dim that it was hard to make out faces clearly. After awhile, a handsome young man came up and asked me to dance. As we moved to the center of the floor, I wondered whether he had just seen my black miniskirt and see-through black lace blouse and, with the help of the bad lighting, he'd mistaken me for a much younger woman. But no. On the contrary, cheek to cheek so there could be no mistaking that I wasn't a teenager, this hunk began kissing me, and with so much warmth and passion that I didn't know what to do.

Since my arrival in America, I had all but forgotten about finding a live sex partner, not least because my low self-esteem made it hard to imagine that any man would be interested in me. But here within a few minutes all those complexes seemed to vanish. Gian, that was his name, overwhelmed me with his spontaneity. It happened so fast I don't know how we ended up in my apartment. What I do know is that it was beautiful.

Gian and I spent three dreamlike days together in 1995. But the fact remained that there was an absurd difference in our ages. He was only 32 and I was quite a bit older. The first time I'd ever had to face such a humiliating dilemma. But as rationally as I put this reality to him, he wouldn't accept our going our separate ways and he kept calling me. Finally he prevailed upon me to allow him to visit me one more time. My attraction to Gian began to be so abnormal that it started to surprise me. I don't recall to have ever had such strong sensations of attraction, which turned to anxiety. I began to believe that Friar G. was pushing me into Gian's arms just to shake me from my emotional indifference.

Up until then, I hadn't made too much of Gian's constant requests for money since he was just getting started in the film business. If anything, I remembered how difficult it had once been for me in Italy searching for a job and how much help Max had given me when I needed it. So now I felt it was time to give back what I had received. Therefore opening my purse hadn't seemed all that unnatural. But instead of making him a better person, the money only made him more greedy. The mask had fallen away and I saw who he really was. I had never experienced such a relationship with a person who worked his seductions for money.

In the end, I explained to Gian that it no longer made any sense for us to be together. This time he agreed and I never heard from him again.

But no sooner had we broken up than I was overwhelmed again by terrible anxiety. I realized that it was Friar G. who was drawing me to him. If Friar G. were seeking someone with whom to identify, he couldn't have picked a better person than Gian. When it came to whoredom, prostituting oneself for money, it was Friar G. who was the real prostitute but with one significant difference: He prostituted for God. Getting right down to it, hadn't Gian been merely one more victim of Friar G.s? Hadn't he merely been one more tool for Friar G. to maintain his control over me?

I told myself that the only way to escape being used by Friar G. was to stop obsessively thinking about Gian that actually it was imposed on me. That was when I had a revelation. Gian was tall, and so was Friar G. Gian's name began with G, and so did Friar G.'s. I had used the words "I love you, I love you, how beautiful you are!" with Gian exactly as Friar G. had been forcing me to use them with him for years. None of that could be mere coincidence.

Friar G. had debased my entire union with Gian. Rather than being content to exploit my pain to achieve his ends, through Gian he had moved on to exploiting my pleasures for the same objective. It was all of a piece. Once again I had been led down the primrose path by the monk. I was deeply hurt even though Friar G. kept creating a terrible anxiety in me over Gian until my heart ached so much that I had the sensation it would break. I desperately desired to put an end to that anguished love and exhausting anxiety. After I protested vehemently, the torment stopped. This peaceful interval confirmed once again that Friar G. wanted to use this love for his purposes.

I was being forced to repeat Gian's name constantly. His name echoed inside my head, intensifying my anxiety. Friar G. suggested obsessively that Gian love me and miss me. I sought refuge in meditation, but it wasn't easy. Friar G. continued to fill my mind with images of Gian. The more I thought about it, the more I was convinced Friar G. must have been pleased by my love story, which also distracted me from insulting him. For another, in his incarnation as Gian, he was able to present himself as somebody brimming with love and that in turn, represented one more chain for keeping me bound to him. To protect myself, I decided to go back to insulting Friar G.

I began to analyze the word "love." If I say "I love you," does that mean I'm responding because of sexual attraction or because I feel protected financially? Wouldn't this be mere gratitude? And if I eliminate those reasons, what remains? The bottom line is that I want to love for love alone, to be loved no matter why, because the love in me needs to be recognized and released in pure joy.

Once I discovered that I retained a *joie de vivre* despite all the torments I had been through, I realized all of us are potentially ecstatic with our capacity to love, which is next to the joy of innocent happiness. And with that central insight I had progressed to analyzing all the mental and physical symptoms caused by Friar G. looking for any and every possible meaning behind my possession. At the risk of sounding arrogant, I came to suspect that it is my life's mission to help others avoid the destructive forces I have been subjected to, which can only kill our joie de vivre and our spontaneous capacity to love.

Chapter 19

My Encounter With Gurumayi

Whether consciously or unconsciously, I was always looking for any way that I could to free myself from Friar G. One day I fell into conversation with a young man from the Italian Consulate in New York, who told me he was a disciple of an Indian religious figure known as Gurumayi. He said she had exceptional powers that included healing the sick. I was intrigued and wanted to meet her, my hope being that her powers, if they existed, would rescue me from Friar G. Gurumayi was then presiding over the Siddha Yoga ashram in the upstate New York town of South Fallsburg.

After meeting with her, I was invited to attend a seminar at the ashram. I use the word invited generously. The cost of this two-day seminar was almost two thousand dollars, and that was merely the beginning. During the retreat we were also encouraged to buy her books, CDs, and videotapes. But I told myself the cost didn't matter, that if she could free me, it would be worth every penny. On the other hand, I didn't spell out my problem for her. If she was as good as everyone said she was, I thought, she should be able to figure it out herself.

While at the ashram, I met a lot of devoted young people who spent a great deal of time collecting money for their guru. Rather than thinking about themselves or planning for their futures, their minds were set only on remaining close to the so-called incubator, Gurumayi. As for the incubator herself, she proved adept at getting her followers to cook and wash dishes for two thousand people. When they weren't working in the kitchen and the mess hall, they were selling dresses donated by famous American designers, a fund-raising initiative that netted more than $200,000 in two days.

Through all this menial and commercial labor the disciples couldn't talk fervidly enough about the great spiritual gifts they were convinced they had received from Gurumayi. All of them were hypnotizing themselves with the strong belief of Gurumayi's extraordinary power and recounted experiences of having seen her in their daily routines even when she might not actually have been there. According to these acolytes, Gurumayi's predecessor, Guru Swami Muktananda, had transferred his spirit to her after his death, inspired her to assume his personality even his voice and gait, and continues to live on within her.

That sounded very much like the supposed relationship between Padre Pio and Friar G. to me. And the similarities didn't stop there. Like Gurumayi, Friar G. preached to the public, and invaded their brains and spirit. Like Gurumayi, he commanded his followers to attend his services, and never with empty wallets. Like Gurumayi, he was forever talking about the vanity of acquiring worldly goods while passing the collection basket.

Of course, I also had to admit a couple of differences between the two of them. In contrast to Friar G.'s coarseness, ignorance, and unkempt appearance, Gurumayi was attractive, charming, and well-educated. She also behaved more prudently with her public, undoubtedly in part because she didn't want any problems about being allowed to stay in the United States.

From what I picked up at the ashram, she and her brother had been accepted as disciples by Guru Muktananda in their infancy and raised by him very strictly. Their polished education included the English language. The brother, from what I was told, was expelled from the Guru's ashram at the age of 18 because of some sex scandal. But Muktananda himself had also been reputed to entertain his female followers in his private quarters when he wasn't preaching to them. Maybe he lured them to his room by promising them a speedier road to enlightenment. Gurumayi was said to have been one of these women.

When I was involved with her, Gurumayi's sect was flourishing. Part of its success was owed to its savvy exploitation of technology. One student, for instance, told me that she had flown from England for the seminar after hearing Gurumayi via satellite; moreover, she had invested all her savings in the trip and the retreat. I suspect that Gurumayi, and other so-called spiritual leaders like her, are able to manipulate people and begin the process of possession at a distance, through the power of their voice or image alone.

Unfortunately, my hope that Gurumayi would be able to release me from Friar G.'s power proved groundless. I knew that the day I was listening to her speak about God and His beauty. Like the others in attendance, I began to chant. Soon I was weeping hysterically. All my despair over the wasted years of my life welled up inside me. But all of a sudden I was hit by a shocking recognition: I wasn't freeing myself from Friar G. at all. Quite the opposite Friar G. was trying to empty me of my unhappy memories and bad feelings about him just so he could retain his power over me. He was using Gurumayi and the charged atmosphere at the ashram to tighten his control even further.

I decided I needed to talk to Gurumayi. But it wasn't easy getting an appointment with her. The closest I could get was to an assistant, and once she had heard me out, she simply asked if I had been to see a psychiatrist. I suppressed asking her if Gurumayi, said to be possessed by Guru Muktananda, had ever sought out an analyst. What good would it have done? The tactics of all these people were the same. First they possessed you, then they told you that you belonged in an insane asylum if you protested. Educated or not, Gurumayi was no better than Friar G. She was the last one who was going to help me get rid of him.

It wasn't too long after my experience at the ashram that I was waiting for somebody outside Trinity Church of Manhattan. Gazing up at the cross atop the church, I became indignant. The longer I had to wait, the more incensed I became about what had been done to me. Was this the great truth of Jesus Christ? The ruin that passed for my life?

Finally, my rage propelled me through the doors of Trinity, the first time I'd been in a church since Friar G. had driven me away from his in San Vittorino. Mass was under way. As I watched the priest elevate the Host, I addressed Christ. How, I demanded, could He have allowed Friar G. to deceive me, to vent such hatred against someone who had never harmed him? Why hadn't He intervened at some point over all these years? Had Friar G. been beyond even His control?

There was no answer. I asked again and again but there was only silence. The silence became so maddening that I did something Friar G. had already warned me not to do and mumbled obscenities to Jesus. I called him a son, of, a, bitch for being part of Friar G.'s schemes. I went on in that vein, "Jesus, you are full of shit. You are a dirty pig. You are worse than Hitler. You *are* a Hitler."

But my insults got me no further than my entreaties. Worse, I was sure, they would bring down the wrath of God on my head, as Friar G. had warned. You just didn't go around calling God a piece of shit without expecting severe punishment, maybe even death. But in the end I didn't care if Friar G. had been right about that or not. Yet I didn't care because I felt that I had already been flung into the abyss.

Of course, I did, I realized. Wasn't it already telling that God and Jesus hadn't reacted to my insults? They had demonstrated neither offense nor anger. There had only been more silence.

God and Jesus might not have been offended, but when I let Friar G. know that I hoped he would die like a piece of shit, suddenly my private radio was on again. "Don't worry," he cackled, "I'm going to die as a saint!" There it was. Even my vulgarities to him weren't half as important as his demented confidence that nothing would get in the way of his beatification one day.

From the moment my life became associated with "God and

Jesus," it became a miserable disgrace. I took stock. I had never shown any particular interest in self- mortification, I had never entertained visions of nailing myself to a cross or provoking any kind of miracles. But if that was the notion that God had of love, His kind of grace, then count me out. For me that kind of so-called grace was only a curse that has had centuries of dire consequences for humanity. And with that awareness I could no longer tolerate the most common acknowledgements that people make of an alleged Divine Power.

I would see a church and I would walk in the opposite direction. Somebody would say "God bless you" in the most unthinking way, and I would get the shivers. God, as is usually construed, was not a benediction, I reminded myself, but a malediction. Reduced to fear and subservience before this classic concept of the Great and the Unspeakable, not just I, but untold zillions of people over the ages, had been reduced in one way or the other to the writhing state that had been my existence. The church loves to claim, for the purpose of subjugating and humiliating mankind, that devils and miracles exist and that Jesus sacrificed himself for our sins. The church is based on these dishonest teachings about the existence of devils and miracles, which in turn, would seem to confirm its supernatural authority.

As the Scottish historian and philosopher David Hume has noted the religions of the world have established themselves upon miracles, which contravene the laws of nature. These acts are called false miracles. Hume says that all men must die and that once a human limb has been amputated, it does not grow back. If someone you know told you they were traveling in Spain and came across a small village where they were told of a holy man who had rubbed an amputee's limbs with a certain oil and that the man's legs grew back, would you believe it? Is it a miracle? All the villagers believe it to be one. Such reports are either lies or cases of collective hallucination.

The people love to be deluded and to believe in the truth of the creations of their own passions and heated imaginations, as in the absolute truth that the miracle really occurred. The miracle cannot be believed without abandoning a basic principal of empirical knowledge that laws of nature cannot be violated. The dead man cannot stand up and walk.

I took further stock. What I had encountered in the Roman Catholic Church, it became obvious, was nothing more than a variety of voodoo. A saint is proclaimed a saint because he has performed a miracle; otherwise he or she is not a saint. And so it is that prospective saints have to go treasure hunting for ready-made miracles.

More specifically, I learned one night from the Voodoo Encyclopedia while I was surfing the Internet, it was an example of the Pier-Loa Possession. According to the encyclopedia, when a Loa, a spirit of the world, possesses a person, that person's actions, thoughts, and attitudes become exclusively those of the possessor. The possessed person cannot be responsible for his actions because it is no longer really that person, only a physical container of that being.

I was convinced by now that Friar G. had afflicted me with his vulgar habits through "magnetic passes" first associated with Franz Anton Mesmer in the 18th century Mesmer who lent his name to mesmerism, claimed to heal through the transfer of his magnetic energy into his patient. Yet there was none of Mesmer's avowed healing aims in Friar G's manipulation of me. However it might have looked to me, he hadn't even used me as an intermediary for curing Paolo but just reduced me to being his container without even any need to apply to a supernatural power.

That poor Marlboro vendor, too, had been incidental. Everything had been done only for the monk's sanctification. If he could have done without his sectarian vision of God to reach his objective, he would have done that, too. But of course that was the one thing impossible for him because it was precisely that sectarian vision of a deity, with the Catholic Church behind it, that endorsed the whole enterprise from the start.

It should go without saying at this point that not even my awareness of what Friar G. had been up to all along, and how it had suited our ignorant culture about God got this vulgar pig to stop molesting me. Every night he kept me awake, forcing me to speak his words as though they were mine: "I beg you. Stay with me. Don't leave me. Use me. I want to be sick. I'm happy only when I feel the pain and weight of Paolo's paralyzed body in me. That way I feel close to our Jesus who loves me so much because I am close to his cross."

With all this mesmerism he wasn't able to distort my love and respect for truth. He never followed the truth even with the stigmatas on his hands and Jesus's declaration that He was the truth. What a weird story. Jesus and the Holy Ghost didn't defend their truth so corrupted by Friar G. s lies.

This almost superhuman resolve to try to heal this one person nonstop for such an enormous span of time always amazed me. Friar G. was very proud of his determination. Any ordinary killer with equal determination could easily abuse sexually and then kill his victim in a moment but not for a period of time lasting twenty-seven years, day in and day out.

Helpless before these invasions, I could at least go on cursing the hypocrisy that motored them but at that point, with intention to finally provoke some reaction from our superior saints, as were a mantra or a rosary I continued to curse God, Jesus, and the Holy Spirit with the vilest language that occurred to me. But after three more months of this, there was still only silence from Them. Dare I admit it that, even as I had my growing proof that God did not exist, I was also sorry for that fact in one sense? For if God did really exist and Jesus had truly been resurrected, I thought, they would never have allowed all the blasphemies that have been carried out in their name over the ages. Starting with what Friar G. had been doing to me for close to 30 years.

But I wasn't finished yet. Call it the trouper in me from my days as a traveling dancer. If I couldn't get God to answer me, I decided, why not the one person on earth who, in the view of millions and millions of people around the globe, was his very special representative?

That's right. I turned to the Pope.

Chapter 20

The Letter to the Pope

The true story of the horrors I went through after I first visited St. Vittorino was so complex and peculiar that the letter I began to write to the Pope became longer and longer, and soon it evolved into this book. While looking through old documents, I discovered that I had met Friar G. in 1972. Then in 1980, I started to make some sporadic notes about my experiences. To my surprise, I realized that my feelings and my situation were exactly the same after so many years. Now I was trying again to write the same letter to the Pope. I was shocked and saddened to discover that in 1980, after eight years of anguish, I was asking myself where I would find the courage to move forward, the same question I was asking twenty-seven years later.

Every night, when Friar G. awakened me, I would write my story on paper. This seemed to cause Friar G. to finally stop using the disgustingly mocking phrase, "Jesus loves you," meaning that he was nailing me to Jesus' cross.

Why did we need a clone of Jesus? Wasn't the original enough? And who was this Jesus in the bleeding hands of Friar G.?

The stigmata of Padre Pio and Friar G. can have only one explanation: the power of mental suggestion. The psychiatrist, Dr. Spitza, says the remarkable power of mental suggestion occurs in a graver forms of hysteria and can provoke permanent scars.

All I've tried to do is understand the reasons for my painful experience. Certainly my story is nothing to be proud of, quite the opposite, embarrassing and shaming me. In fact, I wonder how I could have allowed myself to be so deprived of my humanity. I feel as if my brain was split in half and only one part was communicating. It sounds quite impossible but each time Friar G. intensified the healing of the paralyzed man on the left side of my body, my right brain felt as if it were numb and not reacting to any kind of information but remaining in a state of unconsciousness. I have to always repeat one word as a mantra, otherwise I would lose touch with reality.

Actually, Friar G. is attempting to achieve his miracle by solely using my biological system without there being any supernatural intervention such as the Holy Spirit coming to heal me.

He is manipulating my whole system depending on his needs. If he needs to stimulate my appetite, he whets me with such hunger as if my stomach were completely empty. I wake up famished in the middle of the night, eventually resulting in a weight gain. But not always; sometimes the reverse happens and I find that I have lost five pounds. Another side effect that I experience is the incredibly strong impulse to throw up along with painful stomach contractions. He is able to stop my biological functions or increase them to such a degree that I have to urinate constantly. Moreover, knowing that whatever action I take will be used to heal the paralyzed man, I would even love to stop my daily fitness routine. It is so degrading to be used against your will for the cause which you hate and which disgusts you to the depths of your heart.

He can became even more offensive when trying to arouse me sexually. While I am writing, he overwhelms me with a terrible kind of lassitude, as if I was going to swoon. This feeling of repose can turn into a sexual sensation so profound that it becomes orgasmic. He stimulates me through my hormonal glands and nerves. He is trying to excite me so much, in fact, that I am ready to jump on any man I see. He is looking for any opportunity to stir up my emotions. He needs me to be in love, to suffer anxiety and frayed nerves.

I was being pushed towards an older man I recently met. I have to admit that he was a nice enough person, but no matter how good of an imagination I had, I could never think of him as a romantic lover. Even so, Friar G. was trying to make me attracted to him, arousing such sexual desire in me that day and night I was being forced to repeat this man's name, Alfred. I fought him, I refused to repeat his name. He insisted, suggesting that Alfred loved me and could not live without me. With all my will, I fought against those imposed feelings with all anxiety by repeating constantly as a mantra a harsh curse against Friar G. Like a predator, Friar G. was just waiting for me to meet a new man so that he could use me and stir up my emotions all over again

He needs my anxiety and nervousness; he needs to release them by sharing them with me. He needs me to be in love. The sense of well-being particularly from sexual relaxation is helpful for releasing the tension in my muscles and tendons and allowing my blood to circulate in all the parts of my body which was affected with the symptoms of the paralyzed man.

We know that the most powerful energy that exists is sexual since it produces the beginning of all life. The most charismatic spiritual leaders, like Friar G. and Padre Pio, are endowed with that very intense energy which abnormally increased their human capacities. My reflection over this has led me to understand that to love and to be loved, the impulse never dies as long as we have consciousness. Consequently, sexual energy can be stimulated to the maximum and through breathing reaching every part of the brain and exciting its capacity through our electric nerve energy. This explains why Friar G. kept me in a state of constant sexual tension which was released inside my spinal cord.

For further understanding, I have referred to Sigmund Freud's *Three Stages About Sexuality* in which he states that the sexual instinct is not limited only to genitals but extends also to the rest of the body and involves the whole psychological system. Sexual instinct can lead to sadistic tendencies, which are based on an aggressive element, a residual of the cannibalistic appetite for domination. Sadism and masochism are interrelated. The person in the sexual act who receives pleasure by inflicting pain is able to achieve orgasm and is equally able to receive pleasure from pain inflicted on himself. Freud affirms that pathological behavior often develops the tendency to sublimate the object of attachment into sexual fetishism. Those who reject the natural sexual instinct or fail to transform the same energy to the other meanings become neurotic and hysterical, consequently developing highly morbid attachment to the object. An perfect example of this is the crucifix that becomes a fetish symbolizing pain which is transformed into sexual sublimation.

In order to achieve a deep meditative state, mystics must empty their brains of all thoughts and focus only on one word at a time, like "God" or "love." This intense focus magnifies the word in their minds and allows for the deepest penetration of its meaning. Friar G.'s reflection led him to conclude that to perform miracles and to carry out his purpose he had to hate me; he had to reduce me to a repetitive animal-like life.

To be successful, he had to reserve the passionate love only for God and the paralyzed young man, while forgetting my humanity.

As I write this, I am feeling terribly offended and angry. At the same time I feel frustrated because I'm unable to cry out and tell the entire world what has been done to me. Even if I could, I don't know whether anyone will ever be able to understand the extent of my heartbreak. The same paralyzed man, the same feelings over and over again, constantly being susceptible to anxiety, irritation, and depression.

I can only ask in the name of truth and justice that the actions of those saints be all together taken as an extreme insult to human beings and that such actions be forever eradicated from the world. So now the big question is, what remains of the Church's true foundation, since it is based on this fanatical obsessiveness for proving nonexistent miracles. Particularly, after I came to understand that all healing is not the result of supernatural forces, but of the stimulation of our biological system?

The only thing keeping me alive is the prospect of finishing this book. What's amazing is that it is Friar G. who is writing this book, because if he didn't wake me up every night against my will by the involuntary movement of my head as well as a strong pulsation in my numb legs and in my spine, I would not be inspired to write a truthful and honest description of my experiences.

To avoid the repetitiveness so characteristic of Friar G., I will no longer discuss my own experience but rather will continue my reflection about my deteriorating relationship with Jesus and God and the difficulty in believing in their existence. In my last will I made a donation to Mt. Sinai Hospital. I have specified that I wish my funds to be contributed to research in Alzheimer's Disease and to the study of longevity. This confirms my belief in the human ability to achieve miracles, through science and not God. I have also asked not to have my life sustained artificially. My body parts that will be useful I have donated, and the rest is to be utilized by the Mt Sinai Medical School for dissection.

The second part of the book covers research, which, I feel, will offer some explanation for the existence of this invisible yet nevertheless very real phenomenon known as spiritual possession, and hopefully, how to avoid it.

I fervently hope that by the end of the second part of this book, I will have the good news to announce that Friar G. has finally stopped with his obsession and given me my freedom.

All I can do is to beg you, my reader: DO NOT LET ANYONE EVER POSSESS YOU.

Part Two

Introduction

In determining who my reader is, I asked myself, "What is his or her age? Is this a self-improvement or self-awareness book?" Then I thought to myself that from the very first moment of our coming into this world, our growth proceeds under constant impositions from different points of view. The first imposition came from our parents, then our teachers and friends. As a result, we are not given any chance to develop our own vision about the world. When we are young, we are so taken up by so much learning and discovery that there is no time to know our inner selves. What is worse, we are not allowed to choose our own beliefs. Being born and baptized under the traditional beliefs of our parents, we are burdened with them all our lives since we do not understand anything about them.

Usually, at maturity, between the ages of thirty-five and forty, we begin to feel a void inside us, a missing component to our completion. The attribution for this cause is the giving of too much importance to the practical and materialistic necessities rather than to our inner lives. As we begin our gradual search to fill our emptiness, we unfortunately come across a fatal encounter that can destroy our lives forever. A perfect example of this is my experience—how I have been forced to live against my will. This has happened before to others and can happen again.

Our lives mature, thanks to a package of many experiences. Each new experience that we absorb can open us up to new understanding, particularly when we deal with what is more than mere materialism—our essence. Consequently, reading my story could be helpful in avoiding such an unhappy experience as mine. I recognize that I allowed it to happen because of my ignorance.

The lack of knowledge is our greatest enemy by keeping us from recognizing our greatness. It makes us weak by instilling doubt which can subject us to many destructive forces. I believe that we can find a number of solutions from the knowledge derived from our biological system. I have referred to many medical texts that could explain how I could be manipulated and reduced as a container for such a long time. I have also searched other texts for explanations about universal energy and its forces. If anyone wishes to follow me in this attempt at rediscovery, then perhaps we could serve as one another's guide by going forward courageously and honestly, recognizing the truth and love that we have for one another.

Chapter 21

The Very First Discrimination

I began to search for references about God since my possession was initiated in the name of God. So I started to visualize energy as the most powerful and mysterious force to have originated all life, consisting of procreation and proliferation. This very energy has many different expressions that create constant oppositions: love that becomes hate, sympathy becomes rejection; and selfishness becomes greed and jealousy. The opposite of selfishness is generosity.

Since the greatest energy is based on procreation, which in itself is an act of donation, our essence is based on the natural energy of love. Only we can consciously feel love or hate in all its variations and give it meaning. And only we have the power over this most powerful energy to direct and redirect it wherever we want, whenever we want, however we want. We are the most wonderful and unique creations in this universe, and I crave for people to finally recognize our genius and to accept mankind's inherent goodness and generosity.

At this point the question arises as to what changed our natural spontaneous energy of generosity... It was our consciousness which slowly grew within us and created our selfishness!

Selfishness based on jealousy and greed developed the consciousness for power. Power requires discrimination and hierarchy and hence the need for kings and pharaohs. Since humans are mortal and no one should ever oppose or doubt "the powers that be," power itself has to be immortal, invisible, untouchable and indestructible.

How do we classify such a power?... We classify it as supernatural—the supernatural that rules the universe and rattles the world!

We will call him God and in the name of power God was created.

God has to be above everything; therefore, everything has to remain under His power.

Humiliation and discrimination are the most effective forces that can keep the supernatural God above all.

This is the only explanation I can give to justify the inconsistency of the God introduced to us through the Old Testament, as well as the very first discrimination committed by God.

The God who was created by this supernatural power automatically created himself the very first discrimination and division at all levels.

The first was between man and woman, Adam and Eve, who were prohibited from eating the forbidden tree. Even though they were lacking the knowledge to distinguish right from wrong, they were still unjustly punished for being deceived by the serpent for violating God's prohibition. From that moment Eve, as the mother to us all, had automatically stained us with this original sin. Consequently, all women since then have been, and are being discriminated against and humiliated even today. Women were legally subordinated to men in all societies with the assent of God.

By the research of William Edelen, St.Paul, in his writings, went on to command that women should be submissive to husbands... should not speak in church... and he reminded them that *"women were created by God for men..."*

"I will greatly multiply thy sorrow and thy conception; in sorrow thou shalt bring forth children; and thy desire shall be to thy husband, and he shall rule over thee." *Genesis 3:16*

Likewise, Clement of Alexandria, a Greek Christian theologian (150-220 AD) refers to women thus, "Every woman ought to be filled with shame at the thought that she is a woman."

The founder of Western theology, Tertullian said, "Each of you women is an Eve. You are the gate of Hell, you are the temptress of the forbidden tree; you are the first deserter of the divine law. "

John Wesley of Methodist fame wrote his wife: "Wife. Be content to be insignificant. Of what loss would it be to God or man had you never been born."

The early church fathers of the 3rd, 4th and 5th century said in clear language: The female, as a symbol of the Goddess, was from Satan. There was a Goddess in every woman that had to be crushed.

When the Christian church really went full steam ahead in their destruction of women, the female and the Goddess within women was during the Great Inquisition. Marija Gimbutas, the author, is a Professor of European archaeology at UCLA and the curator of the Old World archaeology at UCLA's Cultural History Museum, quote:

"Women were called Disciples of Satan" and this period was one of the bloodiest in history. The witch hunts of the 15th to 18th centuries were the most satanic events of European history. The murder of women accused as witches escalated to MORE THAN EIGHT MILLION. The burned or hanged women were mostly country women who learned the lore of the Goddess from their grandmothers.

In "Woman of Age, Wisdom, and Power" by Barbara G. Walker, the number of witches slaughtered was estimated by scholars to be 7 to 9 million also. Will Durant, in his 12-volume, History of Civilization, sets the figure at an estimated 9 million.

A woman named Sonia Johnson was recently booted out of the Mormon church for being too blunt and questioning the dogmas of the church. Her departing words were these: *"My Fantasy . . . Is That Next Sunday . . . Not One Single Woman . . . Anywhere In The Entire World . . . Will Go To Church."*

In addition to discriminating against woman, God has also sought to divide man from the land to the extreme of flooding the earth. He instructed Noah to gather together all living creatures into an ark while killing all other remaining life. God even admitted his error: "I will never again strike down all living beings as I have done." Genesis 8: 21.

Noah and all his descendents thus became the first to be blessed by God. In order to distinguish Noah's descendents, Abraham was commanded to circumcise all males. All those not circumcised were considered unclean and impure. This created discrimination and division between peoples and nations.

God in all his discrimination sharply separated Egyptians from the Israelites because the Pharoah refused to let the Israelites go. He had the Israelites mark their houses with lamb's blood in order for him to pass over them while striking down every first-born Egyptian male.

However, when the Israelites disobeyed God, he had a punishment ready and waiting for them. He sent the most powerful nations on earth, Babylon and Assyria, to destroy the Israelites with the mission of killing their sons and raping their daughters. Furthermore, God killed innocent children for the sins of their parents.

As if dividing families were not enough, another discrimination was created, which was the indictment against touching "unclean" things. This was deemed a sin as well as a serious crime.

Yet another serious offense was the withholding of information: "If any person refuses to give information which, as a witness of something he has seen or learned he has been adjured to give, he thus commits a sin and has guilt to bear." Leviticus 5.

More discrimination and division between man and his neighbor could not be achieved. It seemed that God was intent on pitting every man against another and making him his brother's spy. I couldn't believe that this could be an omniscient and omnipotent creator who pits man against man with such vindictiveness as to kill the first-born sons and rape the daughters.

This contradictory God, who is always presented to us as vengeful, will even admit to his own errors, such as destroying all life on earth. Furthermore, many of the strict laws that he established are not even relevant today. For example, the rules which deal with methods of animal sacrifices or the execution of witches are no longer applied, as well as abstinence from eating certain foods on particular days. And there are many more such examples.

It is so obvious to me that for political power the human hierarchy invented God, and that this cunning manipulation was calculated from the very beginning, starting with Eve.

Discrimination didn't end with the Old Testament but continued in the New Testament. Jews who didn't recognize Jesus as their king, demanded that He be killed and that Barabas be spared. This gave rise to the Christian persecution of the Jews for not acknowledging Jesus as the Son of God. From that time onward, all successive Popes have consistently persecuted the Jews, leading to the Inquisition and its continuation thereafter. Moreover, in order to create the fiercest adversity against them, Christians spread vicious rumors that the Jews were evil murderers, not only of their Divine Savior Jesus Christ, but also of Christian children to satisfy the insatiable need for Christian blood for the Jewish Passover celebration.

The Christians claim that only they are in complete possession of the true living God, consisting of three persons: Father, Son and the Holy Spirit. And for this belief they will fight forever. All Jesus's apostles and the early Christians have "brainwashed" others with these claims.

The Catholics, through the intercession of Virgin Mary and their saints, believe in the manifestation, even the creation, of miracles. This belief is rigorously proclaimed and they fight for its protection. To confirm absolute domination, the Vatican state was created, with the Pope at its head, giving him "infallibility" in matters of doctrine.

The Protestants, believing only in Jesus's divinity, do not believe in the intercession of Virgin Mary or the saints and do not recognize Papal authority. Moreover, they don't consider him infallible. This has led to a centuries-old conflict between the Protestants and the Catholics for which there has been bloodshed up to the present day.

Christians believe that anyone who is not baptized in the name of Jesus and who does not follow the Bible will not partake of eternal life, since we can be accepted only through Jesus who washed away our sins. Where do we put the followers of other religions? Will they remain in a sinful, godless, animal-like state?

In the Book of Matthew, we are told that:

"The angels will go out and separate the wicked from the righteous and throw them into the fiery furnace where there will be wailing and grinding of teeth."

All these fanatics who contradict each other are ready to kill the people who do not share their beliefs, so far as using biological weapons in the name of God, as if the "angels will go and separate" the rights from the wrongs. Hitler had already attempted to purify humanity from impure races, by committing genocide of the Semites, and made himself out to be that "angel."

The Christians who fight for the right-to-life are of the same cloth as those who have led the inquisition against the Jews, which was the result of a longstanding atrocity known as anti-Semitism, of whom Hitler was the greatest practitioner by his killing of millions of Jews. And yet at the same time, Christians preach forgiveness and compassion.

The search for truth can only lead one to confirm in what terrible ways the name of God has been used, even to the extreme that such groups as the "Army of God" have been organized and have taken credit for bombing abortion clinics and gay bars. Is our God so feeble that he needs to have armies to defend and protect him? Who is behind this brainwashing that incites these militants of God to assassinate abortion doctors and plant bombs in clinics?

The terrible irony is that they are fighting death by bringing death to others. They protest the destruction of the embryo, yet do not hesitate to use a gun against a grown human being with a history of education, family and career. It seems it is always easier to kill in the name of love for one's God or one's country than it is to truly love another human being. But as long as it is done in the name of God or Ideology, they are heroes.

Religious beliefs have become more important than human beings to such a degree that even school children are being urged to kill in the name of religion. Hate groups, which seek to demonize Jews and others, are growing at an alarming pace. They are inspired by religious theology and their aim is to create a white Christian nation that has no Jews or minorities. The central thinking of "Church of Jesus Christ, Christian Aryan Nations" seems to adhere to a religious-styled racist philosophy called Christian Identity. It states that Jews are evil and that white Aryans are God's chosen people.

They believe that in order for Christ to return to Earth, the globe must be swept clean of satanic forces, including Jews and homosexuals. These groups are found under many different names, one of which is the Phineas Priesthood of Christian Identity. They follow the prohibition stated in the Old Testament against marriages between Jews and gentiles. And they promote a form of Nazi Christianity called Hitler's Christianity, The Church of the Knife.

In much the same way that the various Gods were invented for a particular purpose and domination, many religions were also created, each of them ending up by discriminating against the other. Judaism, Christianity (which includes both Catholicism and Protestantism), Islam, and Hinduism—each pretends to monopolize God.

As for Islam, its founder, Muhamme, having become acquainted with the Jewish and Christian religions and traditions, started his own religion after the Angel Gabriel's apparition to him in a dream. In this way he is considered the last prophet. He was of a highly nervous temperament but with a retiring disposition. He often shrank from bodily pain and was subject to epileptic fits. In fact, some Christians believed that he was close to "a paroxysm of cataleptic insanity." Muhammed was also gifted with great powers of imagination even if he was taciturn. He was addicted to prayer and was austere in the practice of his religion. (Though, after the death of his wife he begin to practice polygamy taking perhaps as many as a dozen wives.)

Interestingly enough, the Angel Gabriel who appeared to Mohammed was indeed the same who appeared to Mary and announced to her that she would conceive a son named Jesus. He would be called Messiah and Lord, and God the Father would call him "the Holy Son of the most High" and would give him the throne of David, his father.

Muhammed, emboldened by the Angel Gabriel, began his active career as a Prophet of Allah and the Apostle of Arabia in 613 a.d. Christians, to impose the new faith, found it necessary to practice persecution. Mohamed, too, followed this same tradition and provoked persecution against his enemies by conquering Arabian, Jewish, and Christian tribes, uniting them under the one emblem of a monotheistic Islam. This monotheism violently rejects all religions other than Islam, leading one to suppose that intolerance would be the first and most fundamental pillar of Islam. Fundamental Muslims reject Trinitarian Christianity as well Hinduism, which they consider to blaspheme the true religion of the one and only Allah.

The goal of Muhammed was to extend Islam by subjugating the entire world to the Muslim faith and its strict rules found in the Koran. After Muhammed's death, his successor, his father-in-law Abu Bakrs, succeeded in conquering and converting to Islam a great part of Saudi Arabia and the surrounding region as far as Indonesia in the east and Morocco in the west.

Centuries later, the Crusades were undertaken in the West as a solemn vow to deliver such Holy Places as Jerusalem from Islam's tyranny. Christians had considered what is today called Israel to be their holy land which, in 1095, was controlled by Muslims.

The original crusades was a political union of all peoples and sovereigns under the direction of the popes. The pope called for a "War of the Cross," or Crusade, to retake the holy lands from the unbelievers. After pronouncing a solemn vow, each warrior received a cross from the hands of the pope or his legates, and was thenceforth considered a soldier of the Church, according to the will of God.

Preachers of the crusades appeared from everywhere as a disorganized, undisciplined, and penniless army, almost destitute of equipment. They plundered as they went East, murder the Jews in Germany among many others and arrived at Constantinople in 1096.

Since then, the meaning of the word *crusade* has been extended to include all wars undertaken against not just Mohammedans but infidels, pagans, heretics, or those under the band of excommunication. The continuation of the crusades was more brutally enforced by the barbarian Inquisition. Yet the end of the golden age of Islam came about not by the crusades, but by the Mongols and their leader, Genghis- Khan.

The conflict between Muslims and Christians in present-day Yugoslavia is a continuation of this same conflict between Islam and Christianity which, as always, is sanctioned by the will of God. Serbs, who are Orthodox Christians, hate Croats, who are Roman Catholic, and both groups hate Muslims, leading to the mass murder of Muslims by Christians. In retaliation, the Muslims murdered thousands of Roman Catholics and Serbian Orthodox, giving rise to a bloody civil war involving mass genocide. All discriminations and divisions have developed over time into a deep, festering hate that took root from God's example.

God's name is always invoked any time a war is about to be launched or other people exterminated. The name of God has always been associated with despotism and tyranny. Many Islamic fanatics who call themselves Hezbollah or "Party of God," have announced their readiness to die in a *Jihad,* a holy war, intended to eliminate those who they believe are the enemies of God.

Recently, Muslims declared a Holy war against the United States. On September 11, 2001, a group of well-trained fundamentalist Muslim terrorists on suicide missions, hijacked four airplanes that crashed into the Pentagon and the World Trade Center, causing the Twin Towers to collapse in New York, killing almost 3000 people. And yet Muslim leaders declare that Islam is a peace-loving religion. Similarly, Christians believe themselves to be messengers of love, while in Belfast Protestants and Catholics continue to kill each other, leaving 3,600 people dead.

Muslim fanatics continue to persecute the Hindus (who believe in many deities) and Sikhs (who believe in ten gurus and one God), and all others who do not believe in the Prophet Mohammed and do not follow the Koran, because they are considered not to have any value, therefore can be killed since they are infidels. They do not belong to humanity and are worse than animals.

Communist China has killed Buddhist Monks and destroyed Tibetan monasteries. The Afghani Taliban destroyed archaeological sites of the Buddhist statues, because they do not accept idolatry in any form.

Certain religious teachings contain resources in encouraging their followers to make violence or to be involved in radical fundamentalist movements. Even the scriptures of some religions tell their followers that killing non-believers will take them to heaven. Still others teach their followers to fear other faiths. Christians try to convert Muslims and Jews to Christianity and vice versa. In fact, the Russian Orthodox Church recently accused the Vatican of trying to pilfer its members in order to convert them to Catholicism to establish an alternative church, speculating that if they were to appoint an alternative Pope in Rome, what reaction would the Vatican have? All in all, this is considered by the Russians to be an unfriendly act which violates canonical principals. Hopefully, this will not lead to another war. As long as fanaticism is being praised by religious believers, a peaceful world would be difficult to hope for.

Shouldn't we teach in schools the history of all religions rather than religious indoctrination? This might be more useful in understanding that the dictatorial impositions of every believer has no difference with those of Hitler or Stalin and many others.

It is difficult to say that God's teachings are a good example. The deeper I have gone into search for truth and meaning, the more have I been amazed to discover in what terrible ways the name of God and his teachings have been used over the centuries and how many victims have been made to suffer under his name.

Speaking about victims as such, I need to understand why and how I could be so persistently manipulated and brainwashed, as well as the meaning of the word, "possession." Since my possession originated in the name of Jesus, it has become necessary for me to reflect and question everything regarding Jesus and Christianity. I am most dismayed by Jesus's consent to my suffering, especially in such a dishonest and untruthful way, since He claimed that He was the Truth. Yet, how can I possibly believe this if Friar G. used Jesus's stigmata to lie? In Christ's name, Friar G. even used my husband's health as an excuse to pursue his own devious mission.

There is one thing I cannot tolerate: lies. Of all the insults to humanity, the greatest is the evasion and the perversion of truth in which real human dignity resides. If God and Jesus do not respect truth, we really do not need them. We humans excel at deception enough as it is. If God and Jesus's cruel method of accomplishing their designs for the world is governed by the principle of the end justifying the means, then we do not need a God. We are already putting this principle into action without the help of any divine authority. And if God and Jesus are not the guardians of truth, why are they so much better than us? Obviously they are not.

By the same principle of the end justifying the means, Jesus in choosing his apostles planted love in their hearts until they burned with undying fervor for him. It had to be that way. The apostles had a mission: to establish and confirm Jesus, God and the Holy Spirit, and to build the Christian Church.

I wonder whether Jesus's extreme love for his apostles didn't turn into despotic hate. Just as great love can turn into hate, it follows then that great hate can also turn into love. If you see the world as hopelessly evil, you begin to dream of good. If you dream of death, and death is approaching, your dream turns to life. When you are so full of sorrow that you are exhausted by it, you will dream of happiness. If your happiness is boundless, you think of sadness. Only those who touch the root of sadness can appreciate joy. Every form is eternal, yet the level of our conscience is perpetually evolving and changing into its opposite. After all, didn't God sacrifice His only son for our love by putting him on the cross in the most merciless manner?

I don't understand why Jesus, the apostles and Friar G., endowed with such extreme power, decided to exercise that power so inhumanly and abusively. I believe they were originally simple, good people, fishermen and peasants, but once intoxicated by power, they turned into fanatics and began to behave in such an inhuman and insensitive manner that it can only be considered despotism. Motivated only by their unbridled passion, they were driven to pursue a mission that was so all-consuming that they were not allowed to reserve any love for themselves. They blindly followed the example of Jesus who was filled with such extreme love of God that none was left over for Himself and others. As Jesus said in John 14:

"The words that I speak to you I do not speak on my own. I do nothing on my own, I say only what my Father taught me." Jesus inculcated this same obsessive love in his apostles. In John 7, Jesus says: "Did I not choose you twelve?"

Jesus is confirming that he is possessed himself; his own existence has completely been annihilated just as he has annihilated the existence of his apostles.

With much sadness I began to see the similarities between Jesus and Friar G. The Gospel, according to Matthew 10, confirms that Jesus was also "possessing" his apostles. We read that Jesus told the apostles:

"Do not worry about how you are to speak or what you are to say. You will be given at that moment what you are to say. For it will not be you who speaks, but the Spirit of your Father speaking through you." And, in John 18, Jesus says: "Father, I wish as you are in me, that they also may be in us, I in them, and you in me."

At last I was discovering the historical religious precedents for the possession that was being inflicted on me.

The apostles' fanaticism caused them to suffer a martyrdom every bit as cruel as Jesus's. In fact, at the beginning, the Romans were generally quite tolerant of the first Christians. Only after they began to create social and political unrest did the Romans turn vicious and start to persecute them.

The Apostles also adopted a very brutal attitude toward any new convert who would not follow them blindly. Ananius and Sapphira refused to share their goods with other Christians. They were persecuted within the Christian society and mysteriously died.

The central question was: Did the apostles live in Jesus? The answer is: No. Because of my experience I suppose that Jesus transferred his power to them as Friar G. has been doing to me. Jesus had also the power of bi-location, meaning that he was capable of existing in more than one place at the same time or at least give this illusion. Therefore, it was no wonder that the apostles believed that he had, in fact, been resurrected.

I believe that the spirit can survive only in a living person. Real eternal life exists in memories we leave behind or in the legacy of our deeds. And so long as the New Testament is read and remembered, Jesus's legacy will be kept alive. Strangely enough, this kind of eternity has nothing to do with one's morals. Someone like Hitler, for example, has achieved a kind of sinister eternal life because of what he has left behind. Friar G. affirms that the spirit of Jesus cannot be found in the physical church, or in the challis of the Holy Ghost, nor can He live inside the Cross, which is just a piece of wood. This is self-evident. These only serve as reminders.

Throughout spiritual evolution, mankind has forgotten the motivation behind creating plural Gods which were then unified in one God. The common acceptance that God's existence is real has been integrated into our lives so much that there was never any doubt about it. It became the convention that God was the only pure essence. Automatically, we as ordinary humans, are tainted creatures at birth. All we can do is to acknowledge our impurity and inferiority with such lamentations as those that I was forced to recite: "Have pity, have pity, have pity"...then beg for forgiveness and offer life to God.

I keep asking myself with undying desire to understand, "Could there really exist the possibility of God, or is He just one made by our selfish desire for power?" And in the hopes of getting some response, I continue to beg for liberation, referring to Jesus's words, "Whatever you ask for in prayer with faith, you will receive." (Matthew 21)

As usual, the only response is silence.

How strange that, in the Old Testament, God is constantly speaking, teaching, and educating the people. And yet, when I implored him, He never answered me. There was always silence. Nor did He answer Jesus on the Cross. When Jesus cried out, "My God, my God, why have you forsaken me?" He, too, received only silence for an answer.

It is amazing that at the most crucial moments, God never answers anyone. Certainly not in my life has God or Jesus ever answered me. All my research, all my analysis, all my questions are still waiting for answers.

I do everything possible to find proof that God exists. Unfortunately, no such proof has been forthcoming. And it has become increasingly difficult to believe in such a deity or in an eternal life after death. Therefore, I cannot believe in the resurrection of Jesus.

If God is omniscient and omnipotent and nothing moves without His will, how could he possibly accept the kind of horrendous miracle that I was forced to participate in? And how could He possibly need such a miracle? Couldn't He perform it alone? Strangely enough, I received the usual extrasensory answer from Friar G. "He does not hear you, he does not know yet." I was quite surprised because in the New Testament, Jesus says, "Your Father knows what you need before you ask Him." (Matthew 6).

Isn't God supposed to know everything? I asked myself. The thought that my life is being cannibalized for such a vile purpose as Friar G.'s self-glorification deeply mortifies me.

In Matthew 10, Jesus says, "Be afraid of the one who can destroy both soul and body." But what if, in the name of Jesus, someone like Friar G. exploits and abuses your soul and body? Yes, I am afraid.

Even if all this suffering were meant for God, I would feel no less pain, as I loathe the idea of doing anything for a God who needs constant affirmation by false miracles done at the cost of innocent lives.

The Dalai Lama was once asked about his belief in God. His response was that Buddhism doesn't include the concept of a creator, but that the mind is the only Prime Mover. This leads me to conclude that since the human mind is continuously creative, it is we who decide our destiny. And it is only we that have a conscious and creative mind, in contrast to the unconscious mind of the universe in its repetitive action. Thanks to our creativity, only we are creators of a constant, new energy and vehicular transmitters of this energy to all the universe. Our creativity is a regenerator of energy and, as such, the sustainer of life in the universe. Buddhism teaches enormous respect for human life, as the expression of genius, thereby winning it a deep respect for the only evolving creature in the universe.

Unfortunately, the greatest fraud committed against man is the false belief in God's existence and His miracles. From the very beginning this has dramatically distorted the image and destiny of human beings by reducing man's existence to one not of merit or worth but one filled only with sinning. As a result, we live without mutual respect for each other. Our destiny was changed from one of potential happiness to one of infernal suffering, through which only, we are told, true happiness can be reached. I believe that the God created by humans was inspired by Egyptian history.

Chapter 22

Who Possessed Jesus?

Three thousand years before Christ, the Egyptian culture was the most advanced on the planet. The pharaohs were considered Gods. The ancient Egyptian priests were very knowledgeable and powerful. Their responsibility was to keep the population under control, to force the people to respect the pharaohs as divinities. They studied the astral movements, eclipses, lightning and the processes of death. These priests were clairvoyant and practiced a variety of occult arts. Foremost among their beliefs was a strong orientation toward reincarnation and all paranormal phenomena. Through meditation, they began to acquire spiritual power and develop the first scientific approach to the study of the universe. In doing so, they enhanced their reputation and authority so that they were considered prophets capable of attracting thousands of disciples.

In order to accomplish their objective, the priests instilled fear in their worshippers and punished unbelievers. If the people failed to contribute money to the pharaohs, these Gods punished them. Natural disasters such as floods or bad harvests were seen as retribution for a lack of contributions. People lived between promises and punishments. The Gods would perform miracles if the people were obedient; if not, they were threatened and intimidated. Everything happened in the name of the Gods.

The Gods that humans had created became more and more inhuman, and more and more vindictive. Tyrannically, they ruled by terror and castigation; human beings were turned into slaves. Denied any autonomy, they were forbidden to declare the words, "I am."

Since man was still afraid of natural events and perceived earthquakes, floods and tornadoes as acts of forces beyond his control, the number of divinities kept growing, each one representing a particular phenomenon, often taking on human attributes.

During the 18th Dynasty, the pharaoh Amenhotep III renamed the sun god from Amen to Aton, an ancient term for the physical solar force. His son and successor, Amenhotep IV, instituted a revolution in Egyptian religion by proclaiming Aton the true and only god. He changed his own name to Akhenaton, meaning, "He who is devoted to Aton." This first great monotheist was so iconoclastic that he had the plural word *gods* deleted from monuments. At first, the king built a temple to his god, Aten, immediately outside the east gate of the temple of Amen at Karnak, but clearly the coexistence of the two cults could not last, therefore, he proscribed to close the cult of Amen. He then sent his officials around to destroy Amen's statues and to desecrate the worship sites. We don't know for sure, but it is possible that Amenhotep III only did this because the power of the priests of Amen was too big. These actions were so contrary to the traditional that opposition arose against him. The priests of Amen must have been really furious, not only because the living god Akhenaten now started to worship someone else, but also because Akhenaten let all temples burn down. From now on it wasn't allowed to worship any other god than Aton. Of course, no one really worshipped him; they all still worshipped the ancient gods but now secretly, and as a result, Akhenaten relentlessly persecuted the priests of Amen.

Akhenaton's sun religion failed to survive, and Egypt returned to the ancient, labyrinthine religion of polytheism after Akhenaton's death. His mummy has never been found and the new religion and cult completely died with his city. He has been called "the first individual in history." The population ended up with two hundred gods protecting them against the vindictive gods who had been instigated against them by the priests.

Egyptian culture gave enormous importance to life after death. The funerary rituals and equipment became the most elaborate the world has ever known. The Egyptians believed that the vital life-force was composed of several physical elements, of which the most important was the Ka. A duplicate of the body, the Ka, accompanied the body throughout life and, after death, departed from the body to take its place in the kingdom of the dead. It, however, could not exist without the body. Every effort had to be made, therefore, to preserve the corpse. Bodies were embalmed and mummified according to a traditional method supposedly begun by Isis, who mummified her husband, Osiris. Ka was judged by Osiris, the king of the dead, after arriving in the kingdom of the dead,

Ancient Egyptian wisdom was taken from the Book of the Dead. Most of them were written in the intermediate periods, when it was normal to rob or kill someone.

Ten of the 42 commandments were written 1500 years before Moses.

I have not done inequity.
I have done no murder; I have done no harm.
I have not committed fornication.
I have not defiled the wife of any man.
I have never cursed or opposed Neter.
I have not polluted myself.
I have not acted with insolence.
I have not stirred up strife.
I have not plundered the Neter.
I have not spoken lies.

The highly educated Hebrew Prince Moses grew up in the Egyptian court and studied magic and astrology; he undoubtedly learned of the strange pharoah Akhenoton who proclaimed the idea of one God. So it appears that the mission of creating a universal monotheistic God fell on him. As a result, the Hebrew population was told that this new God spoke to Moses face-to-face and that through him, God chose the names of priests and princes for each of the twelve tribes.

The political life of Israelites was organized around the tribes. Each of them had a different function in the communal life. The priestly tribes were the Kohamin and the Levites. The names Cohen and Levy survive to this day as reminders of those ancient tribes.

All the learned and wise prophets in the Old Testament certainly appear to have been influenced by the aristocratic Egyptian culture.

If a priest were also a prophet as Ezekiel was, he would be higher than a simple prophet. The prophet who was not a priest, such as Amos, could belong to any social category. The priests were the most powerful class; even the King could not have political authority without religious legitimacy. Kings were chosen by the priests and were directed by the prophets. If the king lost the support of the prophets and the priests, he would be in trouble. King Saul had a falling out with a priest, the prophet, Samuel, who had elected him as king. As a result, Saul was forced to give his power to another king and it was David, who was supported by priest Shilohm. Later, King Salomon was supported by prophet Nathan. The subjects were obliged to strictly observe all rules and religious rituals that the priests and sages decided on. If they dared disobey, they would risk severe punishment, even death.

Hebrew priests would anoint certain individuals as prophets. Many of these prophets were brainwashed to the point of being annihilated from their ego by powerful priests and hence acting as the Voice of God. The prophets would threaten sinners with impending doom if they failed to change their ways.

The God of the Old Testament was also a vindictive God. A father's transgression could put a blot on his whole tribe, and the punishment was automatically passed on to his children. The purpose of the sacrificial tradition was to expiate transgressions. Thus, God spoke to Moses, saying,

"I, The Lord, am a jealous God, inflicting punishment for their fathers' wickedness on the children of those who hate me."

We, who are possessors of our invented God, have had to keep him alive with the partnership of wise and shrewd priests, philosophers and Egyptian astrologers who know how to read the process of human evolution. Anyone who ever spoke as a voice of God was in perfect symbiosis with our evolution. The Hebrew population was advised not only that Moses alone could speak directly to God, but also that God spoke to the people through him. However, it is believed that Moses utilized the Ten Commandments written in an ancient Egyptian wisdom Book of Dead and "interpreted" God's instructions for his own empowerment. In fact, no one ever got to see God in any form, because, as we discover in Deuteronomy 5, Moses told the Israelites that they had seen "no form at all on the day the Lord spoke to you at Horeb from the midst of the fire," because "I stood between the Lord and you at the time. The God who spoke with Moses and through Moses is the only God."

So now poor mankind was saddled with only one jealous and furious God who spoke often in anger. The question arises: "Who is this 'God' speaking through these possessed prophets?" God spoke with them day and night, constantly imposing his teachings.

In Ezekiel 2, we read: "I heard a voice that said to me: Son of Man, stand up! I wish to speak with you. As He spoke to me, a spirit entered into me and set me on my feet." This is another example of possession.

Each prophet was spiritually possessed, indoctrinated by his predecessor, just as Friar G. was possessed by Padre Pio.

In Jeremiah 1, we read: "The word of the Lord came to me thus: Before I formed you in the womb I knew you... A prophet of the nations I appointed you... Whatever I command you, you shall speak... To whomever I send you, you shall go... Have no fear—because I am with you... The Lord extended his hand and touched my mouth saying: See, I place my words in your mouth."

The poor prophets, unable to free themselves of the possession of the spirit of a powerful priest, began to lament their plight. So Jeremiah cries out:

"O Lord, I am an object of laughter. Everyone mocks me. Whenever I speak I must cry out; violence and outrage is my message... Cursed be the day on which I was born!"

In Lamentations 3, the prophet again asks despairingly, "How long O Lord ? I cry for help but you do not listen. Destruction and violence are before me." And again in 17, "My soul is deprived of peace, I have forgotten what happiness is; I tell myself my future is lost."

Reading these particular lines I am reminded of my own life!

So, where is this omniscient, omnipotent God, whom no one can see? He manifests himself only as a voice.

As a matter of fact, the laws governing moral behavior, supposedly dictated by God, proved so harsh that the same priests and prophets who were responsible for creating this supernatural God became fearful themselves.

Inevitably, the supernatural God was thus exploited in order to advance political objectives, as well as to frighten the population into submission. But the population was so enslaved, so humiliated and so scared of God that eventually it turned to idolatry. So the priests and prophets who invented God "decided" there was a need for a new God, a God of Love to replace the vindictive God of the Old Testament. This new God, of course, was Jesus.

The prophets consulted astrological charts announcing the birth of a king of the Jews, and thus prepared the populace for Jesus's arrival. A star guided the Magi from Persia to Jesus's birthplace. It was the Star of Bethlehem, the brightest star in the sky. Centuries before this, the pharaohs navigated by the same star. They built their pyramids always facing towards it, so they would have a fixed point in the heavens to guide their souls back to their burial place on earth.

Important new events were always preceded by some terrible tragedy, some act of atrocious cruelty, so that people would remember the event very clearly. And so, the birth of Jesus was marked by much bloodshed. King Herod, threatened by the prophets' foretelling the arrival of a newborn king, deemed that each first-born son must be killed.

John the Baptist announced the arrival of Christ, saying, "The

One who is coming after me is mightier than I. I am not worthy to carry His sandals." (Matthew 4) John the Baptist himself behaved very severely towards the people of Judea, calling them unclean, a "brood of vipers."

It was important to create a genealogical tree for Jesus, which was done by Matthew. By claiming that Jesus was a direct descendent of Abraham, his followers wanted to underscore the continuity of God's providential plan, starting with the Creation and culminating in the birth of the Messiah. According to the bible, Jacob, the father of Joseph and grandfather of Jesus, was a direct descendant of David, fourteen generations removed. And by choosing a direct descendant of King David, the early Christians could emphasize Jesus's right to be considered as a king. But, of course, Joseph isn't Jesus's real father because Jesus was conceived through the Holy Spirit. So, Jesus, conceived by the Holy Spirit, is more than a human of royal descent. He is a God. So, from the human point of view, He is a king, and from a religious point of view, He is a God.

In contrast to Jesus's detailed lineage, his mother. Mary, is provided with no genealogical tree at all. The story of her life begins only at the moment of Jesus's conception through "The Holy Spirit." Like many other humans in the Bible who were humiliated by God, Mary's role is reduced to that of a container, an object to be filled up and used. This is one of the methodologies of possession.

Joseph, too, was used, his sole function being that of providing Jesus with royal lineage. He is put to shame in front of his peers. Joseph must have been brainwashed by the same priests who played a role in the development of this mysterious God. The Angel of the Lord, the same one who revealed to the Madonna that she would be covered in the name of the Holy Spirit, said to Joseph, "Son of David, do not be afraid to take Mary, your wife, into your home. For it is through the Holy Spirit that this child has been conceived in her. She will bear a son and you are to name Him, Jesus, because He will save His people from their sins." (Matthew 2)

A similar phenomenon was announced in Egypt many centuries prior to Jesus's birth. When no male heir to the pharaoh's throne was available, his daughter, Hatshepsu, became the very first female pharaoh. The Egyptian high priest, decided to justify Hatshepsut as the new, female ruler to the masses by portraying her as an emanation of Divine Power. We can see the same conception in the doctrine of the Church which appropriated Egyptian mythology and other early religions for its own purposes.

God's words in Jeremiah 1: "Before I formed you in the womb I knew you…" confirms my belief that the birth of Jesus was planned by erudite priests, prophets, magicians, and Egyptian astrologers and that Jesus was possessed from the very beginning.

"I knew you before I formed you." Luke 2.22. "He was named Jesus, the name given him by the angel before he was conceived in the womb." It can also be said similarly that the Virgin Mary was chosen far in advance of Jesus's birth and was also possessed as preparation for her mission in that she could have easily confused a select prophet for the purpose of physically overwhelming her as vision of the Holy Spirit in the form of an angel. In effect, Jesus was conceived by the most powerful of prophet-priests whose energy remained in Him forever.

Jesus appeared in public at the age of 12 and astonished many with his knowledge of sacred scriptures. I posit that the prophet-priests whose energy lived in Jesus transmitted the sacred scriptures through him. Jesus reappeared in public at the age of 30, prepared for his mission by austere prophets and Indian gurus.

It is well-known that in India the gurus, having developed their inner power know how to control other human beings, in order to manipulate them, and make them behave as commanded. Jesus Christ, too, was endowed with this power, together with incredible determination. The spirit of the prophet that dwelled within Him made Him feel that he was God Himself and that He would be sacrificed out of love for God. This love that was instilled in Him was so exaggerated that Jesus believed that He possessed God's power. It was necessary for Jesus to believe wholeheartedly that God was living within Him.

In John 8, Jesus says, "I am the light of the world". In John 13, Jesus cried, "Whoever believes in me believes not only in me but also in the one who sent me, and whoever sees me sees the one who sent me." And, in John 6, He says, "I am the bread of life; whoever comes to me will never hunger; whoever believes in me will never thirst... whoever eats my flesh and drinks my blood has eternal life . . . remains in me and I in him."

I sometimes wonder if the apostles might have taken those words a bit too literally, since, after Jesus's death, His body was nowhere to be found. After all, many ancient civilizations, including the Incas, believed that by consuming the flesh of leaders who'd died, they could inherit their power. It was also a way of honoring their memory.

Throughout the history of the creation of a supernatural God, we come across many instances where magic and miracles were used to keep the population spellbound and in awe of Him. Jesus also had to promise protection to his followers and perform miracles, otherwise people would not believe in him.

Even though He was supposed to be the God of Love, He exhibited a distinctly human authoritarian streak of didacticism in his teachings. He tended to frighten and humiliate his audiences, accusing them of living in sin and inhabiting a darkness full of devils. Jesus's mission turned into one of exorcising devils from peoples' heart. He even accused ill and infirm people of being possessed by the devil.

In fact, he caused people to become obsessed with devils. "All the people who saw Him were amazed, 'What is this? A new teacher with authority. He commands even the unclean spirits and they obey him.' (Mark 27)

The whole town followed Him as He exorcised numerous demons and cleansed spirits. Then Jesus spoke directly with Beelzebub, the Prince of Demons, and drove him along with other demons from the tombs whereupon He thrust the legion of these unclean spirits into the sea. There were about 2000 of them altogether and they were all drowned.

People were right to be amazed. They had never seen so many devils, and they had never imagined themselves to be so terribly unclean.

In Matthew 5, Jesus says, "Do not think that I have come to abolish the law or prophets. I have come not to abolish but to fulfill." Yes, Jesus fulfilled us with legions of demons. God came to free us from the darkness of sin, and Jesus came to free us from demons. Raising the specter of demons offered a new way of enslaving and terrifying people.

Gradually, Jesus pushed the people to become completely dependent on their belief in God.

In Matthew 6, Jesus says, "Therefore, do not worry about your life, what you will eat [or drink], or about your body, what you will wear. But seek first the kingdom [of God] and all these things will be given you besides."

Jesus, and those who spoke for Him, like Paul, also encouraged the population to remain enslaved rather than to pursue independence.

In Timothy 6, "Those who are under the yoke of slavery must regard their masters as worthy of full respect."

And to keep people under His power, He also tried to persuade them to remain illiterate. He spoke strongly against the pursuit of human knowledge and voiced hatred for the Greek philosophers. "Do not worry about how you are to speak," He said. "The Spirit of the Father is speaking through you." This means that there is no need to study or read any books.

Jesus's devotion to God was excessive and blind. In John 15, Jesus says, "Whoever loves father or mother, son or daughter more than me is not worthy of me. Whoever remains in me and I in him will bear much fruit, because without me you can do nothing. Anyone who does not remain in me will be thrown out like a branch and wither; people will gather them and throw them into a fire and they will be burned."

These cruel threats are completely contradictory to the idea of a loving God. I suspect that the same clever priests, who used to speak through Jesus's mouth the same way as they had done with the prophets, couldn't help to reveal their fierce determination to control and manipulate their audience.

If a psychiatrist were to examine Jesus today, he would very likely arrive at a diagnosis of insanity. Imagine, Jesus would seem to be a man full of fury. He would see devils everywhere, violently commanding spirits, claiming to be God, insulting the population, frightening people who refused to renounce their lives for Him. A man acting and speaking like this today would be locked up.

In John 8, even his fellow Jews said to Jesus, "Now we are sure that you are possessed."

Of course, in those times, no thought was given to the terrible psychological consequences that such accusations of uncleanness could cause in people. It's possible that we have Jesus to thank for provoking neurosis like phobias and a sense of persecution in mankind. Shouldn't these "God-appointed" holy men who, like Jesus, were deeply convinced that they had been given divine instructions, be psychoanalyzed and sent to some place where they can't harm others?

Today we can see how history repeats itself. Padre Pio's energy keeps living in Friar G. who, like Jesus, insults and humiliates people, possesses them and reduces them to the same role of "container" that the Madonna and the apostles held without ever asking their permission.

Nothing can stop Friar G. By transmitting his thoughts to my consciousness, he suggested that the reason he couldn't be stopped is that Padre Pio, his mentor, is inside him, commanding him. It is frightening to think that the Church recently announced Padre Pio as the last saint of the Roman Catholic Church. Padre Pio died as a saint; shouldn't we then conclude that he is now in heaven, united with Jesus? But if so, why do he and Friar G. continue to inflict their shameful torture on me in the name of Jesus and in the name of the truth?

We learned from Padre Pio's case how difficult a procedure it was to canonize him a saint and what pains were taken to ascribe miracles to him, not only during his lifetime but also after his death, for purposes of beatification. What great effort was expended and what great convincing it must have taken to force people to admit to the miracles that they supposedly received. A saint can be proclaimed as such if, and only if, he or she has performed a documented miracle. The church, by legitimizing Padre Pio's stigmata, attempted to affirm not only the sanctity of Padre Pio but also the resurrection of Jesus. In both cases, miracles are needed since the church is nothing if not for its saints and their miracle

My advice to all those who wish to become the next Jesus, or think they are already Him, is that instead of senselessly enslaving others for their own personal gain, why don't they just start with their own crucifixion?

Chapter 23

Does The End Really Justify The Means?

After seeing all types of discrimination perpetuated in the name of God, I have come to believe that from its inception, the Catholic Church has been, more often than not, enveloped in scandal. The Inquisition is only one example of the persecution it waged against heretics and disbeliveers who were only searching for knowledge and trying to find answers to many questions. The church has opposed scientific and social progress, pretending to be the sole possessor of the truth. The moral code that the Bible imposed on us is strictly administered by the Vatican and is filled with taboos and prohibitions. The most important activity, procreation, was fostered in a perverted way ending with a completely distorted and sick approach to sexuality.

This creates a sadistic and violent approach to life. Modern society is rife with violent sexual abuse, which in many cases has led to murder. Certainly it remains one of the gravest problems in our society. Many of these problems can be traced to the tendency to humiliate and sadistically shame women. These have been cultivated with fervor by the Church.

The Catholic Church chooses to shun any kind of truly pleasurable sexual activity between men and women, keeping them enslaved to the concept that the only purpose of sex is reproduction. Sometimes I wonder whether ultimately the church wouldn't prefer to see humanity turned into a unisex species, like the famous leaping lesbian lizards that caused such controversy among scientists. These lizards are called parthenogenic because the females do not need to mate with a male in order to reproduce. What was even more shocking, at least to some people, was that the female lizards were observed courting and mating similar to a lesbian relationship. This phenomenon left many scientists baffled. In the case of the lizards, touching stimulated and developed the reproductive system of the female.

However, the Church has chosen to ignore the enormous human need for touch, a need that has even a scientific basis. As a matter of fact, researchers have documented what happens to infants who receive very little affection from their mothers. They almost literally wilt. In some cases, they die.

What the church failed to take into consideration is the fact that each atom in a living being emanates electrical energy and impulses which radiate enormous power whenever touching occurs. In some fish, for instance, the electrical cells have such a strong capacity that they emanate electric shocks that kill the fish on which they feed.

Sex is the wonderful and mysterious energy that creates constant tension and attraction between opposites. There is no doubt that the most powerful possession that happens is through sexuality. The feeling of love, including our spiritual love for God, is rooted in sexual love. It affects our spirit and intellect and becomes the powerful energy that spurs all cosmic life.

Since it is the most important life-affirming energy in the universe, I wonder why it has been so debased and vulgarized. Shouldn't sexuality be honored as a most tender human expression? Shouldn't we instill it with noble value and regard it as the most meaningful aspect of life? Every sexual encounter should be turned into a wonderful ritual filled with respect and admiration for the beauty of nature and the body. All nature has a sexual connotation, directly or indirectly, in one way or another. Even when the rain falls into the hungry womb of the earth it makes mother earth pregnant, and we try to read something evil into it.

Unfortunately, the Church vulgarizes this most noble aspect of life, teaching people to look on it as a dirty act. This attitude results in a lack of respect for a fundamental human activity that ridicules men's needs and turns women into whores. The wife becomes the mother, and the mother is seen as a Madonna, therefore untouchable. Men then go to prostitutes for satisfaction so that sex is turned into a vulgar commercial exchange. At the same time, they suffer such an enormous sense of guilt that they often become depressed and unstable.

Hypocrisy has long characterized the church's attitude towards its followers. The Popes, declared to be infallible and holy, built underground passages to the whorehouses of Rome during the Renaissance. It is not necessary to go so far back to find church hypocrisy with its emphasis on the secrecy adopted by Roman Catholic dioceses. Over the last two decades, dioceses have reached more than 1,000 settlements in cases involving sexual abuse by priest many of them sealed. Furthermore, Pope John II has ordered that the tribunals for clergymen accused of child molestation be held in secret. They will use secret ecclesiastical courts and the proceedings will not preclude civil or criminal prosecutions. They will be overseen directly from Rome. Obviously, the Roman Catholic Church is trying to protect potential perpetrators, rather than the victims. In decades past, priests accused of pedophilia were allowed to go to confession, get counseling and be transferred to other parishes, where they found new victims.

Finally, at the beginning of the third millennium, the news media is extensively reporting on the serious problem of sexual abuse in the church that for a long time has been kept secret. The archbishop, Edward Egan, who was bishop of Bridgeport, Connecticut, was accused of suppressing a series of sexual-abuse lawsuits involving six priests and 26 adults, who charged that they were abused as kids. The suits, in which the church acknowledged some guilt, were settled with a multimillion-dollar payment. Connecticut lawmakers then proposed a law to strengthen sex-abuse laws and allow for the prosecution of molesters years after the crime, but the Egan-led church reportedly crushed it. It is no surprise to Connecticut politicians that New York's Egan-led archdiocese is now opposing another such law.

But this time, Archbishop Edward Egan wasn't able to stop the trial of a former priest, John J. Geoghan, accused of molesting young boys sexually. The Roman Catholic archdiocese seemed more preoccupied with avoiding a scandal involving a pedophile priest than making sure the priest had no further contact with children. The church knew of the priest's pedophilia but moved him from one parish to another for 30 years.

More than 130 people were to testify against John J. Geoghan for molesting young boys. The mother of a then nine-year-old-boy testified that Mr.Geoghan slid his hand up the boy's swim trunks and significantly squeezed his buttock during a swimming lesson. The incident took a few seconds but those few seconds were forever emblazoned in the memory of the young man and permanently emotionally damaged her son.

Many letters were written to Cardinal Medeiros about seven boys who were molested by Mr.Geoghan and received blessing in his bedroom. The letters complained that Bishop Tomas Daily had been urging relatives of the boys to remain silent. Mr. Geoghan was also accused of raping a seven-and a ten-year-old boy.

In stark contrast to the secrecy, the Archdiocese of Los Angeles has dismissed up to a dozen priests involved in past sexual abuse cases. Bishop Anthony J.O'Connel of Palm Beach, Fla., resigned. He acknowledged that he had inappropriate contact with a teenager. The victim reached a secret settlement with the diocese of Jefferson City for $125,000. But Archbishop Edward Egan obstinately continues to maintain the secrecy of sexual molesters and also allows them to keep their jobs and even sends them to different parishes.

The most common lure for engaging the boys was a theological brainwashing that consisted of explaining to the boys that the conjunction of two bodies, namely that of his with that of the altar boy, would be an ideal way to reach unity with Jesus. What came next was to have them massage his back, and then other parts, ending in an oral sex and forced masturbation. The boys were also introduced to pornographic magazines and videos. At that time, they were only 9 year-olds and severely intimidated.

Another such case is that of 74 year-old Pastor Davis, who was also accused of sexually abusing teenage boys over a long period. Thus far, only twenty have come out to denounce Pastor Davis for sexual abuse that occurred during his ministry. Of course, Pastor Davis, using his divine mission as a disciple of Jesus and as a voice of God remains untouchable. He claims that he is protected by the Bible. Which part of the Bible protects him? I would love to know. He still maintains his position as a respected pastor that allows him considerable influence over his parish, including the collection of monies.

And again, history repeats itself. He is in the process of building a new church. How familiar it sounds to me. These self-made saints are always building monuments to their eternal memories. Extending his power far and wide, he has been accused lately of abusing a small boy in Tijuana, which, again, he denied. How many unknown cases occur in which priests and nuns abuse young boys and girls?

Meanwhile, the ordinary clergy is forced into self-repression, which is a source of many emotional and psychological problems. But because it is so difficult to deny nature's instinct for sex, it is almost inevitable that most clergy turn to masturbation or end up in mental institutions. So in order to help them in their mission of sanctity, shouldn't there be help to keep them from falling away from their holy path?

I am reminded of a molester of small boys who, facing his imminent release from prison and worrying about his ability to control himself in the outside world, requested that he be castrated. This may seem rather harsh, but should it be denied that even men of such standing as Pastor Davis, Geoghan and Bishop Anthony J.O'Connel and many others are nevertheless just as human as a common molester, and therefore equally susceptible to the same sexual urge? The suppression of sexuality by the church creates psychological disorders in those who are called to serve it. The church is filled with pathologically sick people, such as this, who pretend to teach us and to be our good example.

I will never forget one cardinal whom I used to know, who lived in a beautiful apartment in the Vatican City with three bedrooms and an enormous living room. His servants complained about how hard they had to work because the cardinal was constantly entertaining. Actually, one of the servants became his lover. The cardinal began calling her the Holy Madonna. He even tried to convince people of her holiness, citing as evidence the many sacrifices she made in caring for him.

This results in guilt and masochistic suffering, followed by psychological, spiritual, moral and sexual complexes. Our sense of guilt causes the development of fears which hide the truth and change our behavior from a normal to an occasionally pathological one.

The church's moral code, which applies to us while excluding the clergy, doesn't merely stop at the distortion of human sexuality but keeps on distorting all knowledge as well. Today the division seems to be between religion and science. Science is supposed to deal only with factual reality, and religion is supposed to have the only authority to mandate human morality. The Church, far from being perfectly infallible in moral conduct, continues to sow opposition to progress by interfering in scientific inquiry.

First, the Church divorced philosophy from theology, then it went further and segregated science as well. When Galileo expounded upon Copernicus's theory that the Earth moved around the Sun, he was tortured and put in isolation. To escape death he was obliged to repudiate his theory, though he knew it to be true. Giordano Bruno went even further when he proposed that the universe is infinite and denied the existence of a center of the universe. For that reason he was executed by the Inquisition in 1600.

According to modern cosmological thinking, the universe has been in continuous motion since the Big Bang. Far from being static, it is in a dynamic state. Scientists have long since proven that there is no center to the universe. Rather, it is composed of billions of galaxies, each with billions of stars that are constantly expanding.

For centuries the church denied that the heavens were in constant motion or that such extraterrestrial phenomena as meteorites or supernovas could possibly exist. Even though scientists believe that the big meteorites which fell to earth 65 million years ago were one of the causes for the extermination of the dinosaurs, the church adamantly asserts that this could not be true.

Darwin's theory also contradicts the moment of God's creation by affirming that such moments do not exist. His theory states that life arose as a result of natural selection of the chemicals in the earth's shell. The church still insists that we should not inquire about the Big Bang theory, but maintain the belief that creation was an instantaneous moment of God. The church refuses to take into consideration that creation is an evolutionary process.

So, Darwin's theory of evolution was greeted with skepticism by most Western religions, including some Protestant Christians. How could man descend from apes? People scoffed. Of course, many people even today are opposed to evolution insisting that they are a creation of God. That is what they have been taught in the Bible. The most recent breakthrough confirming Darwin's theory of evolution states that the genetic code of the human is about the same length as that of the mouse.

To the great disappointment of many, instead of having DNA packed with tens of thousands of new genes that make people radically different from mice, fruit flies or even worms, it seems now that we have a much closer kinship. Before we were human we were apes, and before that sea worms, and even before that, just living cells from which all life derived. The repeated elements in the genome, over and over again, look like guideposts to evolutionary history that we can put together into a family tree.

As far as moral instruction is concerned, the only thing of value left to us is the Old Testament. The question begs to be asked, Who wrote the Bible? So far as Richard Elliot Friedman is concerned the question all along is not "Who inspired the Bible?" or "Who revealed the Bible?" but rather the question is "Which human beings actually composed it?" It is known that the first five books, the Torah, which means instruction, were written by Moses. But medieval scholars suggested that the larger portion of the text was written by someone other than by Moses. The Book of Lamentation was written by Jeremiah and half of Psalms were composed by King David.

What we learn about the formation of the bible is inseparable from the writer's own background and historical context: when they lived, why they wrote, the relationship between what they wrote and the events of their world. Since most writers were priests, with religious authority they taught law and tradition, and having access to documents they could promulgate or disseminate the documents and put them together.

One such Aaronid priest, Ezra, had all this power. He had enormous authority and political backing and was authorized to enforce the law of God. Ezra fashioned the five books of Moses and his authority was directly linked to a scroll that identified him with "the Torah of Moses."

Since the Old Testament was written by priest-prophets and kings who were seeking enlightenment while tightly holding on to power, it makes perfect sense that the God introduced to us in the Bible is autocratic and inconsistent. In the Bible God kills innocent children for the sins of their parents without remorse. The Book of Job describes the autocratic behavior of God when he conspired to kill ten of Job's children. God himself being a killer, he spared Cain punishment when Cain murdered his brother.

Abraham, who is supposed to be an example of virtue, had three wives: Sarah, Hagar and Keturah—but to protect himself, twice offered his wife, Sarah, for sexual pleasures. He presented her as his sister to those who threatened him. Since kings and priest-prophets are endowed with divine authority, they are God-like. Polygamy appears to be normal. Moses had two wives, Jacob had four wives, Esau three and Salomon seven hundred concubines. Thus, they are never at fault and are free to pimp their own wives, sisters, daughters as sexual commodities for their own defense.

They believe that their families are their property; consequently, they can prey on them whenever the need arises. Throughout the Bible, woman is considered by God to be less moral than man. Since the Bible is written by male prophets and kings, obviously the man is favored by God and the woman dishonored and humiliated.

Ephesians 5. 22. 23: "Wives should be subordinate to their husbands as to the Lord. For the husband is the head of his wife just as Christ is head of the church."

The male is considered equal to a God, since Jesus presents himself as a "God," and a woman is just a container without contents equal to the Madonna without history.

It was common practice to use all kinds of astute tricks to gain advantage, not only with women but with all others as well. For example, King David, already married with eight wives, had his friend and commander of his army, Uriah, killed in order to get his wife.

Throughout the Bible, we are instructed on various sorts of vindictive crimes that people committed against each other by sundry tricks and deceits. The sexual chicanery and rapes used for becoming pregnant were all part of the usual rituals that were engaged, particularly by the descendents of God's chosen people. So, there is nothing extraordinarily unusual in the spurious pregnancy of Virgin Mary.

The most recent evidence that the sacred books aren't as divine as commonly thought was reported in the U.S. News & World Report, December 24, 2001, which stated that from the archaeological point of view, the latest discoveries have not found any archeological evidence described in the Bible. Thomas L. Thompson, professor of the Old Testament and Archeology at the University of Copenhagen, is affirming that today we no longer have a history of Israel, we can no longer talk about a time of the patriarchs, a united monarchy under David and Solomon, or the Hebrew prophets as historical realities.

The magazine continues that one prominent archaeologist, Israel Finkelstein, also described the biblical saga of Israel as not a miraculous revelation, but a brilliant product of human imagination. Modern archeology has found nothing from the middle bronze age, 2000-1500 B.C., directly associated with Abraham. Ancient Israel as described in the Bible never existed. It belongs to the fictional characters of Hebrew mythology.

Then there is the New Testament, which is actually a record of the eternal pain of human sacrifice in which all humanity is invited to follow the example of the crucifixion of Jesus. Most Christians claim that God Almighty came down to earth in the form of a human being and died for our sins. John 3:16: "God loved the world so much that he gave *his only begotten Son."* John tries to prove that Allah or Jehovah came down to earth to die for our sins. The Apostles profess that because Jesus is the *only begotten Son of God,* that He, too, is God which ultimately leads us to the conclusion that Jehovah is Jesus.

Most of the Old Testament is adapted to establish Jesus's royalty as the son of God and of David. Jesus was called the "Son of God," the Son of Man," as well as the "Son of David." (Not forgetting that Jesus came at least 1,000 years after King David!) Is David divine since Jesus is his Son?

Following is just a brief sampling of how the New Testament adapts passages from the Old Testament in order to prove Jesus's divinity.

In Exodus 4:22:" "Thus saith Jehovah, Israel is my Son, even my Firstborn,"

"Even my firstborn" refers to Israel but John 3:16 uses it to refer to Jesus. Here we see in this verse that Israel is not only God's so called "Son" but also his first-born ! Does this make Israel divine? Does this mean that Jehovah is Israel or that we must worship Israel as Jehovah or Allah. as we do Jesus?

The entire Bible, corrupted and mostly filled with man-made laws, is only to be believed by blind faith. In any translation, we clearly see that the Jews and Christians have appropriated scriptures for their own purposes. And if we add Islam, how is one to know which faith contains the most truth?

Samuel introduces us to the evil and lying God:

In 1,Samuel 18:10: "The next day an evil spirit from God came over Saul, and he raged in his house."

In 1, Kings 22:23: "So now, the Lord has put a lying spirit in the mouths of all these prophets of yours, but the Lord Himself has decreed evil against you."

Since Scriptures are the product of human imagination, so the idea suggested to us by Samuel and Kings that we have also an evil and lying God is more acceptable. It is easy to see that the Bible, which is supposed to be our moral guide, instead teaches us about the immoral behavior of our predecessors presented to us in the preceding examples. Among other things, it continues to persecute and disrespect women, as so many religions have throughout time.

For example, the Jews, who by following the Old Testament are protected by a rabbinical court which gives the men the right to disrespect and subjugate women, namely their wives. Under Jewish law, only the husband has the right to apply to this religious authority which issues a decree called Heter Meah Rabonim, the equivalent of a marriage annulment, without even informing the wife in some cases. The Heter Meah Rabonim allows the husband to declare his wife as incapacitated or recalcitrant thereby allowing him to marry again. In fact, some rabbis have been accused of impropriety in religious court procedures. Similarly, fanatical Muslims still practiced this terribly disrespectful attitude towards women by not recognizing any of their basic human rights, so far as to refuse necessary medical attention, as well as education itself. Women live in such a marginalized condition that even at home the windows are covered with black curtains to indicate their presence.

Humankind is not allowed to discover its greatness. Only a select few who hide behind God and who speak in his name are allowed to be recognized as such, but in most cases, they are possessed by others and in turn they themselves become the possessors, pronouncing apocalyptic prophecies by which to subjugate humanity. Thus the ordinary man is reduced to beggarliness. In the end, taken together, the Old and the New Testaments promote religious intolerance, which, in turn, rejects human rights. In fact, how many people have been killed in the name of God's love! Where is the morality that the church pretends to uphold? Can the church still pretend to be a moral guide?

Interestingly enough, up to the present day, each president-elect of the United States or any one about to swear to the truth in a court of law, swears on the Bible to vouch for his honesty and integrity, instead of doing so on the constitution. What credibility does the Bible give us? Should politicians be free to use the same deceptive tricks as the Bible teaches us to gain advantage, not only with women but with all others as well? Why then was Clinton's conduct so offensive? After all, he swore only on the Bible which itself is a travesty of truth!

We can only conclude that the morality of the biblical God was totally incompatible with the unconditional love taught by Buddha and Confucius. Therefore, the Catholic Church has dismissed Buddha and Confucius with the excuse that their teachings do not constitute a religion, but merely a philosophy. The philosophy which invites people to love and respect each other for our greatness is in opposition to the humiliation imposed by the God of Abraham and Jesus Christ.

Fortunately, they lived 600 years before Jesus. Otherwise, perhaps they, too, would have been accused of having demonic powers and been put to death. The only exception is Socrates, whom the church honors as a precursor to Christ. Since he sacrificed his life for truth, this is seen as a confirmation to the church's belief that if there is no sacrifice of life involved, then life has no meaning. Of course, the first and only divine messenger of love, according to the church, was Jesus Christ.

And again, the church contorted truth to suit itself, since Socrates didn't die for truth but for rights and the rule of law. He gave us the dialectic method—a method of questioning the rules of others, of cross- and self-examination. He was a symbol of the rational thought of the Greek philosophers.

The same attitude distinguished Confucius. Therefore, whenever somebody asks me what my concept of morality is, I always refer back to Confucius's saying, "Do not do to anyone what you wouldn't like to be done to yourself." Its simplicity is so profound and yet it encompasses all morality. It is easily comprehensible and adaptable for everyone in every moment of our lives.

Confucius's teaching, however, doesn't coincide with the church's own morality. Instead, the church has perpetrated countless abuses against humanity over time, including those who were high and mighty.

For example, Emperor Theodosius, who, after converting to Christianity and recognizing the rights of Christians, put a stop to the persecutions against the church. He fought against paganism and promoted accord between the church and State throughout his empire. In spite of his devotion, an archbishop of Milan accused him of being guilty of old sins and forced Theodosius to make a public confession in the main square of the city. His death marked the end of the Roman Empire. The empire's dissolution fulfilled the wishes of the Catholic church, which wanted to create an empire of its own.

Chapter 24

The Catholic Church And Its Approach To Sexuality

What I have come to realize is that almost all of these so-called saints, prophets and mystics affected by stigmata, who are able to bi-locate and perform magic miracles have one trait in common: They all suffered from extremely poor health from childhood onwards. They remained very frail both physically and psychologically, and suffered from many complexes which resulted in irrational, unstable personalities. To survive, these individuals often turned to God, developing a highly sensitized, hysterical relationship with religion and spirituality. They transformed their own human suffering into a morbidly pleasurable and highly sexualized kind of suffering, which allowed them to justify their sadomasochistic behavior. They could then assert that they were elected by Christ. To maintain this exalted relationship, they needed to feel intense, passionate love for God.

However, since it is impossible for human beings to experience true love for an abstract entity, this fierce passion could only be expressed through the mid-brain, (animal brain) which needs constant stimulation either by means of the imagination or through physical contact. Contact produced prolonged sexual fantasies, which released stimulating hormones similar in effect to amphetamines, which trigger the release of dopamine. This most powerful energy could produce many sensations about an illusionary God.

I observed that once men became endowed with strong spiritual power, most were arrogant and driven by enormous sexual passion. Instead of turning into holy, kind and generous people, they could be very dangerous. Since they had to contend with their own abnormal amount of passionate energy, as well as the energy they absorbed from their environment based on raw sexual power, the combination can become positively combustible.

When this mixture explodes within the individual, it often causes him to try to impose his dogmatic convictions on others violently. This has the effect of stimulating the autonomic nervous system of their mid-brain involuntarily. The stimulation is so extreme that they easily become impatient and tense. Therefore, only this illusionary God can help them to transform this stimulation into human suffering that produces pleasurable sensations.

I began to wonder whether the irrational suffering imposed on me by Friar G., which caused me to roll on the floor crying for hours, was actually sexual in nature. It occurred to me that this was, in fact, the case and it explained why human beings so often seem to love to suffer.

It is difficult to remember any of Friar G.'s followers ever receiving any kind of grace expressing happiness, love or joy. The only grace bestowed on Jesus's followers was suffering and pain. Inspired by the example of Jesus on the cross, pilgrims were obsessed with suffering and their life experience was reduced to a competition as to who was suffering more.

Such pathological behavior occurs when devotion is so extremely passionate that people confuse their spiritual feelings with their sexual ones. As I mentioned before, if our attitude towards sexuality was healthier, humanity's approach to life wouldn't be based on suffering and expiating guilt.

In their wisdom, the priests are fully aware of the fruits of their own humiliating indoctrination. They realize that as a consequence of their teachings, people love to suffer. The followers of the church are happiest when they are rolling on the floor and undertaking pilgrimages on their knees, bleeding and crying.

For Friar G., no days were more glorious than those preceding

Easter known as Passion Days. When Easter itself arrived, Friar G. would make a triumphal entrance into his church, carried on the shoulders of four strong men. At such times, his face would be completely contorted in pain—that was to be expected since he was supposed to be reliving the martyrdom of Jesus. Yet at the same time, his eyes were full of pride because he was carrying the sins of all humanity, just like Jesus! On that occasion, the church was invaded by a very strong scent of gardenia. It was the persistent perfume that always emanated from Padre Pio's stigmatized hands, in exactly the same way it did from Friar G.'s, as a testimony of the presence of God.

But the scent wasn't exactly miraculous: I was present on the day Friar G. picked the heady lily and rose extracts from a number of samples offered to him by one of his minions! I believe that both he and Padre Pio had the power to intensify this concentrated scent to an enormous degree. They also had the ability to transfer it to a gigantic distance. Of course, they used it as a subtle psychological manipulation since most of their naïve followers believed that it indicated their presence even when they were not visible. As a matter of fact it confirmed their supernatural powers.

During these manifestations his followers became massively excited at the sight of "Jesus" in pain, and inebriated by the strong perfume. Some even began to cry exclaiming, "Poor Jesus, how he is suffering for us!" Others, observing Friar G. would say, "This is real life. We should all live this way!" Of course, their euphoria was tempered by a sense of humiliation and guilt. This man, in whom Jesus lived, was also relieving them of personal responsibility by assuming the burden of their sins. Through this show of devotion, Friar G. also succeeded in making them more willing to donate money to his church.

Since people need to identify themselves with the suffering of others, the crucifixion turned out to be the most successful ritual of the church. In the crucifixion, people find a God who is human like them and who can make them feel cleansed by their own tears. I believe that with a strong will, it's possible for someone to channel the energy from such enormous suffering into physical manifestations like the stigmata.

The last great "design" of our man-made God was Jesus's crucifixion. God had made himself visible and sacrificed himself for the salvation of humanity, and in his generosity he appropriated our sins and crucified himself in the form of Jesus. A greater design couldn't have been invented; the entire history of humanity was now sealed for eternity with Jesus. That was the ingenious scheme of the church: to eliminate the importance of the prophets by creating Jesus on the cross and concentrating on that single person (God) and all humanities as one. Therefore, all humanity should find its identity only in Jesus. And to that purpose, the priests didn't mind crucifying Jesus, asserting that it was the only way to seal all humanity to a church as a symbol for our "salvation."

The crucifixion appears to have been intensely sexual for all those who identify themselves with the visceral suffering of Jesus. I think Jesus anticipated Freud's idea that all creations are based on sexuality. When the pain is as agonizing as it was for Jesus on the cross, it can become transformed into a kind of masochistic sexual pleasure. By possessing our sexual energy, he has nailed us to the cross with him. More to the point, the only thing that Jesus left us as a legacy to the world is the example of his crucifixion and the elevation of suffering as a virtue.

Even today in the Philippines some faithful women, as a protest for the church's ban against women priests, reenact Jesus's suffering and death on Calvary every year. They do this by undergoing the same carrying and nailing to the cross for the salvation of the world, accompanied by an exultant public following.

This doctrine inspired hundreds of groups to consider pain necessary for salvation. Self-hatred and a belief in self-sacrifice were particularly noteworthy among them. The Russian Old Believers practiced a religion so severe and punitive that only the most fanatic adherents could abide by its tenets. In imitation of Jesus, believers would don a crown of thorns and nail themselves to a cross, declaring that they were sacrificing their lives for the sins of the world.

The belief in the perfection of the spirit requires them to practice such methods of self-torture as flagellation, clitorectomies and self-mortification. They believed that through these painful practices they could transcend their mortality, achieve complete annihilation of the will, and transform themselves into Gods. Absolute faith was crucial. "There cannot be doubt," they asserted. From that moment, they would become a living God and, because God can't be criticized, their behavior, no matter how extreme or immoral would be venerated. They were beyond sin and could not be judged by mortal man.

This doctrine of self-inflicted torture made a U-turn to glorify the body's pleasure. Now extremes of pleasurable behavior were regarded just as effective as extremes of bodily pain. Then they would indulge in ritualistic dances and sexual orgies to achieve spiritual enlightenment in the belief that once they were sufficiently stimulated, they could transcend their bodies and thereby open the doors for the Holy Spirit to enter them. In their religious ecstasy, their bodies would convulse and they would speak in tongues and supposedly utter prophecies. At this point, spirituality would turn to sensuality and prayer meetings would turn into an indiscriminate sexual orgy among the celebrants. This ceremony was known as the "Love of Christ." And for good reason: They were simply trying to emulate Jesus's example.

When I read about this, I was very confused and embarrassed. Did Friar G. tell me that Jesus loved me so much at the moment he was driving me crazy sexually?

It is instructive to compare how saints and spiritual leaders like Padre Pio and Friar G. express sexual energy with the way it is expressed in the Orient. There is probably no more famous erotic doctrine than that followed by practitioners of tantric yoga. The spirit of tantric yoga is observed by disciples who consider themselves either brothers of the right hand—feminine—or brothers of the left hand—masculine—since all human beings are constituted of these two elements. In fact, the great psychologist, Karl Jung affirmed that our glands are bisexual.

Tantrism can be achieved without the participation of another person. However, the effect is far more explosive when the two elements, one representing the feminine negative symbolized by the moon, and another, the masculine positive symbolized by the sun are combined through mutual respiration. When the two currents of energy join together in the spinal cord, they close the circuit and awaken the Kundalini.

Kundalini is considered the feminine element or Goddess, representing the potential power of men and symbolized by the form of the serpent uncoiling itself. This union produces a great liberation, transcending any limits, allowing the individual to bind with the cosmos.

Keeping the Kundalini's ecstasy awake only with erotic fantasies cannot be sustained for a long time. Therefore, there is a strong need for physical contact which can sustain the Kundalini ecstasy by memories recalling moments of excited and stimulated sexuality. These memories continue to stimulate the already-achieved excitement in order to hold the energy necessary for ecstasy.

This sexual union is achieved through Kundalini which is the first principle of cosmic energy. In tantric doctrine, sexual union is never intended for the purpose of reaching coitus. The emphasis that tantric yoga placed on prolonging sexual stimulation recalls to mind the practices that Rasputin proceeded with his female followers. Curiously, there are some people today who, for whatever reason, consider Rasputin a great saint.

Somebody to whom I gave my manuscript to read came back surprised that I have mentioned in it the healing technique which consists in not achieving orgasm but in holding back that energy and redirecting it to the brain. He told me that he conducts lectures on the subject and that he has read about it in the book, "The Multi Orgasmic Man," by Mantak Chia & Douglas Abrams, I was even more surprised that he was. Rasputin, presumably a potential saint, used this practice a long time ago not only to become a multi-orgasmic man, but because his redirected sexual energy was stimulating the neurons of his brain.

Owing to my painful experience, I am very much against the practice of supernatural healing. However, I do believe in the incredible power of our bodies, particularly when our electrons are awakened through the stimulus of a great sexual relationship, accompanied by the proper sound of repetitive, rhythmical music. It stimulates memories and all neurons, creating a healing warmth which gives rise to miracles.

These rituals are usually accompanied by proper musical sounds. As an example, in the Orient, bells are used with magical sounds. In the West, Gregorian music is used in the churches. All genres of music can stimulate our visceral memories and reawaken our dormant neurons. This can be misinterpreted as a miracle, but it is always our biological system that is reacting to smell, sound, and touch.

Whether for sexual stimulation or for any other reason, this terrible experience of mine should never have happened. Just because of one moment of distraction, of not listening to my innate desire for fulfillment, and using silent meditation in order to find my father's roots, my whole life was destroyed. Instead of relying on myself, I put my life in the hands of somebody else, giving more credit to him than to myself. Not only did I not find my identity, but I actually lost it.

How could I expect that I would be so horribly abused, so brainwashed in San Vittorino, the legitimate Catholic church recognized by the Vatican with the Friar who followed Padre Pio who was declared as the last Saint of 2000? After all, this wasn't voodoo!

Chapter 25

The Untouchable Truth: The Story of Padre Pio

By chance I came across a book on Padre Pio, Kaos Publications' *Blessed Imposter* by Mario Guarino. I learned a shocking revelation about Padre Pio that I found difficult to believe.

He was born in Pietralata, a village with a population of around 3000 in the south of Italy. Most of them were peasants and shepherds who believed in medieval superstitions, common in a culture of predominant illiteracy. Pio's mother was devoted to Saint Francis of Assisi; thus he was named Francesco. The small Francesco used to cry all night. One night, his father in a fury screamed, "A devil was born in my home instead of a Christian!" He took the baby and slammed him upon the bed so forcefully that the child bounced onto the floor. His mother sought a fortuneteller to have the "evil eye" removed from her son, as was the common practice for people in villages like Pietralata to do. Therefore, between benedictions of the church, and the magic rituals of fortunetellers, the town felt more secure.

After the mishap with his father, the baby never cried again. At the age of four, however, Francesco started to have various visions of deformed devils, showing menace and violence. Whenever his mother shut off the light, the devils would appear, and disappear when it was turned back on. His mother was shocked one day to discover the nine-year-old Francesco scourging himself with the heavy chains, exclaiming, "I must beat myself like the Jews did to Jesus, and make myself bleed!"

His parents then decided to offer him to the service of God. Only the clergy could read and write, so Francesco was given over to Domenico Tizzano, who not only taught him to read and write, but also told him the story of Saint Francesco of Assisi. The future Padre Pio was so impressed by this saint's stigmata that he couldn't stop asking whether the wounds were real or not, and if they bled exactly as if they had been caused by nails. He wanted to be told the story over and over again.

Often sick with heavy fever and migraines, Francesco was bathed in cold sweat so much, he was often observed in tears, and was prone to many fainting spells. His visions of devils during the night were so intense that often the sound of breaking furniture and screams would be heard throughout the town.

At the age of 15, Francesco was assigned an essay, asking what he would do if he were king. His answer was that if people refused to lead a true Christian life, he would prescribe very severe punishment, including exile, imprisonment, and even capital punishment. Praying in isolation for hours, he severely flagellated himself until he bled, manifesting his fanatical approach to a religion filled with hysterical superstition.

When he finally became a priest, his masses would be held for hours, until ultimately at the end of each mass, he would arrive at a state of semi-conscious ecstasy. As time passed, successive masses would run longer and longer, his own ecstasy growing more intense. He eventually achieved stigmata in 1910.

In 1916, he decided to move to St. Giovanni Rotondo, a town much like his own Pietralata, where illiterate superstitions dominated. Padre Pio's violent nocturnal fights with the devils and bleeding stigmata generated curiosity around the population, elevating the collective hysteria.

Padre Pio was known to have a weakness for women. It was reported that he chose 12 of his young female followers to be his "spiritual" daughters. Surprisingly, perpetual prayers were performed even during the night in his bedroom. His detractors accused him of engaging in sexual "fusion" with them at bi-weekly encounters.

Whatever the truth of the matter, his involvement with these women stirred up a great deal of jealousy among other women in the parish. According to one biographer, Padre Pio's capacity to love women was so profound that his heart "bled" for them. For example, here is Padre Pio's letters to one of his young "daughters," Cleonice:

"Here is our union, here are our chains, which the tighter they bind us, the more joy and freedom they will give us! Their strength is levity, their violence sweet, keep me then very tied to you and do not worry about having any other thoughts in your head."

Padre Pio also, like other powerful mystics, did his utmost to alienate his disciples from their families and friends, so that he could more easily brainwash them into blindly loving their teacher. There is no need to point out that their chosen victims were never asked for permission. Such was the case with Clotilde, whom Padre Pio was able to estrange from her own mother. When her mother died and the young woman expressed guilt about being absent from her deathbed, he reassured her that he was in constant contact with the dead mother, who approved of their secret meetings.

Apparently, Padre Pio had come to the conclusion that women could serve both as objects of love and as symbols of donation: women were the givers of life, embodying all the sweet manifestations of love. That gives more reasons to use them. Padre Pio, mentor of Friar G., uses the same rationale that lying in the end will be justified.

I thought that such lofty passion of all mystics was based on stimulating their sexual energy for the purpose of healing or reaching a different dimension of higher spirituality. It seems to me that the only thing that separates a prospective saint from the common man is his power of redirecting his ejaculation and using it for different reasons.

It is well-known that most great mystics suffered from the burning flames of passion. History offers us many examples of "holy couples."

Some of the most noteworthy were the apostle, St. Paul, and the legendary St. Tecla; St. Theresa of Avila, the mystic and a doctor of the Church, bound by an extraordinarily intense "affection" to St. John of the Cross, St. Francis of Assisi with St Catherine, the beatified Jordan of Saxony and the beatified Diana of the Anjou conducted a correspondence overflowing with smoldering, tender words.

"Your love, with which you strongly and sincerely embrace me, certainly confirms that I, too, love you, according to God living in Christ," wrote Jordan. "I know, however, that you love me much more intensely than I love you." Letters like these, filled with expressions of almost conjugal devotion and amorous longings, are not unusual. The history of saints and mystics offers many similar examples.

It appears that Jesus also felt a deep, passionate love for women. Some of them like the Samaritan woman and Mary Magadalen developed an especially close attachment to him. In the Gospels, we learn that Jesus cried rarely in his lifetime? one such occasion was upon hearing the news of Lazarus's death. He then rushed to comfort Martha and Maria, Lazarus's sisters. He was fond of both women, but it was Martha to whom he opened his heart. In fact, whenever he was tired he used their house as his retreat.

As Padre Pio understood that women could serve both as objects of donation and as symbols of love, it seems that Jesus also loved in this same way. The woman as object of donation—Maria? was used for the purpose of healing; the other as spiritual symbol of love—Martha? remained a confidante.

Perhaps the person most responsible for causing Padre Pio's fall from grace was Padre Gemelli, a world-renowned scientist and one of the church's most respected spokespersons. A remarkable intellect who had studied medicine, Gemelli was the author of many authoritative books and articles on philosophy, unusual psychological phenomena and theology. It was because of his fame and prestigious position in the church that in 1924, on the occasion of the seventh centennial of the stigmata of San Francis of Assisi, Padre Gemelli was commissioned to examine Padre Pio's stigmata and provide his assessment.

A Franciscan monk himself, Gemelli was generally skeptical about the phenomenon of stigmata and speculated that even St. Francis's stigmata might have been pathological in nature. Gemelli contended that those who came after St. Francis—however saintly or mystical—were, in effect, false claimants, their stigmata evidence not of divinity, but of hysteria.

His opinion of Padre Pio was especially harsh. Gemelli called him "arrogant, a psychopath, a self-wounding man." Gemelli rendered his assessment against Padre Pio and declared that the priest had abused his power and brainwashed his followers, to such an extent that some of the young women gave him perfumes and other gifts in exchange for his attention and caresses.

In addition, he was accused of intimidating parishioners during confession. He would practice a form of emotional blackmail, preying upon his more vulnerable and credulous followers so that they would attribute miracles to him that he had never performed.

All of these charges were documented and agreed to by some of the most important members of the Catholic hierarchy. The report, now filed away in the archives of the Vatican, created an enormous controversy once it was issued. Supporters of Padre Pio called the report "Satan's masterpiece." In spite of their protests, Padre Pio was officially banned from the church in 1923 with the accusations of spirit-possession and taking advantage of devoted women and forbidden to have any contact with the public.

In 1933, however, the Vatican granted him permission to return to the church, but without, however, formally retracting any of the accusations against him.

A huge organization grew around Padre Pio, which arranged buses to transport pilgrims to San Giovanni Rotondo. Eventually, the flow of pilgrims became so great each passing day that in the end there was no time to pray.

Padre Pio himself organized his own clan consisting of such luminaries as Lieutenant Francesco Morcaldi (the so-called Ciccillo), his best friend the notorious Mason Cesare Festa, and his cousin Giorgio Festa, a devout fascist. Padre Pio's favorite, however, became Emanuele Brunetto, who was married but living with a girlfriend. Brunetto was known as a dishonest manipulator of money. He was the only one permitted to go to Padre Pio's room, often removing the bleeding bandages of Padre Pio and selling them as relics for $25 or more.

In 1920, a new election was held between two parties: one a liberal-popular conservative faction, which consisted mostly of peasants, the other a neo-fascist faction which received the blessing of Padre Pio. His benediction was to no avail, however, as the socialist party won the election. Divine intervention failed to materialize. Even so, Padre Pio remained a great supporter of fascism, and with his friends he organized a completely new group of fascist clerics called the "Fighters of Christ," who used the fascist black flag with the pontifical coat of arms.

During this political disorder, the pilgrimages continued, including nobility like Queen Zita of Austria, Duke Eugenio D'ancona (with his wife Lucia di Borbona), and the Archduke of Austria, Roberto Adelaide Marchese Napoletono.

Due to the enormous amount of money, the cloistered lifestyle was no longer observed, and the vow of poverty was disregarded as well. These Catholics were more reminiscent of pagans, and their belief in God was eclipsed by their idolatry of Padre Pio.

Even as the accusations against Padre Pio charged him with being an obscure and dangerous charlatan with questionable stigmata, Pope Benedetto XV declared Padre Pio a great propagandist of the church and Catholic faith, therefore deserving of special protection.

In 1922, Pope Benedict XV died and was replaced by Pope Pius XI. The new Pope was quickly informed by Monsignor Gagliardi, a strong opponent of Padre Pio, about the terrible pagan idolatry surrounding Padre Pio.

The Vatican world turned against Padre Pio to such a point that it ordered an examination. Doctor Bignani, a university professor, concluded that his bleeding stigmata were caused by nitric acid, with a tincture of iodine and both substances were found in his room. He declared that the stigmata were actually psychosomatic manifestations of a neurosis.

The enormous amounts of money that began to flow into San Giovanni Rotondo, however, became more important than spirituality, and the declaration of the luminary professors was no match for religious fanaticism. The superstitious masses they were up against discredited the professors as miscreant pagans.

Padre Pio asked Emmanuele Brunatto, his favorite trafficker, and his devoted women's prayer group to write a false declaration against all the priests who accused him of abuse. They were able to arm themselves with the priests' dossiers, using them to prepare cunning traps so that some of the priests ended up in prison charged with false testimony.

This holy war waged by Padre Pio and his followers reached as far as the Vatican. Emanuele Brunato even wrote a book under the false name of John Willoughby entitled *The Antichrist in the Church of Christ*. Padre Pio not only won his war against the Vatican, but also was able to accumulate enough money to build a hospital that was his dream.

Emanuele Brunato was a very active Nazi collaborator, whose activity with the Germans resulted in three and a half million francs being sent to the hospital of San Giovanni Rotondo called Casa di Solievo. The League of Nations, which in 1943 was providing assistance to the countries devastated by the war, strangely enough provided the just-born Casa di Solievo with 250 million lire and shortly after, it made a second donation of 400 million lire, and the Casa di Solievo was built.

It brought in so much money, though, that there was no time for introspection. Little wooden sheds turned to luxurious hotels, shops and lavish homes and large factories. Emanuele Brunatto's propaganda ended in a great triumph of spirituality that was sold on every street corner as "the really only truly great miracle." For example, one photographer, the spiritual son of Padre Pio Vinelli Giuseppe, was selling souvenirs and photos from inside an old car sunk in the ground; in a very short time he built his own factory, hotel and shop valued at over 100 million lire.

Often, the handicapped, after being declared miraculously healed, were later seen in wheelchairs. The blind still required assistance from relatives.

Most of Padre Pio's friars owned their own cars, far away from the promised poverty of Franciscan life, including Padre Pio himself, who was chauffeured around in an expensive luxury car. The fights between friars became routine, when they started to make dangerous speculations in real estate.

The Vatican once again tried to isolate Padre Pio by prohibiting him from confessing and having contact with the people, but the populace and the Franciscans fought this decree violently, declaring that he was theirs and no one was going to touch him. The people's own beliefs were mixed: They were undecided whether they were fighting for Padre Pio, or for all the income that his presence continued to bring.

The final decision of the Vatican was that all of Padre Pio's property, along with Casa di Solievo, would be transferred to the Vatican. Brunetto, the favorite son of Padre Pio, started a worldwide movement against the Vatican.

In Geneva he organized an international association for the defense of Padre Pio. With the six famous attorneys and public appeals to the United Nations for human rights, Brunetto presented himself to a new Pope, Paolo VI. He suspended the isolation of Padre Pio from public interaction but did not revoke the charge of being an imposter. Padre Pio became a moneymaking machine even after his death; the commercial veneration and idolatry, surrounding him grew to even greater proportions than before.

One problem remained when Padre Pio died: He died as an impostor, and could not be declared a saint. The God of Money performs more miracles than any spiritual God could, and thanks to the revenue of hundreds of billions of lira, Padre Pio was declared the last saint for the year 2000, who even after his death is still performing miracles under ambiguous circumstances. The Roman Church has been reduced to an industry of "souls" that have given a vote of fidelity to the God of Money.

After the sanctification of Padre Pio, San Giovanni Rotondo continues to grow in the style of Las Vegas, with new churches and refuges for pilgrims, which are sustained by state contributions of multiple billions of lire. And with continuous public funding the Vatican Banks happily grow, with more and more conviction that Padre Pio really was a great saint.

The same Italian company, Kaos , that published the book about Padre Pio has also published a book named *The Merchants of The Vatican* by Mario Guarini, which gives another shocking look at events in the Vatican during Pio's time.

In February 11, 1929, Mussolini and the Cardinal Pietro Gasparri signed the "Patti Lateranensi", an agreement between the Italian State and the Vatican. The Italian State now recognized Vatican City as a new state which was to be exempt from all taxes, including importation taxes and duties and was to receive an indemnity of $85 million, as compensation for papal lands that were confiscated when the Vatican was not yet independent.

Pope Pius XI gave the money to the financier Bernardino Nogara, and created a special administration, a "Religious Works Opus." Immediately, Nogara with the profits accumulated during the Mussolini regime made himself a black market shareholder, participating and taking control of all Italian institutions like communication, utilities, insurance and a munitions factory as well. As a result, when Mussolini needed ammunition for the invasion of Ethiopia, Nogara would purchase a great quantity for the Vatican, which was then passed on to Mussolini.

The second agreement between Germany and the Vatican included the notorious ecclesiastic tax known as "Kirchensteuer," which, in 1943, consisted of an income tax amounting to $100 million flowing into the Vatican.

In 1939, after the death of Pope Pius XI, Eugenio Pacelli was named Pope, and renamed Pope Pius XII. He was also known as the Pope of Hitler since he never opposed the torture and the killing of more than six million Jews. Finally, the worst church inquisition for centuries against Jews had been achieved.

Hitler admitted that he was inspired by the Vatican in his inquisition against Jews and had branded them from the rest of the population the same way that it was done in Papal history. This was done in a way similar to what was mandated by church Councils over six hundred years, by marking them with yellow hats and badges on their clothes, as well as imprisoning them in ghettos.

This coincided with the outbreak of World War II. From 1939 to 1945, the conflict stained the continent with the blood of millions of Europeans and Jews. The hundreds of millions of Swiss francs that were sequestered by the Nazis from the Jews, as well as from all the nations invaded by Germans, ended up in Vatican banks, due to the extraterritoriality and neutrality of the Vatican.

The Criminal History of Christianity, which encompasses ten volumes, was written by the German historian, Karlheinz Deschner, in which he analyzed the possessions of Pope Pius XII. At the end of his life, Pious XII was in possession of 80 million gold deutschmarks.

In 1942, Pope Pius XII transformed the special administration of the Christian charity Institute of "Religious Works Opus" to the (IOR) Vatican Bank, managed by Nogara. As a result, the IOR begins to establish ties with the leading financial institutions of the world, including Morgan Guaranty, Credit Suisse, Chase Manhattan and the Chicago-based Continental Illinois.

Soon, the Vatican was gobbling up interests in corporations involved in steel production, agri-business. The Vatican also bought a

15% interest in the giant real estate, giving IOR a piece of the action in everything from the Watergate Hotel in Washington DC, to resorts in Mexico. Working through Chase Manhattan, the Vatican Bank also began purchasing stock in General Motors, Gulf Oil, Bethlehem Steel, TWA, IBM and other major companies.

Nogara retired in 1954, died in 1958 amidst relative obscurity, and during his lifetime, had pyramided the money given to the Vatican by Mussolini's regime to nearly $1 billion.

The flood of blood was engulfing the world with millions and millions of people of all kinds who were tortured and killed by Hitler, while millions and millions of all currencies from all over the world were flowing to the Vatican. This was truly the most magnificent and glorious time for the Vatican

In 1958, Pope Pius XII died. Under his successor, Pope John XXIII, the Vatican continued to flourish with the legend of a good Pope. With his death in 1963, the new Pope, Giovanni Montini, named Paul the VI, became more aggressive in questionable business practices, like the Vatican money invested in weapons manufacturing and even in a pharmaceutical firm that produced birth control pills.

The enormous earnings the Vatican was making through the IOR attracted the attention of the Italian government, which proposed lifting tax exemptions which had been granted by Mussolini, but the Vatican objected and in 1968, Pope Paul VI refused to honor the new legislation.

The Vatican consulted the financial planner, Michael Sindona, who was also a conservative, a fervent Catholic specializing in fiscal evasion. His clients were Mafia bosses Joe Doto and Vito Genovese, the international drug smuggler and boss of the New York crime family founded by Lucky Luciano. Sindona was also trusted by the Gambino-Inzerillo family.

Pope Paul VI delivered the signed document himself to Sindono, entrusting him with all Vatican money in foreign countries. While under suspicion of drug trafficking, Sindona transferred money illegally out of Italy with the assistance of Monsignor Marcinkus, the president of the Vatican Bank.

The bank controlled 38 percent of the real estate, valued at 30 billion lira and paid for by Sindona in U.S. funds. Marcinskus transferred the other part through suspicious speculations to Luxembourg.

Most of the bank's shareholders were church-controlled institutions and one of these networks of "Catholic banks" was Banc Ambrosian where Robert Calvi was a manager. Later, he reached a dead-end and his patron became Michael Sindona who introduced Robert Calvi to the Vatican, along with the other conservative Catholic Masons, such as Lucio Gelli and Umberto Ortolani.

They took care of the Italian real estate sector of the Vatican—which in 1967 had a value of 202 million dollars, excluding the money from the "Ratline" which transported Nazis to Argentina, Canada and elsewhere with passports procured by the Vatican at the end of World War II.

Sindona's career as a Vatican consultant led to a union with David Kennedy, president of the Illinois Bank, and Richard Nixon. Sindona transferred 22% from his own Private Financial Bank to Illinois Bank. Richard Nixon, after being elected President, entrusted the Treasury Department to Sindona's partner, David M.Kennedy. The partnership of these three men was supported by International Masonry.

Luccio Gelli was the Grandmaster of a Masonic secret lodge? the most controversial character known as P-2 lodge with links to different groups as Argentinean General Juan Peron, and the most powerful functionaries in Italy, like Prime Minister Gulio Andreoti. Cardinal Paolo Bertoli introduced the members of the logia P-2 to the Vatican, where the pact to accelerate Calvi's career up the ladder at Banco Ambrosiano was established. Sindona would serve as Calvi's business partner, Marcinkus would represent the Vatican bank in this new arrangement, and Gelli and Ortolani would handle political details.

The Ambrosian Bank became so powerful that it could easily compete with international commercial banks. Clandestine transfers of money between Luxembourg, Switzerland and the Bahamas allowed it to become a fiscal paradise. However, this would have been too difficult to prove since Sindona was constantly recycling and creating new anonymous accounts.

The Vatican and Calvi had made fortunes from Sindona and their mutual associations. For instance, in one transaction, in 1971, the Vatican sold to Roberto Calvi's group 37. 4% of the stock, and received the equivalent in today's dollars of $1.15 billion.

In 1973, the Federal Bureau of Investigation began to understand the mechanism of the illegal trafficking, but progress was halted once they discovered that the Vatican was involved in this criminal activity.

In 1974, Sindona found himself close to a complete financial crash, and his last hope lay in the hands of the Christian Democrats, represented by Andreotti, (even giving two million American dollars to Andreotti's campaign against divorce).

After the Democrats lost the 1972 election, America had to confront the difficult Watergate crisis, and when Richard Nixon resigned from the White House under the pressures of the scandal, Sindona was ruined.

In 1978, Pope Paul VI died, and Albino Luciani, who became Pope John Paul I was elected later that year on August 26. Pope John Paul I received open letters from the newspaper "OP" titled, "the Gran Loggia Vaticana". It published the names of 121 Vatican Cardinals affiliated with Masons, such as Marcinskus. In early September, Pope John Paul I requested the immediate substitution of Marcinkus by Monsignor Angelo Abbo and an investigation of the presence of Masons inside the Vatican. On the 29th of that September, he was found dead; it was assumed that he was assassinated.

On October 16, Karol Wojtyla, John Paul II, was elected, and left things the way they were; Marcinkus would continue to direct the Vatican bank, while Calvi and Ortolani were free to continue their fraudulent affairs for him.

In 1981, Pope John Paul II promoted Marcinkus to Cardinal, while Calvi, president of the Bank Ambrosian, was facing total bankruptcy. The IOR Vatican Bank lost much of its investments.

John Paul II had to intervene and single-handedly recover the losses incurred by proclaiming 1983 the "Overtime Saint Year," producing an immediate financial windfall at the hands of faithful pilgrims, rather than waiting for the appropriate date, the year 2000.

The Vatican real estate was being used to make all types of speculative deals in which billions and billions of lira were at stake, even to the point that Assunzione, the most prestigious Catholic college, was transformed into a hotel. Finding lodging for pilgrims was more profitable!

The teachers were fired without any warning or without any compensation from one day to the next. When they applied to the Vatican for employment in some other Vatican institution, the Vatican, feigning to be completely unaware of the situation, denied any knowledge of the closing the institute.

Calvi was later found dead, hanging under the Black Friars Bridge in London. The Court of Milan called Marcinskus to appear, but Pope John Paul II, referring to Article 11, stated that the Vatican City was independent from the Italian State, thus protecting Marcinskus and the Masons along with him.

For two centuries, Masons had been excommunicated from the church to the point that whoever belonged to Masons were considered to have committed a cardinal sin and could not receive Communion. In 1996, Pope John Paul II became a staunch supporter of the Masons, holding them and their tenets in high esteem, their existence no longer being a sin but rather an honor.

That same year, Manuel Noriega was accused of trafficking narcotics. The Vatican tried to extradite him from America, because the Panamanian dictator was recycling money from narcotics trafficking, which eventually found its way into the hands of the Marcinkus-Calvi-Sindona triumvirate.

The spokesmen for John Paul II tried to contradict this accusation while the Pope himself adopted the casual posture of a modern superstar, concealing his medieval beliefs in an effort to increase money for IOR. By using the media to show him frolicking in swimming pools and skiing, he conveyed his romantic love of life through film, portraying himself as strong, handsome and modern with a *joie de vivre*. He became a famous pop superstar, since he could not commercially promote products by himself.

After his visit to the United States in 1995, for the first time in the history of the Vatican he authorized products licensed by the Vatican, bearing its official seal of coat-of-arms on such items as jewelry, watches, post cards and T-shirts. It was also the first time it could be promoted in advertisements on commercial television. Its success in the U.S. was acknowledged by the Wall Street Journal to bring in 20 million dollars each year for IOR.

In 1984, Pope John Paul II gave his consent to make a commercial spot in which he walks in a Canadian forest with the rosary, praying in Latin with the Vatican chorus behind him, promoting the CD named "Giovanni Paolo II, the Pope of the Rosary" a special edition that comes complete with a free rosary and a photo of the Pope inscribed with "The Saint Pope is praying with you in your home," available by sending the coupon to Post Office Box 4384, San Guliano, Milan with a payment of 79,000 lira.

This modern Pope is a businessman, who participates in show business while he is intolerant of divorce and abortion. He rejects prophylactic contraceptives as well, and excommunicates homosexuals other than his clergy, 50% of whom are homosexual. He won't accept women as priests. In the meantime, the same Pope, is the majority shareholder on the Italian Stock Exchange, owning 51 percent of the company, worth 93 billion lire.

In 1996, John Paul II was spreading the New Testament wisdom through the Internet, complete with benediction and a special CD-ROM, a high-tech confessional appropriate for all kinds of penance and sins produced by a German company "Society of Lazarus." The CD-ROM also gave addresses and names of the priests to contact.

The CD-ROM biography of the papal superstar was formatted for Windows 95, and made available for 59,000 lire. Available in eight languages, there was Papal information about the Jubilee, historical information, plus an on-line access charge of 15,000 lire.

After only two weeks, over two million people from 70 different countries hit the site and made 4,678 e-mail requests to find out where the Pope would sing to prepare for Jubilation, the conversion of hearts for the year 2000, which would be a multi-million-dollar business venture capitalizing on those who had never seen the Pope.

As an added incentive, the special edition of the CD-ROM could be purchased for 69,000 lire, instead of 90,000 lire, and as a bonus you would receive the CD-ROM "Discover Christ" for free. The Italian state would give the Vatican 200 million lire every day.

If I kept on discussing all the shady speculations in which the Vatican has been involved, not to mention all the billions and billions of lira made during the Jubilee, it would still be only a drop in the bucket.

I only wish to implore people not to fool themselves with superstitious beliefs and to resist their being exploited as the revenue source for the Vatican's bank, whose only interest is power and money. All these inventions of the church, indulgences, confessions, devils and saints like Padre Pio, are for the sole purpose of keeping and manipulating people.

In all this complexity and intriguing financial speculation that was conducted by the Vatican, as well as Padre Pio, I didn't find even one little light of spirituality in Padre Pio or in the Vatican; both pretend to be only one possessor of God through Jesus.

Where is God? Where is Jesus who proclaimed, "Again I say to you it is easier for a camel to pass through the eye of a needle than for one who is rich to enter the kingdom of God?"

Where then is Padre Pio, who lost the vow of poverty? I know he found eternal life here on our planet, but did he find the eternal life promised to us by Jesus? And the Vatican, the supervisor of our lives in truth and honesty, has even become a highly skilled merchandiser of God.

Where then will we end up with the promises of "beneficial" indulgences for our sins, along with eternal life? If the Vatican itself is the chief executor of the Ten Commandments, then what about "Thou shalt not steal?"

In the not-so-distant past, the same sins, for which today you can receive indulgences over the internet, brought about the demise of thousands. How many people were killed for the inconstant truths of the Vatican, not only during the Inquisition, but now, with abortion clinics being the new forum where Catholics choose to fight and kill their opponents, even in the face of grave deformity and genetic diseases?

In 1999, Pope John Paul II, forced by incontrovertible evidence presented by the media, expressed a brief apology for both the Church's indifference to the plight of European Jews and Pius XII's personal complicity in Anti-Semitism.

What terrible truth have we learned? Money, money, power, power. Today, the power to help hungry people is of less consequence than using that same power to throw up another monument to religion as a symbol of eternity, whether it be a cathedral or a pyramid, or investing in another Padre Pio money machine, and then granting it sainthood.

I would just like to ask if it is possible for any of us to still believe in the existence of God and Jesus if the custodians of God and Jesus do not have time to think about Him, due to the heavy pressures placed upon them by their serious involvement in the international political, and stock market currents, and in the same breath, they have the temerity to tell us they are the apostles of truth. What an irony!

Why then should I be surprised about the dishonesty of Friar G., if the Vatican is based from the very beginning on the false premise regarding Jesus's conception from the Holy Spirit, consequently arrogating to be the sole possessor of the living God? And why then should the Vatican worry about its own honesty, if the only thing that really counts is political power? This is why politicians hide behind Jesus Christ and God, since the most powerful religious organization is Christianity, overseen by the Vatican. All political and financial transactions the world over, one way or another, lead back to the Vatican, which decides their outcome. God was invented only for political power for maneuvering people all over the world.

Chapter 26

My Last Revelation For The Third Millennium

The most fitting conclusion to be made in this, the third millennium, is one that would strongly deny the existence of God, the greatest fraud in human history. We should finally mature and accept the idea that the God introduced to us was a God invented by human beings for political power? even going so far as to put Jesus on the Cross—the finale in this sordid scheme, diabolical drama, to humiliate humanity, and seal us to the cross for eternity.

It is understandably difficult to live without an idea of God; we are so accustomed and so enamored of the concept of a supernatural power that governs our lives. Naturally, it is much easier to put our responsibilities on God's shoulders or on those of someone else in the belief that our problems will be resolved automatically. This belief only takes from us our will power to react and to create our destiny and our history, which are created by us and not by God. Would it not be better to live without illusions and instead embrace the truth that could be the mighty engine for our perennial power to run our lives?

However, if we humans still feel it is necessary to retain the idea of God, then it should be in a wholly different form than the way Christianity envisions Him. I far prefer the ideal of Aristotle who defined God as the "Essence of essence, knowledge of knowledge, in contemplation of Himself." But he does not intervene in our daily lives. Our lives belong to us, and we humans are the only owners of this world. Even so, I wonder whether Aristotle's God makes sense. After all, is knowledge a static thing, unchanging, for ever the same from the beginning of time? Just because it is the "essence of essence" doesn't mean that it contains all the knowledge that ever was or ever will be.

I recently had a very strange dream. I was dying and about to breathe my last. At that very moment, I felt as if my every fiber was being sucked up into a powerful vortex, spiraling down at incredible speed. And all around me I sensed the presence of thousands upon thousands of shades of varied energies of wills and desires. I suddenly understood that they corresponded exactly to the nature and degree of desire we feel at the moment of death. Our energy is immediately reabsorbed through electromagnetic waves by the exact same level of energy of our wills in the universe.

What my dream revealed to me is that if there is a God, it has be a God utterly devoid of will or desire, an unchanging God. When I woke up, my mind filled with vivid images and sensations, I began to ponder the nature of God. Could God be space? No, because space is in continuous extension. Could it be energy? No, because energy is movement caused by vibrations. But then what causes vibrations? Could that be God? No, because if vibrations need to be caused, a will is needed. So the question remains: where is God if He exists?

Unfortunately, it is we who created God, furious and vindictive, and now we are fearful of Him. We also created the atomic bomb and now we are afraid of it, too. But, if we loved and respected each other, we wouldn't have any fear, since our mutual respect towards everyone would preclude the use of such weapons. And there would no longer be the need for fearing God, nor a need to possess each other.

The dominant theme of the Old and the New Testaments is possession; in the first, the prophets are possessed by someone that played the rule of God, and in the second, Jesus Himself was possessed by the same fictional God, and in turn, he possessed his apostles. This history seems to repeat itself: Friar G., claimed to be possessed by Padre Pio, and Gurumayi by Muktanand. The same phenomenon of spiritual penetration applies to the leaders and gurus of various other cults who often take their inspiration from Jesus's example, causing their followers to feel extreme love and devotion towards them.

I was sure for a long time that no one would believe the painful and unhappy tale about my possession. Nowadays, we Westerners are skeptical of such phenomena as possession and annihilation of the ego, as well as the reduction of another human being's existence to that of an empty container, susceptible to manipulation. But then to my big surprise, the world woke up one morning not long ago to learn of the mass suicide of the members of the Heaven's Gate cult in California. Marshall Applewhite, the leader of Heaven's Gate, preached to his followers that before Easter, when Jesus was resurrected from death according to Christianity, they would be taken by UFOs and brought to another planet to start a better new life. For this belief, 37 persons took their own lives. Before the mass suicide, Applewhite expressed his solidarity with David Koresh and the Order of the Solar Temple.

This event shocked the world, of course. But more than that, it revealed that even educated, professional people can be subjected to manipulation by powerful leaders to the extent of apparently possessing them. And imagine how I felt when it was discovered that they called themselves containers. While this term was hotly debated in the media, journalists didn't seem to understand its meaning. I felt like shouting at the television screen: "Read my book, find out about my story, then you'll understand!"

I wondered whether they ever understood what their own lives were about in the here and now, lives that they were so anxious to discard in the belief that heaven was waiting for them. All religions followed Jesus's teaching, which brainwashed people that this life here is not important, that only the future eternal life in heaven counts. As a result, the suicidal fanatics are dying happily since they are convinced that God is waiting for them with a reward.

David Koresh was another false messiah, who gathered his followers, many women and children among them, into a compound in Waco, Texas; he declared to his followers that he was speaking in God's name and predicted that the day of judgment was at hand. When Federal authorities tried to arrest him on charges of possessing illegal weapons, Koresh seized the opportunity to fulfill his prophesy by provoking Federal Authorities to exchange fire with him and attack his compound. All the disciples that followed his orders not to surrender were killed, while Koresh died at his own hands.

Later, Timothy McVeigh justified his bombing of the Federal building in the Oklahoma City that killed hundreds of innocent people as a protest against the actions of the Federal Government against David Koresh and his disciples.

Jim Jones's cult, based in Guyana back in the late 70s, is a famous case of mass brainwashing. He claimed to be Jesus and inspired such "love" for himself among his over 900 followers that when he feared that U.S. authorities might arrest them, they "willingly" took a poisonous drink and committed mass suicide. Those who resisted were shot.

Based upon anxious inquiries by relatives, U.S. Congressman Leo Ryan and Senator Jackie Speier went to inspect the Jones compound in Guyana. While there, Ryan was killed by Jones's disciples. These people were mentally manipulated by Jones. Senator Jackie Speier was also shot, but luckily, she survived. Recently, as a guest on a television show discussing cults, Senator Jackie Speier mentioned thoughts similar to what I have expressed about sexual abuse, saying that there are indeed extreme forms of spiritual harassment. Spiritual possessors are potential killers, just as sexual abusers are, if not worse, because spiritual molestation is not recognized in our courts.

The use of arms and domestic violence are adjudicated under State and Federal laws; however, there is no legislative protection for the spiritual and religious abuses of one's individual rights. Spiritual and sexual abuse under the guise of religion is a taboo subject. Everyone is afraid to touch what is sacred, even if what is sacred is morally incorrect.

When we talk about possession within the Catholic Church, even the police hesitate to investigate. Isn't it time that the legislature provides protection, so that the massacre of 900 people in Guyana by Jim Jones or of 37 people in San Diego at The Heaven Gate cult massacre will not happen again? Right now, Kim Miller is holding thousands of people separate from their families. Who knows what end they will meet! They are all dancing and singing, while they were probably preparing themselves to die.

The stories of mental manipulation repeat themselves. Similar to the Solar Temple was another messianic cult, which committed mass suicide in Canada and in Switzerland on the same day.

In Japan, the same phenomenon reoccurred when Shoko Asahara, leader of the cult Aum Shinri Kyo (the Supreme Truth), brainwashed his disciples, directed them as if under hypnosis and reducing them to dummies, forced them to plant containers of Sarin, an extremely toxic gas, in five subway cars in Tokyo. Twelve people were killed and another 5,000 injured in the attack. Shouldn't such manifestations be considered an offense to the meaning of life and be stopped for ever?

Now that the millennium has come, we can expect ever more to see new prophets purporting to rescue us from darkness, but ending up killing innocent people in the name of God. Inevitably, they will model themselves after God or Jesus, voicing apocalyptic threats about the End of the World, and offering visions of a Promised Land. They have already built underground bunkers all over the world, using money donated by members of their cults, once again making the Promised Land extremely expensive. Many strange new cults formed in the name of God are constantly appearing. These fraudulent operations have two goals: to rob their adherents of their money and their spirit.

I hope to bring this issue to the attention of the U.S. Supreme Court. I believe it is time for our legal system to recognize how serious spiritual harassment is, and how many lives have been negatively affected by cult affiliations. This is an invisible brain manipulation, which integrates the most vulnerable part of our entire existence. People who are sincerely searching to fill their void of love are often ready to unquestioningly submit themselves to some unrealistic dream, which they think will lead them to a higher level. Instead, however, they are spiritually kidnapped, the kidnapper representing a spiritual symbol which allows him to abuse the victim by their tacit consent.

This offense is on par with physical kidnapping or sexual abuse except that these are without consent of the victim and therefore, are less cruel. In contrast, spiritual abuse takes over the whole existence of the unprotected victim, resulting in a more sophisticated and a more cruel possession, killing the entire being. Unfortunately, this phenomenon is rapidly extending its grip as each day goes by. Perhaps legislation could do much toward preventing deaths that result from the mental manipulation of these cult/religions.

Even though freedom of expression is given to all religions, as is freedom for democratic expression, there would still be justice for anyone crossing the line and offending the freedom of democracy. That recently happened when fanatical Muslims, the so-called "Soldiers of the God" had killed 3000 people by attacking the Two Towers in New York. The offended democracy rightly declared war against the extremist Muslims of the Taliban, but for diplomatic reasons it is not a war for human rights and democratic dignity, but is called "The War Against Evil." What is evil? What do we mean by evil? Why do we not courageously face the truth and recognize that all religions and ideologies are based on an ambitious overpowering of the world, thereby ending in evil?

The irony of evil is that it reconnects us to the time when America was fighting communism and the office of President Carter called the Afghan army, "Soldiers of God". The Carter administration declared that God was on their side and affirmed their rights by supporting them with all kinds of weapons. When America didn't need them, any more, the Soldiers of God were abandoned and left to fend for themselves. They kept fighting communism because the communist philosophy contradicts their established beliefs; it instead teaches them equality, to treat all people alike, equally. This was seen as a great offense to God, because only God is supposed to decide who can be rich and who can be poor. In the meantime, fundamentalist Islam has spread to the extent that Osama bin Laden, under the protection of the Taliban with the same weapons given to them by Americans, declared a war against "capitalistic infidels," the Americans. And as usual, some poor people were enlisted for suicidal attacks being lured with the promise of compensation from God for dying for a just cause. Today, the same Soldiers of God are called "evil" and God is no more on their side!

This is an example of how far fanatical believers of all religions and ideologies will go, as well as how easy it is to be brainwashed or possessed, in the name of God or any ideology in which innocent people lose their lives.

A 16 year-old, John Walker, who was innocently searching for spirituality, was totally brainwashed, became a fanatical Muslim and joined the Osama bin Laden camp. Today, he is a prisoner and is judged as a traitor of his own country, America. But he, for one, still maintains that his heart remains with the Taliban and he feels very sorry for them. Instead of pursuing his path of spirituality, his innocence led him to be so radically manipulated as to become incurable today. He can no more distinguish what is right from what is wrong. He has become a puppet of someone.

A similar story about Herve Djamel Loiseau, age 28 and well brought up, has come out of France. His body was found frozen and unnourished as a member of "the Foreign Legion of Al Queda." He died as a French Muslim, fighting on the side of Osama bin Laden. His parents remember him as a very kind, sweet boy, who wouldn't hurt a fly. He was a good student who used to watch American movies with his father and had a girlfriend who would go with him to night clubs. But after serving in the army, he came back home completely transformed. He refused to listen to music, watch television, or go to the movies. He got up at 5 in the morning saying that he had to go pray. His father told reporters that he didn't not know who had recruited his son, but, according to rumors he had heard, many other young Europeans were gravitating toward Al Queda. He thought that they were possessed, brain-washed by radical Muslims.

Isn't it time to protect innocent people with a new legislation when the freedom given to all religions goes so far as to manipulate young people to the extent of reducing them to a state of such unconscious acts as becoming executors of the dictatorial will to exterminate non-believers even with their own life? Shouldn't that be opposed tooth and nail?

Politicians should also be more compassionate for the lives of the young people in whom patriotism is injected. Shouldn't they fight only for the human rights and democracy and not for self-serving ideologies in which one day they are part of God and the next day a part of evil?

This reminds me of a time when I was very young, only twelve. In school, I was brainwashed that my only God was Stalin, and then one morning, I saw the image of our idol lying at my feet as a piece of trash that the garbage man swept right into the sewer. It was shocking. I was too young to be involved ideologically just as poor Walker and many others were, the only difference being the various religions, ideologies and time periods.

It is also well-known that all religions, particularly cults, try to recruit young and naïve people in places like schools and universities. Using the pretext that they are seeking information about political or religious views for educational purposes, they can obtain a great deal of personal data which they then employ to target their victims. Thereafter, they proceed to send out enticing brochures and invitations to seminars and retreats carefully composed so that they never disclose their true objective.

Once they get these young people to attend their centers or churches, the brainwashing begins. People are separated from their families and friends and become inducted into the beliefs of the cult, and to bind them completely, are made to feel guilty about their unknown sins. At this point, they have completely lost their own will and have fallen into emotional turmoil.

They are brainwashed to go against their own families to such an extent that they even reject the idea of ever returning home. In reality, they are kidnapped and whenever the parents try to recover them and bring them back home, it is the parents who are accused of being kidnappers of their own children. They even risk penalty or prison by the laws protecting the freedom of religious expression.

Yet these laws do not take into consideration that religious choice is a consequence of brain manipulation. This permits cult leaders to treat their victims as slaves, who are forced to "redeem" themselves from the guilt and, with promises of future reward directly from God, it allows leaders to exploit them in any manner they want.

They induce them to work very hard for the cult. The work may take any number of forms—selling flowers and trinkets or taking on jobs like cleaning, cooking and washing for the cult with the intent to not give them any time to think for themselves. Any manifestation of individuality is stamped out.

In many cases, cult members are also asked to clean their spirits by expunging their homes of all dirt. By "dirt," of course, they mean jewelry... check books... cash... anything that can be covered with "dust." One group, the Church of Scientology, even provides some very sophisticated and semi-scientific auditing and personality testing devices for the ostensible purpose of cleansing its members of their "insecurities."

I urge people to take this problem seriously and realize how these cults are misleading individuals and taking away so many young lives. This is something that can happen to any one of us. Isn't it time we exposed this most insidious and cruel form of abuse and propose laws similar to those protecting victims of sexual abuse? I admit that it's difficult. For one thing, horribly real as the abuse is, the problem is hard to define. For another, there are no laws against spiritual possession.

Perhaps today, after the tragedy of Sept.11, this problem will be viewed more seriously not only in cases of mass carnage when finally terrorists of holy war are severely judged for their destructive acts, but also in those innumerable cases throughout history in which individuals have been singly sacrificed by various fanatical believers of the same holy motivation. Should there not be an equal application of the law?

I have heard that there are already books on the market meant to help victims recover from psychological and spiritual violation. I just hope that recovery from one abuse will not pave the way for another.

One thing that has always struck me about these cults is how much money they rake in. The Catholic Church teaches us that this life is not important; only the spirit counts. It teaches that we must not accumulate wealth in this life because only eternal life counts. Well, strangely enough, the Catholic Church in the end has become the richest church in the world! The cardinals are all fat, arrogant and lazy, doing nothing.

I will never forget the sight of a cardinal in his purple robes, full of self-satisfaction and smug in his privileged role as a high official of the church. When he was approached by some poor homeless man begging for help, he held his ring proudly for him to kiss, reassuring him, "Do not worry, the good God will provide for you."

The model established by the Church was duplicated in turn by the "saints" and any number of occult sects. I wouldn't exclude from this list Mother Teresa of India. I saw her several times at Friar G.'s sanctuary while visiting him. I don't know if Friar G. brainwashed her too, but I know that, like all potential saints, she also has a long record of taking money from shady sources, such as the Duvalier dynasty in Haiti and Charles Keating of the Lincoln Savings and Loan, as well as from KGB agents. All of them generously let Mother Teresa accumulate considerable wealth for her order.

Mother Teresa, under the mask of being humble or reclusive, could indeed be abrasive and tyrannically severe. Her nuns appeared to me to be more like slaves, as they were treated far worse than any vows of poverty would require. The poor nuns lived in fear of being approached by strangers. They were also made to freeze in little sandals during the cold of winter. In the same way Padre Pio also, despite his vow of poverty, became one of the richest saints in the twentieth century. As usual, these ambitious saints, on the backs of others, are preparing for their own eternal glorification, while pretending to be remembered as good and generous.

They are helped in this monetary endeavor, thanks to the old blind belief in the vicarious redemption for our sins in which our sins can be canceled at second-hand for cash. It is practiced vigorously even today, just as evil can be canceled by charitable service to the church. Also, by casting one's sins onto the shoulders of an ethereal being, future indulgences for forgiveness can be secured.

The same concept prevailed in primitive society. It was a practice known as scapegoating, whereby a symbolic animal was loaded with the sins of the tribe, then driven into the desert to suffer on behalf of all. In some societies, it was not an animal but a human being that was done away with in this ceremonial manner.

Children and adults are taught especially by the Christian churches that they can become sinless by casting their wrongdoings onto another person who has the power to take these offenses on himself.

This corruption is on both sides, leading to the sale of indulgences and the merchandising of mercy. This immoral practice by vicarious and fake saints makes us believe that they, in fact, take our sins on their shoulders the same way as Jesus did. This makes them incredibly rich.

Many Indian gurus, for instance, after learning how profitable preaching spirituality is, have found their way into the West, particularly the United States, where they have attempted to win converts.

Taking the path of least resistance, they appropriated the trappings of the Catholic Church and began calling themselves Jesus and their mothers, the Madonna.

They, too, have become extremely rich. Without any scruples, they alienated young people from their families and destroyed many lives, but not before relieving their followers of their savings. Of course, they made sure to stash their money away in private banks in India, which were equipped with more advanced technology than even the wealthiest American bank. The Vatican bank is not too far behind in size!

Recently, it was reported by media that the quickest and easiest way to make money in Nigeria today is to carry a Bible on Sunday and start preaching. The boom of Pentecostals churches is called, "Theology-Prosperity." The electric guitars and dancing allow for a closer connection with God by focusing on the outpouring of emotions. It's like being at a party. The Rev. David Oyededepo, who has modeled himself as a preacher, founded the "Winners' Church." He writes in a pamphlet, "God prospers people here. He will prosper you, too." Pentecostals churches saying only, "It's a divine time." They become a leading exporter of religious business for the rest of the continent and even in Europe and United States. Many young ministers, modeling themselves on the Rev. Oyededpo, pretend even to make miracles and heal people, but for you to acquire a miracle, you must give money so that minister will pray for you. All warehouses are being turned into churches, the only way to become a millionaire here overnight.

Speaking about money, the Reverend Sun Young Moon, founder of the Unification Church, another of many preachers, who was made a millionaire in the name of God, has proclaimed himself a messiah and has indicated that his role is to complete the mission Jesus left unfinished and bring about salvation.

Like most of these cult figures, Moon has built a huge empire, which includes large real estate holdings in Uruguay and a major newspaper in Washington, DC, subsidized by his converts. Although he himself has been divorced, he has made marriage a sacrament of his church and is known for bringing together thousands of couples who have never met before and often may not know each other's language, marrying them in mass ceremonies.

The couples like to believe that the Reverend Moon, through divine wisdom, is far better able to select a mate for them than they could on their own. Once again we see that all sense of individuality is destroyed for the sake of the spiritual leader who thinks and decides for his followers.

Strangely enough, the Reverend Moon succeeded recently in "converting" Archbishop Milonga to his point of view. Milonga had served twenty years in Rome in complete obedience to the command of the Lord Jesus Christ. He was blessed in marriage with Maria Sung and their union was consecrated by the Reverend Moon.

Archbishop Milonga justified his action by the dictum that God has shown him that intimate union between man and woman is a true reflection of the Holy Trinity; therefore, man and woman are called to fulfill their original purpose to reflect God's image. He expressed his sadness that many priests wouldn't be able to reconcile this original longing with their celibate vow, so their commitment has become a hollow shell, an unreachable standard.

He declared that all manner of defilement, including unnatural lust, illegitimate children and other secret horrors have burdened the lives of those seeking to serve God. The increase of child molestation, homosexuality and pregnancy among priests and nuns has become common knowledge.

The satanic blood has flown into God's church. The satanic blood has to be cleansed, since Milonga spent all his life confronting Satan; so now by answering God's call, he will fulfill his real mission; which would be to restore the original ideal of marriage. He will pray day and night to purify the spirit of the church to separate it from Satan.

Meanwhile, the church is praying for the possessed Archbishop Milonga to be rid of the devil. I don't know what the church would do without the constant presence of Satan as the scapegoat. How pathetic!

And why should the church complain, since it has allowed married priests from the Anglican and Lutheran traditions to come into the church, some even with children? It has caused a lot of resentment among committed Roman Catholic priests, who accepted the vow of celibacy. They question, "What happened to the honor of our celibacy and the ethics of the church?" There is no doubt that it all ended up in satanic hands.

The Pope urges people to submit themselves to the power of exorcism which consists of sprinkling holy water with the command for the devil to leave the possessed body. What is holy water? It is regular water that, after having been blessed by a priest, turns to holy water. What proof can he give us that this is holy water; does it have a different chemical composition? How can the priest prove that his holiness has the power to turn regular water into holy water?

Wouldn't it be better for the Pope to start exorcising the entire Vatican, which is full of political and moral corruption that is made worse by its priests, many of whom are molesters of young boys and girls? Instead, the church, in its highly indisputable morality, chooses to protect its priests rather than protecting the young victims. And then the question arises as to the holiness of the water used for exorcising, since the same priests after nightly rituals of auto-eroticism the next morning with the same hands and dirty mind try to turn regular water into holy water.

Isn't exorcism based on the same superstition as that of a fortune teller using the term "evil eye?" The Pope is turning the world into one full of superstitions, since it is easier to manipulate a population under the fear of devils. Predictably enough, it is we the masses, who are called to submit to exorcisms, and not the evildoers of the Church.

The Church has always been concerned that our potential power could be used in the wrong way, as they disregard their own misuse of power. Therefore, it tries to keep us in fear by scaring the population into believing that either the devil will conquer the world or that it will be destroyed by some catastrophe.

Isn't it time to stop this abuse of power? But without a doubt the Church and cult leaders will not stop in trying to subjugate humanity in the name of God, until they are completely empowered and enriched.

Without a doubt, the abuse of power is a popular subject also in the media. While it didn't fare well at the box office, the film *Extreme Measures* made a powerful impression on me, because I was able to relate it to my own experiences. The plot revolves around a doctor, played by Gene Hackman, who conducts research on human vertebrae in an attempt to find a cure for paralysis.

However, in order to pursue his research, he needs to remove the vertebrae of healthy people. So the doctor decides to use the homeless; to justify his actions, he declares that he is helping these unknown people give meaning to their lives. He adds that one day they will become famous for their sacrifice.

Normal, otherwise healthy people are rendered paralyzed, their spinal cords disconnected, their bone marrow destroyed, and their central nervous system separated from their brains. No one has any qualms of ever asking these people if they want to take part in the experiment; they are just collected from the streets.

The parallels with my own life are obvious. I, too, was a healthy person who was seized without being asked if I wanted to devote my life to curing someone else and to being reduced to the state of an animal. I, too, was told that I was helping to serve a very noble mission, and that God would one day know about it. And all this was done simply for the purpose of proving a false proposition: That miracles are possible and that God and Jesus exist. But I wasn't told who was actually hiding behind the image of God; it was the ambitious Friar G. Unfortunately, this wasn't a film but the real story of my life.

In January 2000, on an early morning in January, I received a terrifying call from Italy. "Come quickly, your husband is not well and it would be good if you came." Within hours, I was crossing the Atlantic, returning to the country that had brought me so much pain and yet so much happiness.

As I made my way through Rome's streets with heavy traffic, I knew that this would be the last time that Max and I would share time together. The hospital was an immense labyrinth. As I made my way up to the second floor and into his room, I vowed that he would see only his happy Maria. His face made it clear to me how pleased he was to see me again. It was then I realized that he couldn't speak. With the will of the great Roman patrician that he was, he did his best to keep up appearances, to keep me from being disappointed or upset.

We were together for ten days and I never left his side. I wept inside to think what a sweet person he was, so good and so discreet; he never wanted to inconvenience anyone, not even on his deathbed. He was grateful for any and every little thing that was done for him. I have never known such a wonderful person.

I cried, knowing what Friar G. did to us. He destroyed our happiness just for his own glory. My husband didn't deserve such treatment. His goodness and his generosity should have been recognized and appreciated. While I struggled with Friar G. in New York, my husband, old and alone, had a fall at our home one dark night. He lay there struggling to get up until the early morning hours when his waiter came with his breakfast. This saddened me very much. If I had been with him, would such a thing have happened?

What has consoled me is that my husband, ever since we met, used to say that his death could come at any moment. Yet, he died at the ripe age of 89, and until the last moment, he was completely independent. I believe that in some way my life of suffering and ordeals was helpful to him.

My husband died discreetly and sweetly, a dignified man to the end. Even in my moment of pain and grief, Friar G. capitalized immediately on the void that my husband left by filling me up with the paralyzed man. I was certain that after the death of my husband, my suffering would end since he would not have anyone to hide behind.

Instead, Friar's wickedness not only allowed him to continue as before, but also filled me with even more of the paralyzed boy's sickness. Finding myself with the same symptoms as my husband's, such as a trembling hand and a pain in my neck that spread to my gums, I remarked to myself how strange that my husband had already been resurrected from the dead and with the same symptoms as before.

Friar G.'s unabashed hatred and ill will toward me, my husband, and his family had no bounds, it would seem. I screamed, "Oh God and Jesus, if you really exist, how can you accept such inhumanity?"

Wanting freedom, I began wishing a quick death for the paralyzed Paolo, which automatically made Friar G. suggest that if I kept doing this, he would redirect my ill will to one of my husband's sons. What a vicious disrespect he had for our family, even in the face of death. I would like to shout to the world my disgust from the bottom of my heart.

But after having learned about Padre Pio and the Vatican, nothing shocks me any more. Throughout history, the church has been a vehicle for generating money to aid in its unending designs and manipulations for power. In the same way Padre Pio and Friar G. have hidden behind the name of God, indifferent to the pain and desolation they have caused others, hungry only for their glory. Inasmuch as the Church ignores poor people and their pain, all charity is a front, a mask, behind which greed breeds. The church is an empty place, unfeeling even for its saints.

On the plane, a young priest from Spain sat next to me, as we flew back to New York. I told him I was sorry that he was my accidental flying companion. "I don't believe in God and I have a very bad opinion of the Church." I proceeded to show him a book that I had just purchased in Rome, *The Merchants of the Vatican*.

The young priest immediately became offensive and said, "I see by your face that you are very close to death, perhaps it would be better for you to turn to God."

Once again, the church was attempting to frighten me into submission. No mention of God's love, merely threats, like a mafia hit man. "Not to worry," I said. "I am very healthy and a lot younger than you might think."

He then confided in me that he was an only son. He had left his parents alone in Barcelona to do missionary work in New Jersey. I continued our little sparring match by stating that he would have been better off staying in Barcelona and doing missionary work with his lonely parents. With that, I turned over and fell asleep. He, too, covered himself with a blanket and before drifting off; I heard an unusual amount of activity under the blanket. I thought perhaps he was saying the rosary, praying for me, this great sinner sitting next to him, but no, he was simply playing with his organ!

My own painful experiences that have so shamefully offended every part of my life drew me to dream that just as during the Inquisition, when "witches" were persecuted and burned at the stake, we should begin to hunt for Saints, or anyone identifying with the Holiness of God or Christ. Those who believe themselves to be unassailable, even when corrupting young people's spirits in order to gain power and wealth, should be exposed.

It shouldn't matter what their belief is, whether they look for salvation from a space ship following a comet taking them to a better life, or a miracle making paralyzed people walk. One way or another, these fanatics ought to be stopped. Those who try to destroy others and narcotize them under the opiate of their religion should be arrested and convicted, as they are no different from drug dealers. At the very least, they should be arrested for fraud.

It can be extremely dangerous when uneducated people wield "spiritual power." They often harbor resentments and vindictive feelings that may stem from ignorance and their sense of social inadequacy. Of course, it's easier to deal with illiterate people because they have two qualities that make them easy prey: spontaneity and blind belief. However, I tend to think that it isn't only the poor and uneducated who provide easy prey for possession. Those who are open and free like the young and the naïve, are equally vulnerable.

Friar G. had his eye on young, naïve foreigners, whom he managed to recruit. There were about 30 of them, many from abroad, especially America. Free-spirited and spontaneous, dedicated to their vocation, they were unswerving in their loyalty to Friar G. He was intent on inculcating in them a blind, fanatic devotion to God.

Now I see how dangerous the consequences were; he was brainwashing them to the extreme to put out their ego and their will and to be able to maneuver them as a puppet just as he has exploited me and as he himself was manipulated by Padre Pio. They, in turn, would be sent off to brainwash more unsuspecting people, spreading his spiritual terrorism throughout the world like a virus.

It worries me deeply that these priests are now preaching around the word, still being exploited by Friar G. I can imagine their teaching in schools, passing on his fanaticism to eager, wide-eyed students. Those unfortunate families may discover to their horror that they have a zealot with a powerful vocation in their midst.

I am greatly concerned about this matter because I don't wish for anyone to be possessed, not even by the noblest of causes that Muslims and all types of gurus and others fanatics motivated by various kinds of spirituality, along with the Vatican, are apt to do.

Without failing to mention Padre Pio, Friar G., as well as Mother Teresa, each considers himself or herself a noble cause, while gladly associating with people whose scruples tie them more closely to the world of corruption than the world of honesty and truth. Do they believe their mission is to obscure their base intents with noble phrases and suspect gestures, while all the time defrauding others of money and even their self-respect? They declare miracles in order to achieve self-glorification and if they fail in their intent, their fanaticism is transformed into vindictive sadism.

They reduce their followers to an animal state, by killing their brains and their emotions in the name of God's love. It is no longer carnal violence. Hitler, who was a great ally of the Vatican, massacred people with a new kind of atrocity. Now, with the likes of Friar G., slaughter has become something more subtle and sophisticated in his ever-present desire to kill our inner fabric. Abuse driven by spirituality doesn't make any difference between Osama bin Laden, and the al Qaeda leaders who lived in a luxurious palace, so luxurious that his cows were drinking distilled water, while his soldiers had hardly any water at all.

All religions, having feudalism as their base, never considered human rights as essential to mankind. The sects and cults that use the church's methods to brainwash their followers and rob them of their sense of responsibility are also to blame. I still believe, however, that one knowledgeable, ordinary man is worth ten ignorant saints.

We shouldn't blindly follow any gurus or teachers who seem interested only to create their own image and enrich themselves. We shouldn't accept any kind of manipulation of our inner self. We need neither the church nor any cult. We have to remember that each of us has the potential for greatness. The evidence is right in front of our eyes. We only need to observe what man has created and look at the tremendous knowledge he has achieved.

When I stumbled upon a web site devoted to secular humanism with a declaration drafted by Paul Kurtz and others, I learned what is humanism and who are humanists? I didn't know that secular humanists actually include scientists, philosophers, biologists, sociologists, researchers and medical doctors. I immediately felt connected to them, since their rational heritage was adopted from such ancient Athenian philosophers, as Socrates, the father of Greek rationalism, which in turn was followed by the Renaissance.

And up to the present day only humanists have been searching for truth through dialectic questioning and reasoning. They have always been trying to understand and find an explanation for the naturally dynamic and explosive universe. With scientific discovery and technology, they have been trying to solve human problems in order to improve and better our lives.

For example, modern astronomy and physics have opened up exciting new dimensions of the universe and have given opportunity to all humankind to understand and explore the universe through the possibility of space travel. Biology has given us opportunity to understand our cellular makeup through DNA and the Genome project.

This incredible progress has not only improved our health, consequently increasing our longevity, but very recently, has opened up new vistas for humanity by discovering in embryonic stem cells the possibility of transforming any cell and generating other tissues of the body.

Therefore, by injecting them in determinate parts of the body, they could possibly cure diseases, such as Alzheimer's, diabetes, cancer, Parkinson's and spinal-cord injuries. After injuries of the spinal cord occur, the neurons at the injury site stop functioning, and die quickly. In an experiment in which rats received injections of 1 million embryonic stem cells, they regained the ability to stand on four legs and walk. (Stem cells are the unprogrammed master cells that mature to become different cell types.)

Scientists are excited about the idea that transplants of immature nerve cells may provide a treatment for strokes, and many other neurological conditions. The neural stem cells are able to grow into any of the cell types in the brain and migrate to damaged areas. They can regenerate our cells and improve memory

Unbiased, objective persons will surely recognize science's profound contribution as the only realistic one able to expand human well-being. Even so, as usual, the irrational morality of the church is trying to stop the use of embryos, based on the same concepts on which the church opposes abortion. This means that it is better to keep embryos alive with no certainty of life, rather than try to save the lives of millions of already living people.

The church hides itself behind the name of God and acts as the supreme moral conservative, but, in reality, wants to maintain its power accumulated through the centuries. Thus, it manipulates people through superstition disseminated a long time ago as the best weapon for dominating rational thinking and weakening humanity by taking power over intelligence.

Unfortunately, superstition still today spreads fear among the masses through doomsday prophets calling for supernatural disasters. Their determination consists as usual in stopping progress and not letting people grow in freedom and happiness; they are anti-science, anti-freedom, anti-human. They believe in theologies of despair and ideologies of violence.

On the contrary, it is the secular humanist who finally puts humanity above God as opposed to the church that deliberately relegates human status to the lowest level. Contradicting this, the secular humanist trusts only the superb intelligence and genius of human beings, instead of divine guidance and approaches human reality with realistic and rational methods.

Since the humanist rejects the idea of eternal life and the theories of redemption, his quest is for happiness, optimism and hope in the here-and-now rather than pessimism, despair, fear, guilt or sin. Therefore, the only alternative for blind, ignorant and dogmatic faith is knowledge and truth.

And from a social point of view, people with open minds believe in a pluralistic society and hold that democracy is the best guarantee of protecting human rights from authoritarian leaders. They believe this is done by securing justice and fairness in the form of eliminating discrimination and intolerance based on race, creed, religion, ethnicity and sexual orientation.

For freedom's sake, secular humanists aim to be allowed to fulfill their aspirations, to express their sexual preferences, to exercise reproductive choice, to have freedom of religious expression, and have the option of dying with dignity without any totalitarian oppression.

Those who think rationally, respect and stand up for the human rights of life, liberty and the pursuit of happiness. Such people are intrinsically secular and independent humanists; responsibility, honesty and truthfulness are part of their daily rediscovery; they don't need the imposition of morality or ethics by religion. The morality didn't come from the clouds but is learned from human experience.

Over the centuries, there have been any number of distinguished secularists and humanists who have demonstrated moral principles in their personal lives and works: from Socrates, Democritus, Lucretius, Aristotle, Epicurus, Spinoza, Voltaire, Immanuel Kant, David Hume, Charles Darwin, George Eliot, Jeremy Bentham, John Stuart Mill, G. E. Moore, Bertrand Russell, John Dewey, Albert Einstein, Robert Ingersoll, and others.

Secularists deny that morality needs to be deduced from religious belief or that those who do not espouse a religious doctrine are immoral. If morality were the will of a supernatural being, how would it explain the questionable presence taught to us in the Bible which is at best a vindictive, bloodthirsty God, who introduced polygamy and treated women with disrespect, and laid down capricious laws and severe punishments, among other things?

Therefore, secular independent people believe that any one church should not impose its views of morality, virtue and sin. Our maturity leads us to the conclusion that life can be lived without the illusion of immortality or reincarnation, and, as secular humanists, we believe in the central importance of the value of human happiness here and now.

What I learned about humanism confirms all my beliefs and reinforces my love toward humanity. How can we not love each other in the face of such greatness that we human beings represent! I love humanity immensely and find a great relief that I no longer believe in God as a consequence of my own experience, which leads me to understand that God doesn't exist and is and was purely a figment of our imagination.

My liberation from illusionary God makes me feel free and honored to be a secular humanist. The impressive list of great thinking people, who were labeled humanist, atheists and therefore, regarded with disdain, are free thinkers, who have truly helped humanity by daring to confront the status quo. In their own lifetime, they were called heretics and lunatics; we have seen Einstein make a quantum leap from a public figure of derision to TIME magazine's "Man of the Century."

Today, Darwin's "heretical" theory of evolution has thrown humanity into a big dilemma, as it seems we are no longer a creation of God but simply a product of evolution, starting from the first cell passing to successive forms of life. And yet humanity still refuses to accept the truth that we were once apes. Therefore, a great debate has been taking place in the schools as to whether students should be taught the process of evolution since this would completely deny God's momentous act of creation and existence.

In fact, when students are taught evolution, the religious activists pressure teachers to include creationism, as it is presented in the Bible as part of the science curriculum. The students are forced to repudiate the theory of evolution and those belonging to creationist groups are promised full credit in their examinations. In addition, many biology teachers prefer to believe that they are part of God's creation, instead of being the result of evolution; thus, the evolution theory, if it is ever taught, is taught very poorly.

If we don't start teaching youngsters something more about science, we will find ourselves running backwards into a different kind of society. The majority of students seem to lack a basic knowledge of science. It is sad that they are brainwashed by superstition. Instead, they should seriously apply themselves to learning and prepare for a scientific approach to living.

It is highly probable that, in the future, bio-electronic augmentation and genetic engineering will cause human development to continue its physical transformation. The evolutionary process that began on a physical level with genes will continue in the future, and we humans will be on a journey of discovery, including one of self-discovery, that will allow us to acknowledge the complexity of human behavior. We should avoid thinking in the simplistic terms of good and evil. Our culture urgently requires a radical change. We should adopt a new vision, which is possible from the scientific world alone.

I don't know why we feel so honored to be a part of these believers, since all religions insist that faith should be accepted without question, thereby negating our intelligence and grossly offending all of humanity.

Our lives in the past were based on ideologies, both political and religious. As we survey the third millennium, humankind's new maturity allows us to confront the truth, no longer based on ideologies, which, more often than not, has suppressed scientific truths about our world. I think that as we move more and more into the world of scientific miracles, approving and participating in their great discoveries and innovations, we are all becoming, either consciously or unconsciously, a part of the atheistic world—nothing to be ashamed of since an atheist, when saving neighbor's life, is moved by love and respect, unlike the religious person, whose primary motivation appears to be future reward.

In spite of the odds, evolution has achieved its most magnificent achievement in the human brain. We have an active consciousness and conscience as well as an analytical mind which we can use to guide our choices, making us solely responsible for them. God had nothing to do with the cosmos or with any of the natural phenomena on this planet. Today, our scientists, after having even succeeded in cloning a sheep from an adult cell, are ready to clone human beings and perhaps even defeat death. Finally, eternal life will perhaps be in our grasp and, even if the Earth becomes no longer habitable, mankind will be able to live on by transporting our cells to other planets.

Many scientists believe that the impact of asteroids, each one to two kilometers wide, could result in a collision similar to the explosion of a million megatons of TNT. The heat and pressure caused by such a collision could instantly wipe out life in the region. The huge masses of dust and gases that would be emitted into the atmosphere could block out sunlight for a period of time, long enough to kill significant portions of life on earth.

Hopefully, by such time, we will have resettled on the planet Mars, thanks to the advancement of science. It is high time humanity stopped dreaming about angels and devils and realized that we are the only ones capable of achieving and giving meaning to eternal life.

I trust that by relating my painful experience, I can convince people to stop dreaming about any superior forces outside of themselves. No ideologue or fortuneteller can predict the future or lead us to a treasure. That route is really the road of ignorance! Instead, we must become aware and take responsibility for our lives. Man has been put on this earth to be happy, not to suffer. This is why I love America, because it is the one young and strong country that believes in the pursuit of happiness. Americans are one of the few peoples who encourage others to be strong and to trust themselves.

Chapter 27

Buddha And Confucius

To all the great names of the great thinkers, I would add two outstanding ones: Buddha and Confucius. I would call them the pioneering secular humanists who loved humanity and dedicated their entire lives and died for this cause

Through Lama Anagarika Govinda's *Buddhist Reflection,* as well as through the Internet's Encarta Encyclopedia, I came across the happiest of discoveries, that Tibetan Buddhist philosophy disavows miracles of any kind. Another thing that made me enthusiastic was that Tibetan Buddhism considers wisdom to be the greatest gift in the universe and that wisdom is obtained only in the search for our true self. Yes, absolutely! I believe this wholeheartedly.

How exciting to have a philosophy that encourages us to search for truth in our own conscience and to fuse it with the cosmic essence! The best thing about this philosophy is that it is not spirit-possession, nor is it spiritual or material theft. And how good it would be if our truly achieved awareness could be shared with others, rather than using it to humiliate or dominate others with "superior" knowledge.

Buddha, like all great men, was simple. Born in 623 B. C. almost 600 before Jesus, he taught the value of love and respect for the life of others. What a contrast between Jesus the God and Buddha the teacher, who doesn't pretend to be God or seek to achieve any political or spiritual power. His intention was only to inspire us to seek our innate, natural knowledge, which will then invariably lead us to a state of heightened awareness. He didn't attempt to be a saint or try to possess us with the Holy Ghost and hold us in ignorance, forbidding us from seeking our own identity.

There is simply no place in the Buddhist doctrine for any kind of supreme deity. Self-exertion in doing right is essential to comprehend the true nature of life. "If the world was created by a deity," said Buddha, then "there should be no such thing as sorrow or calamity, or doing wrong or doing right. And if God was the creator of all living things," the argument goes on, "then all living things should silently submit to the creator's power" So what is the use of practicing virtue in that case, Buddha asks? After all, as the creator, God is responsible for all of us and thus, answerable to all of our actions. Such predetermination, at least in Buddhist terms, overthrows the idea of God as a Being relevant to the affairs of man. No one can rely on God to intervene in the world or depend on God.

Buddhism is a non-theistic religion; it is not a doctrine of revelation or a messenger of God. On the contrary, Buddhism encourages people to search for self-knowledge; therefore independence of thought and action is an integral part of Buddhist teaching. He always underlined that he was human, that what he achieved was only the development of his own human potentiality and that he did not receive anything from a higher authority.

His teaching is based on his own personal experience; therefore he taught a method and not a doctrine. He invited all of us to challenge ourselves, because each of us deserves the same development of our own human potentiality. He never referred to himself as a supernatural being; on the contrary, he taught that this achievement belonged to and is attainable by every human being.

I wish I hadn't relied on emotions and sensations to guide me, but on the real knowledge of scientists and philosophers alone, who believe that knowledge can be acquired only when one abandons a state of ignorance. Buddha taught us that even one with a "perfect" open mind would arrest intellectual and spiritual growth the moment one recognizes himself as perfect. In fact, Buddha himself never considered himself to be perfect. Every day of our life is equivalent to opening a new page of a book. If our arrogance doesn't allow us to remain open and humble, recognizing each experience and being considerate toward others, we will not be able to write anything new in it.

I realize now how essential it is to experience each moment of our life with awareness and to connect us consciously with the continuous transformation of cosmic and human life, instead of searching for emotions and sensations. This awareness will bring us a deep appreciation of our lives and awaken our creativity, opening the doors to real happiness. In this manner, we will be able to establish our existence on a firm foundation.

Recently, I found myself at a party where I met some doctors who agreed that all too often our true identity is lost in our professional roles. I was pleased to hear that others shared my beliefs. During our conversation, other guests admitted that they, too, had become so self-satisfied that they were reluctant to embrace new experiences or seek new knowledge. They were aware that their false selves had forced their true selves to stagnate and that we all need to free ourselves from the imprisonment of mental restrictions.

Our old concepts and ideas can be rediscovered and transformed into new understanding, and the best approach to this newly rediscovered knowledge is silent meditation. Meditation trains our minds and develops concentration, and through the power of concentration, we are able to reach new understanding, which, day by day, leads us toward freedom and happiness.

That Buddhism never addresses the idea of God restores my freedom. The abstract idea of God as the basis of any religion terrifies me. In fact, from what I've discovered, any attempt to rely on God for help saps our strength and, far from allowing us to become independent, places us in a condition of dependence.

Strangely enough, most religions could not be accepted unless they relied on blind faith, without which they cannot exist. But because of the burdensome dogmas and contradictory "truths" they promote, it becomes impossible for people to reach a definitive truth. Those who gravitate to any kind of religious practice inevitably find themselves so confused that they are obliged to look for spiritual leaders, whose honesty varies greatly according to their level of moral maturity. Buddhist philosophy advises us never to follow a leader or a religion out of love, respect and certainly not out of blind faith.

Buddhism's honesty invites us to develop our potentiality, since the same potential power of Jesus and the prophets lives inside us; after all, they were human beings like us. Isn't it great to be finally allowed to look upon ourselves not as slaves, but as equals to Jesus and be invited to recognize our own power?

Over the centuries, religious leaders have kept people ignorant of the fact that they possess such remarkable spiritual powers themselves. The priests feared that if the populace developed spiritual powers they would certainly abuse them. From what I know of Friar G, I can only agree, although I don't think they did it for the goodness of humanity, but rather because they were afraid of losing their own political power. And in order to maintain the status quo, they employed the best method they knew, humiliation.

The Buddhist philosophy invites us to reach maturity caring only for the good of humanity. It taught us about love in a more mature and enlightened fashion, it considered love as an independent power, not a dependent one. This was entirely different from the teachings of Jesus, who demanded total submission. Jesus himself says, (Luke 15) "If anyone comes to me without hating his father and mother, wife and children and even his own life, do not come with me." In addition, he said, "Deny even your own life." This amounted to a kind of physical and psychological self-destruction.

On the contrary, Buddhism makes us realize that only through self-respect and self-love of our essential being can we love others and recognize in each person the same potentiality that is in ourselves, but is obscured by ignorance.

To affirm his philosophy, Buddha didn't need to provoke disasters. In Buddhist tradition, we never find a figure like Herod, who was provoked to order the slaughter of all newborn children. Nor did

Buddha ever spread doctrines that would lead to the killing of thousands of people through the Inquisition. If we take into account the announcement of the new messiah, Jesus, we would discover that, from the very beginning, it had no basis in truth. Because truth is self-evident, it doesn't need to be imposed by human will.

Buddha was not the only ancient teacher, who offered his knowledge to the people when or if they wished to receive it. The great Chinese teacher, Confucius, also advocated a doctrine that was based on independent thought and self-knowledge. Kindness and love emanated from Confucius, who lived 551-479 B.C. In a conversation with his disciples, he said, "What you don't want done to yourself, do not do to others." He also said, "Base yourself in loyalty and trust and permeate yourself with justice."

When a student queried, "May I ask about death?" Confucius replied, "If you do not understand what life is, how will you understand death?"

Confucius divided people into two categories—superior man and inferior man. Freedom from anxiety and fear was what it meant to be a superior man. Resolve delusions, he urged, and take care of your responsibilities before you seek knowledge.

He also taught that if you placed honest individuals in positions of power and ousted the corrupt, you will force the dishonest to become honest.

Whatever beliefs are not intrinsically truthful have to be imposed with violence. Which is why I find it so strange that the announcement of a new messiah needed to be accompanied by such an outbreak of brutality.

Without imposing himself on the world, Confucius says: "Speak to your friends honestly. If you cannot, then stop, don't humiliate yourself. If you can't correct yourself, how can you correct others?"

"Do not think evil. If you desire good, the people will be good; superior man is like a wind, the nature of the inferior man is like grass; when the wind blows over the grass it always bends."

He also urged us to ask ourselves every day: "In doing things for others, have I been disloyal?" Again: "Become intimate with good, be honest in speech."

Those two enlightened Superior Minds, Confucius and Buddha, left the world as peacefully as they came into it. They didn't assume the form of God, nor did they humiliate people or accuse them of being "unclean spirits," "serpents" or "broods of vipers." Nor did they pretentiously proclaim, "Your sins are forgiven." And they didn't bind humanity either to the cross or by promoting the non-existing miracles. Yet, Buddha and Confucius probably possessed spiritual power equal to Jesus's, if not greater.

Great teachers are also to be found in the West. Socrates, who died in 599 B. C., also taught self-awareness, asserting that we should always be conscious of our actions and ourselves. The Greek philosopher also said that those who commit evil do so without knowing. Thus, all evil actions can be reduced to one real evil, ignorance. Similarly, all Virtue and Good can be unified in one virtue, knowledge.

This leads us to think that the truth is only one. All important philosophers wish to guide us to self-awareness and advocate the virtue of true knowledge. They urge us not to deny ourselves and tell us that evil is the result of ignorance and not a consequence of being possessed by devils.

Socrates declared that "To know good is the same as to love good; he who renounces superior good doesn't recognize it as his own good.

"All men desire happiness. There are many types of happiness but self-possession is one of the principal, crowning types of happiness.

"Best of all is to be in possession of our own knowledge and wisdom, to have confidence in ourselves and to cherish the liberty of our spirit rather than to allow others to possess or dominate us."

These words took me to heaven. I wish I had been aware of them before my possession. I continue quoting Socrates:

"Man seeks sensation: this is his nature. But sensations are changeable and contradictory; if we base our lives on sensations, we will always be contradicting ourselves. Our sensory thoughts and facts must be organized so that we can achieve mutual understanding through rational thought."

These three great philosophers never mention the name of God, and yet how much more real is the enlightenment they offer the world.

After these profound, peaceful and touching thoughts, I compared them with the Old and New Testaments. And I was more and more convinced that the God of the Bible was of man's own imagination and construction in constant search of his own identity. This is why we can find so many contradictory teachings.

The most amazing thing is if we are indeed God's creation, why doesn't this God respect our lives, instead of making us long for death as a reward for eternal life? And if the world in which we live is also His creation, why does He treat it as merely a repository for demons? And why is Jesus always exorcizing and asking us to mortify our bodies in an effort to expunge emotions and negate the senses? Yet, at the same time, He arouses in his followers such intense passion in their expressions of adoration for him, God and the Madonna. If he displays any love or consideration, it's not for human beings, but only for an imaginary God.

Older generations, who were introduced to this cruel and contradictory God, grew up in fear. They were constantly being punished and were always apologizing for being alive and feeling guilty if by chance they were feeling happy. Is this the kind of God that the Church should introduce to children in schools?

It is obvious that the Kantian and Cartesian saying, "I think, therefore I am," would never be admitted by the Church, which only approves Jesus's constant declaration, "I am because He is in me, and whatever I say because He speaks from me." This is a perfect example of the total rejection of the self.

On the contrary, for enlightened thinkers there is an immense respect for all aspects of our existence, seeking improvement of the self through gradual transformation.

From the very beginning of creation, the truth about God's existence and his power that we were made to believe was so ambiguous that it had to be constantly proven. And why so many tales as the one in which Moses, on God's command, turns a rod into a serpent to prove God's existence to the pharaoh? Throughout history, at least the way it's related in the Bible, we find innumerable examples of supernatural, mystical, extrasensory and visionary communication between Him and his "chosen" possessed prophets. If He is real, why such need?

I felt incredible relief when I put the Bible aside and turned instead to passages from Confucius, Buddha and Socrates. It was like a breath of fresh air. My readings brought joy to me. But at the same time, I felt ashamed for being so degraded in the name of Jesus and for having wasted so much of my life, while my spirit was brutally possessed.

It was Socrates who brought home to me what possession was—in the best sense. "One is to be in possession of his own knowledge and wisdom, with complete confidence in the self, and to be in possession of the liberty of the spirit, and not to be possessed." We have to come by this knowledge on our own, because many of the people who, we believe, possess knowledge and sanctity, turn out to be frauds. Had I known this long ago, Friar G. would have never met me.

All these unanswered questions led me to conclude that silent meditation is the only way to protect us from becoming dependent on spiritual teachers of any religion, from the kind of terrible possession that I experienced. By reflection we can find the wisdom and meaning of our existence to make the right choices instead of acting impulsively and setting in motion events whose consequences may come back to haunt us for the rest of our lives. Everything is subject to cause and effect and not because we fear punishment by God but for our own benefit, for if we do not behave in accordance with the truth, loyalty and responsibility, we will cause suffering to others and ultimately make ourselves unhappy, too.

Our attitude taught by the church obliges us to look outside of us, for we are often given to comparing ourselves with friends or neighbors, becoming consumed with jealousy or envy rather than taking the trouble to discover our own identity. If we did discover it, we would probably feel richer and more important than our neighbors.

Focused concentration helps us listen to our intuition so that we can discern the truth. In this way, we will no longer have to worry that we are making the wrong choices and be able to develop our full potential, which is what all great philosophers celebrate. They teach us how we can become powerful and sublime through an open mind. Real knowledge is what is achieved when we are able to go beyond the physical evidence and embrace the metaphysical meaning. It stands for the capacity to be able to penetrate to the heart of a matter.

No one can give us knowledge. It makes no sense dreaming of UFOs and of life on other planets, as members of some cults do, trying to escape from this world and dreaming of another. We can reach happiness and self-fulfillment only by living in this world with love and respect. And we can discover and develop just as much intelligence and brilliance in ourselves, if we follow the example of great men like Buddha, Confucius and Socrates and many others of equal genius and true introspection, free from the baggage of bias and superstitions. Nothing can come to us without our working for it. No knowledge will dawn on us as a result of some miracle nor will it be realized by escaping into outer space: Everything we want to achieve requires our dedication, discipline, awareness and objectivity.

Our emotions and our dreams have to be controlled and directed. The Tien-Tao philosophy, for example, tells us that desires cause extreme anxiety and bring suffering. All disasters are brought on by emotions and desires. Our real essence is based on truth, but unfortunately our true self is camouflaged by our emotions and desires.

Knowledge comes from freeing ourselves of the idea of God. We are better than God, since our knowledge, which is infinite, is in constant evolution. We have to begin to believe in ourselves and find wisdom within us. Confucius said, "Superior man can make mistakes, but he is very attentive and constantly analyzing where the mistakes have occurred and he immediately tries to correct himself."

Chapter 28

We Are All Children of the Stars

One of the teachings of Socrates, which I consider to be the most important and which exercises a great influence over me, is that "the best of all is to be in possession of our own knowledge and wisdom, and not to allow others to possess or dominate us." I began to try to understand how I could be so easily manipulated without the factors of time and space. I started to learn about energy. Since all life is based on dynamic radiation, which is based on energy, it follows that the logic of energy is a constant movement that belongs to natural motion. Nothing in nature can rest; everything is in continuous movement. This movement, until it is stopped or redirected, will not change. It will keep going forever just as life goes on with the same repetitiveness. Dynamism is the motor for life, since it is the only force that can effect change. In our psychic lives, it corresponds to our will. Change can come about only through tension generated by an antagonistic relationship.

We have three types of energy: The first is based on the antagonistic power that forces the dynamism to develop its potentiality. Each atom is the system between two antagonistic energies and the more that antagonistic energy exists, the more powerful the energy becomes so as to be able to face contrasting forces. There is no doubt that the most potently antagonistic power is nuclear energy. In the psychic world, it can even be said that the whole course of human events is driven by conflict. By nature, human beings are conquerors; the more resistance we find in our way, the stronger we become. Some people are dominant, whereas others are weaker. Nonetheless, if the weaker manage to resist the domination of the stronger, they will become stronger themselves.

For example, if an antagonistic force were to invade our country or the stability of our family, our will would become stronger by opposing the invasion. The seven-year war waged by American colonists against Great Britain marked the beginning of the Declaration of Independence, which was the most important document in American history, confirming the American will for self-determination.

The second type of energy is in contrast to the first. The antagonistic power, in becoming weaker, shifts into a state of relaxation, causing a process of disintegration. As energy degrades, all its components tend to lose their complexity and become more uniform or homogeneous and what is individual, autonomous and meaningful degenerates. The differences between the various elements begin to disappear and at a certain point, the system can lose so much energy that it cannot be reconstructed. This process is known as entropy, and it results in a black hole. The reverse case of this disintegration of energy is a reawakening of the antagonistic power at the last moment of life by regenerating itself into new energy.

An analogous process occurs in human beings when the power of the ego loses its motivation, i.e., its energy, resulting in the regeneration of a new beginning in acceptance of new knowledge. Similarly, the philosophical rules of death and rebirth are followed.

The Buddhist approach may seem contradictory, as regards the two examples already discussed. Equilibrium and harmony prevail in Buddhism, which is the acceptance of opposition by obedience to nature, thereby diminishing the conflict of egoistic energy which dominates the psychic tensions.

A truly enlightened individual will seek to master the psychic tensions that exist in all of us, until he attains a state of complete emptiness, meaning that he has transcended the self and is at one with the universe. Only in this way can one get to creative energy. Man, free in his complete emptiness and silence, is taken to the highest spiritual level of experience. Even though the psychic level is based on memory, which has the tendency to conflict with our ego, especially when our dormant memories are awakened, we can still gain freedom from conflicting tendencies through silence.

In my case, I find myself drained of all energy. I fear I am on the point of being taken to a gradual death without any hope of enlightenment. All through my blank time I was living in darkness, deprived of any capacity and interest in studying. But one day after I got to New York, I had the chance to listen to Michael, an innately meditative Egyptian, aged 45, who works as an attendant at the health club in my building, and opened up a new world for me. I owe a debt of gratitude to him, since it was he who introduced me to the theory of the Big Bang, helping me to understand how our universe originated. I was exhilarated.

Following Michael's advice, I decided to go to the Museum of Natural History on Manhattan's West side. What an unforgettably wonderful experience it was! There was so much new to learn and discover that when I found myself in the Museum bookstore, I was confounded by the incredible number of books and didn't know which book to select. Finally, I decided on Joseph Silk's, *Big Bang.*

As I started to read the book, I found many handicaps. I was already struggling with English, and the hard part was figuring out what the authors of these books were saying. I have no background in physics or chemistry, and the terminology was altogether unfamiliar. When I began to study, I felt that the task was hopeless. How, I wondered, could I ever possibly understand such an abstruse subject?

I was almost ready to give up when I decided that maybe I was going about my research in the wrong way. Instead of trying to understand everything from the beginning, I thought, why not just try to concentrate on what attracts my attention? If something in particular intrigued me, then I would do my best to learn about it. If not, I would go on. That seemed to resolve my problem. This approach is in keeping with my theory about how magnetism works. When we are pursuing a subject that interests us, we are naturally drawn down a path that will expedite our search and be guided toward our destination, even though we may not be aware of it until we reach it.

What attracted me the most about cosmology was the theory of perfect equilibrium advanced by scientists. About 15 to 20 billion years ago, the universe was infinitely compressed into a tiny agglomeration of gas. Then the mass became denser, hotter and smaller. When mass and radiation were in perfect equilibrium and had an identical temperature, they became so dense that no heat or light could penetrate them. At this point the radiation became an absorber of its own radiation and when it reached the state of equilibrium, the Big Bang occurred.

In this same way, the second type of energy occurs. When energy degrades, all its components tend to lose their complexity and individuality, and by becoming uniform, the system is destroyed, giving rise to the creation of the stars. Exploding stars are called supernovas.

When these stars explode, they turn back into dust and gases; in other words, they revert to the very same elements out of which new stars are created, producing a major galaxy with such brilliance that they can be seen for billions of light years across intergalactic space. But sometimes the stars, before they explode, can lose much energy and die. Their mass becomes infinitely compressed and gravity becomes so strong that it can result in a black hole. Any object, even another star, that gets anywhere close will be immediately sucked into and devoured by it.

Similarly, in human beings the process of psychic energy is also based on the irreversible degradation of energy between the successive transformation which can result in the explosion of a new star or in a black hole.

The perfect balance that goes over and over when the rebirth occurs has fascinated me the most. In a similar way, I equated this concept with the idea that the same kind of condensation and equilibrium of energy could be reproduced through silent meditation, unleashing an equally powerful explosion of creativity within us.

It's astounding to realize that stars are not only responsible for the origin of the universe but that each atom in our bodies was already present in them. Just as the first stars consisted of hydrogen and helium, their fusion released energy, and helium burning produced carbon, and carbon produced oxygen, including iron. In fact, our bodies contain all the same elements from the universe, including such gases, as hydrogen in the form of water, and such minerals as iron, calcium and zinc.

Therefore, we are all children of the stars. Once I heard these words, I was very moved. I found great joy in knowing that I was so intimately connected with the universe. Most scientists believe that earth became habitable about 3.85 billion years ago; so this realization that we are all children of the stars gives us a new perspective: Our lives originated in outer space.

After billions of years of continuous changes in chemical composition, which produced the stars, it would seem that the universe was not created in seven days by an unchangeable God, but from continuous dynamic motion through electromagnetic waves and constant chemical transformation analogous to human evolution. Now that the Big Bang theory has scientifically accounted for the origin of the universe and life on earth, we can see why it is such a mistake to follow Jesus's teaching and deny our egos when our egos still have the potential to evolve. It has been ever thus since human beings first appeared on earth.

It was even announced in 1929 that the universe is continually expanding, its galaxies racing ever farther apart, and not static, which conflicts with the church's concept that the universe is a fixed thing. Physicist Michio Kaku, challenging traditional Judeo-Christian thought, said, "If God is omniscient, the Quantum principle upsets the entire apple cart. If God cannot even know where the electron is, he cannot know what a human being will do, or feel in the future. Free will is reintroduced into our world. No book in heaven knows all of the future."

If the universe is in dynamic transmutation and in continuous expansion instead of being fixed and eternal, how then can we combine the idea of an eternally unchanging omniscient God? Even if God were omniscient, He would not know about chemical transformation as He is not a part of this dynamic world.

Only the same two entities, the universe and the individual, can share the same reality. Neither one can be experienced without the other, since we are basically composed of and nourished by the same elements. Any new entity, which is not made up of the same elements that we are composed of, will simply not be recognized. For instance, if we do not acknowledge the planet Mars, then it will not exist. And if we do not recognize the universe in its present form, it will remain without significance. If we fail to recognize God, then God will remain without existence. Who, then, is the real God?

If nothing can exist outside of our space until we recognize it, why then dream about what does not exist? It is so obvious that human dreamers who were imagining a perfect and unchangeable God, as well as the dramatic attempt to have us believe that Jesus came from the Holy Spirit, wrote the Bible. And if the Holy Spirit is not constituted from the same chemical composition as the stars, the same is true for humans, so then from which universe does he originate? How could God become a human if he is not of our chemical world?

Why not, instead, respect our planet, our lives, ourselves? Despite all this incoherence, if we insist on believing that God created this world, why then did this God at least in the Christian tradition, not teach us to revere it, instead of making us aspire to another, eternal world? We do not even know the world we live in very well. In any case, where is this eternal life to be found? Our universe is not eternal, and the stars die just as we do. One day, perhaps, after billions of years, our universe will die, too.

The reality is that only human beings can create another world on a planet like Mars. And if we should succeed, I hope this creation will not be attributed to God, but rather to human ingenuity and imagination.

At this moment in time, our integration with the universe is what is important. My father used to compare our own lives to a microcosm within the macrocosm of the universe. He would treat his patients by teaching them how to focus and integrate themselves with the universe, emphasizing the importance of the cycle of death and rebirth. I'm finally recognizing the wisdom of his beliefs, as I become more and more conscious of how important I am to the universe and the universe to me. I'm now able to understand that the immense expanse of the cosmos cannot exist without me. I'm proud that I originate from the universe, and that within me lies an entire cosmos. This holds true for every one of us. If we do not recognize it, we are rejecting our own essence, dooming ourselves to remain prisoners of our egos.

The feeling of nostalgia and inexplicable sadness that we occasionally experience is due to our inability to reconcile ourselves with the universe. This nostalgia is not for God or any other deity; rather it is for the fact that we do not recognize our own potentiality, just as in life we often do not recognize an ardent lover or loving friend.

The shocking simplicity of how we arrived at such a complex, vast multiplicity of life again made me draw a parallel with meditation. We, as a microcosm identical to the universe from our very beginning, have been continually evolving, and like the galaxies themselves, we are still expanding and developing our natural potential. Therefore, through silent meditation, might be able to cause the same condensation of energy within ourselves, similar to that occurring in the Big Bang. We will be able to create a perfect equilibrium in our biological organism and be able to evolve in the same complex multiplicity of knowledge.

This symbiosis with the universe is based on continuous penetration. Positive energy penetrates negative energy in a manner similar to hydrogen bonding with helium. Perfect balance is difficult to reach, though. One force will usually try to dominate the other. This is also true in relations between couples; one person always has more power than his or her partner. Elements in the universe continually exhaust and transform themselves to avoid an excess of density. So, too, do human relationships undergo a kind of continual penetration, as we strive to establish consistent emotions and achieve balance with those we share our lives and with ourselves.

To accomplish these goals, we need to go through a process of surrender and renewal. Even though we are forced to let go of the things and people we love, there is no alternative if we wish to grow. This is what is meant when we talk about a cycle of death and rebirth. We can experience the same thing in the physical world. One of the most important forces in the universe is gravity. Gravity depends on density; there is more gravitational pull on the sun than on the earth, and even infinitesimally more density will generate an excess of gravity over repulsion. In human terms, the need to achieve balance is necessary in order for us to be able to accept new knowledge. This does not necessarily mean rejecting or discarding old concepts. What it does mean, though, is that we are in a position to transform and integrate them with the new ones.

If I hadn't begun discussing Buddhism with Michael, the health club attendant, and found that enlightening, I would never have had so many new horizons opening up for me. My candid nature and receptivity allowed for a fusion of many thoughts, inspired by our conversations. Thanks to this process of dialogue and integration, new concepts arose in my mind. It was in some way much like the great dialogue we should be carrying on with the universe. This is why integration is essential to achieve understanding of the self and acceptance of the new. The brain can absorb an enormous amount of information and, once codified, it can be transformed into a variety of concepts.

However, if we want to absorb and integrate any new concepts, we must first isolate ourselves and concentrate on our inner-self. But nothing creative will be produced, if one remains isolated for too long. A long isolation can cause any number of afflictions, including self-absorption, when we remain centered only around the needs of our ego. Many psychological disorders can result as well: excessive material desire, jealousy and delusion. Involvement in such petty concerns cuts us off from the roots of life and creativity, often turning into negative energy.

This kind of rot will eventually lead to physical illness and early death without the possibility of discovering our innate power or realizing our potential for happiness. This is why interaction between parties is essential to avoid stagnation and ossification, but instead to allow a better understanding of the self and acceptance of the new.

Chapter 29

Penetration Between Two Entities: The Basis of Life

The perfect fusion is between two people who, every moment of their lives, try to integrate each into one entity, while at the same time manage to retain their individuality. Love should be based on equal physical and emotional penetration, one "dying" inside the other in order to be reborn. When that happens, we call it love. In physics, fusion is defined as the act of liquefying or melting by the application of heat, as the merging of different elements into a union. It is no accident we say that someone's heart melts for that of another person.

Similarly, what happened before the Big Bang is that the compressed gases required the same kind of equilibrium and an identical temperature before the universe could be born. A microscopic clot of blood is all that's necessary to form a prototype for the embryo, which, by emitting nerve impulses, creates the development of the spinal cord. The spinal cord is filled with marrow, which contains nerve cells called neurons. Nerve impulses travel to the peripheral cells called ganglia and then return to the central spinal cord. In this way the impulses permit a continuous exchange of information that keeps the nervous system in equilibrium.

My metaphorical attempt at comparing our biological system with that of the universe sparked in me the idea about how the brain is formed in the embryo and how the same process seems to be at work in the universe itself. As the spinal nerves grow, they need space; it's a package deal. The nerve impulses create a space for different types of cells that develop other tissues, which slowly expand and sculpt themselves in a cranial curve, creating enough space to hold the four lobes of the brain. The brain keeps expanding itself during all of adolescence; this seems to be the same process that is at work in the universe itself.

When the Big Bang occurred, the radiation of the gases, or our embryonic cells with nerve impulses, in the explosion created a space analogous to our cranium that contains matter and gases just as our cranium contains the four lobes. Our brain expands itself during our evolution similar to how the universe expands itself. To stretch the metaphor a little further, think of the ganglia as planets in interaction with the spinal cord as the sun. The universe expands to contain matter and gases which turn into stars, planets, and galaxies as our brain expands itself through the formation of convolutions. This creates a new surface area for neuron growth and enhanced chemical interaction between nerve cells, making the processing of new information possible.

In trying to understand the human anatomy and its metabolism, I confronted the same dilemma I did when I was researching the origins of the universe. What I wanted to do was to see whether I could relate each one of my principal organs to my psyche and my ego to understand the way Friar G. had manipulated specific parts of my body and inflicted illnesses on me for so many years. I was particularly concerned with the brain and spinal cord because those were the two regions where the pain from the paralyzed boy was being transferred onto my body. Of course, it would be presumptuous of me to claim that I was able to acquire a comprehensive knowledge of physiology and neurology in just a short period of time, when it obviously takes years to master it.

Not forgetting Kundalini, which continues to intrigue me even during my research on our anatomy, I visualize, when I close my eyes, the amazing collaboration between the peripheral cells and central spinal cord, intuiting the connection between the marrow and the sacral bone. According to oriental philosophy, the Kundalini, which is the human being's most powerful energy, lies dormant at the base of the sacral bone inside the tail of the spinal cord in the form of a serpent and can be activated through the same process as that of the perfect equilibrium that brought about the Big Bang.

To my great surprise, Kundalini, which is the only power that can trigger the explosion of the Open Mind, is, known as the "Holy Spirit" in the teachings of the Catholic Church. While it is the same energy, it doesn't come from outside, as Jesus and the Church would have us believe by creating three distinguished identities, God, The Holy Spirit and the Son, but from within our own biological system.

I believe that Kundalini is a force that is similar to the power inherent in every element in the universe. When the complexity of the mass of the star is destroyed, the created uniformity will provoke the explosion of the star which will produce new stars and new galaxies. Similarly, the explosion of Kundalini will create in our brain new thoughts, new ideas, and new knowledge.

I was very happy to have it confirmed that it was neither the Holy Spirit nor any other outside forces that enable us to tap into the greatest source of our power and energy. There is only one way in which these individuals who, like prophets and Friar G. could succeed in reawakening this energy. It would be through breathing deeply and systematically that we are able to reach a profound silence, which ultimately culminates in a perfect equilibrium, prompting the opening of the Kundalini inside our sacral bone.

This explosion of energy provokes a great heat like fire, which follows through the sacral medulla oblongata as in a thermometer reaching the lowermost part of the brain flooding the entire brain with essential, powerful energy. It is exactly the same process that is followed when the sexual energy is redirected just before orgasm by breathing up to the brain. Consequently, the excited neuron can transmit stimulation to another neuron,

This gray matter of the medulla oblongata (consisting of nerve fibers called axons neurotransmitters and blood vessels) expands into the fourth ventricle (or cavity) of the brain connected to the nerve cells that constitute the cerebral cortex. The white matter then sends this gray matter further up to our frontal lobe, which is largely responsible for higher brain function, including thought, reasoning and memory.

This explosion of energy generated by the medulla charges new electrical impulses, and these impulses transmit neural messages that augment the capacity of cells that might never have been awakened before. What is happening, in effect, is that the cells of our brain become sensitive and perceptive to such an extent that philosophers categorize this perception as pure intellect or open mind, which extends beyond reason to join with a super-conscious level of wisdom, which allows us to acquire new and superior knowledge.

The frontal lobe is what distinguishes us from animals and makes us human. It is the rational center of our brain, providing us with the ability to codify neural impulses and giving them meaning by creating conscious thoughts, which are translated into words. In my view, it is at this point that our ego comes into play. My imagination led me to believe that the ego has an actual physical location, which can be identified, namely the digestive apparatus beginning from the pharynx to the esophagus, which leads to the stomach.

The respiratory system follows the same passageway and continues through the trachea, which lies below the pharynx to the larynx, leading to the respiratory tract which consists of the lungs. It is a passageway for air moving in and out of the trachea, which is where the vocal cords reside. They are called the voice box. The words transmitted from the brain and received by the vocal apparatus are either accepted or rejected. The mechanism is much like our digestive systems. Food passes through the pharynx and the esophagus and is either digested or rejected.

The same is true with words. We select the words we want to hear, depending on our level of maturity and our capacity to accept the truth. Refusing to face the truth is a rejection of equilibrium. Or to put it another way, it is the cause of the destruction of psychological and physical balance. It can be called a black hole when any object that gets too close is immediately sucked in and devoured.

The same can happen in the case of our rejection of truth. If truth is not accepted it will be immediately sucked into the deepest part of our subconsciousness. And any supernova, any rebirth, will occur since the gravity of our ego will be so strong that neither light nor radiation can escape; only the circuit of the same energy will survive until finally our psychological and physical imbalance completely destroys our system

When we talk about our ego, what do we really mean? Ego is not only a matter of constant conflict between our spiritual/moral selves and our egoistic desires. Ego can also be thought of as a conductor orchestrating how our five senses work together with our sexual and emotional faculties.

The way the "conductor" communicates to his "musicians" is through electrical impulses produced by nerve cells and fibers that extend through the spinal cord and reach into the pituitary gland. This gland produces a number of hormones in connection with the hypothalamus, whose neurons constitute an endocrine gland that secretes hormones stored in the pituitary gland, which is the king of all glands.

The pituitary gland is the stimulator of all other glands, including the thyroid and our digestive processes, which is also controlled by the hormones. These glands not only modulate all digestive, olfactory, and acoustic systems, but also send multiple projections to different parts of the cerebral cortex, influencing our state of consciousness and all our emotional and sexual responses. If these systems are thrown out of balance, all moral constraints like shame and modesty disappear, resulting in anger, emotional instability and uncontrollable sexuality.

From a clinical perspective, if there is imbalance in the pituitary gland and if our ego is not enlightened, we can just as easily turn into monsters. Our only consolation is that by continuing to develop self-knowledge, we will eventually stamp out ignorance. Ignorance is like a black hole in space, an infinitely small mass devouring anything that comes close to it.

I began to understand that brain activity is characterized by a continuous interaction and collaboration between the right side and the left side. I perceive that the right side is more intuitive and creative, influencing the left side of the brain. Once codified by the frontal lobe, sensory input received by the brain is first transmitted to the right side; this means that the right side is stimulating the left side and vice versa. Therefore, the left side has the capacity to translate this input into words, even though they may not actually be expressed.

There is a continuous dialogue between the two hemispheres: the left side with its representational memory and the right side with its more abstract and intuitive capacity. When we apprehend an idea such as space, it is initially perceived by the right, intuitive side of the brain. Once it is interpreted by the left, rational side of the brain, the word space becomes figurative, an intellectual concept.

I was convinced that the left part of our brain is the rational side; like a computer, it is capable of accumulating all kinds of data in forms that we can use to paint images. The images that reflect themselves in the left brain are not endowed with any emotion. Any judgments the left brain renders are based on facts, not on emotions. This is why I think that abstract painting, for instance, which requires intuition and creativity, belongs primarily to the right side; anyway, they link to each other in continuous symbiosis.

Recently, however, I came across a book, *The Brain Pack,* by Ron Van Der Meer and Ad Dudink, which takes into consideration that our brain works in a crisscross fashion. It contends that the right side of the brain controls the left side of the body and the left side controls the right side of the body. But what really is important is that my painful experience in which I could only live connected either with the left or the right part of the brain, but never with the two in tandem, correctly led me to intuit ideas that have been confirmed by recent research on the human brain.

I further came to believe that many of my intuitions deduced only from my living experience weren't so far from the real evidence, which actually confirmed them. From this, I conclude that while we are thinking, talking, or writing, we are constantly pronouncing words. Words automatically pass through the throat glandular system and ultimately find their way to the "heart," so long as the word is accepted or found "digestible."

According to the book, *Emotional Intelligence,* by Daniel Goleman, particular importance is given to amygdala, a component of the brain, which is responsible for our emotional memory. Emotions are processed by amygdale, which maintains a constant communication with the endocrine system, one of which is the adrenal glands. When stimulated, the adrenals secrete the hormones, epinephrine and norepinephrine, that cause a strong "fight or flight" reaction, facilitating retention of these emotional memories for recall, when, once again, confronted by the same stimulus.

The thyroid gland, in particular, exerts a powerful influence on our psychological state. Amygdala plays such an important role because the right side of the brain is influenced by the emotions attached by amygdala. Whether these feelings are valid or not; these impressions and judgments do not always correspond to the truth because they are often influenced by our own desires. Only the left brain can supply the data necessary to make correct judgments by means of logical reasoning. Otherwise, there's no way that we can establish the truth.

If I say to myself, "I am tired," this would involve the right side, because I cannot decipher the meaning of an abstraction since it registers emotional feelings. The left side of the brain cannot understand my feelings, but can translate the abstract concept charged with emotional feeling into words.

So why do I insist on believing that the left side of the brain is the more realistic and truthful part, while the right side is the more emotional and intuitive? Here is my reasoning: I believe that people who rely more on their intuition instead of their rational thinking use the right side. The right side is the part of the brain which compels us to talk; in fact, when people talk too much, they do not have time to analyze situations or even pay much heed to the words they're using. It is the left side that interprets concepts and allows us to express them in a coherent way.

I believe that prophets, gurus and "holy men" like Friar G. only listen to their amygdala, because they believe that they are in communication with God and no other voice is necessary to attend to. They are so driven by their desires that they never take into consideration the logical part of their brain. And so they pull people along with their falsehoods about the end of the world, space ships, and redemption in the next life, officially acting in the name of God but, in reality, motivated by their own desires. Thus, the existence of God was invented

Friar G. seeks to rob me of my emotional memories and I have become aware of the methodology he uses to succeed in this barbarian intent. For instance, at times, I would suddenly become very emotional and often start crying for the most trivial reasons. Even watching the news on television could make me cry. Why should I react so strongly to accusations against Clinton's behavior in office or weep over Boris Yeltsin's heart surgery? Ordinarily, such events wouldn't have had such a strong effect on me. Friar G. was trying to erase all the scars by cleansing my heart, actually my amygdala, and negating my memories. Since he is so determined to take all of my emotions, it occurred to me that the emotions are what keep our memories alive.

As a matter of fact, I wish to remember everything I went through, but in the absence of feeling, I cannot. Because our bodies are inextricably connected with our five senses, any intense sensation, whether pleasurable or disgusting, is memorized by our bodies once the sensation is recorded. The memory in the brain is reinforced by physical reactions, which strengthens the retention by intensifying the emotional response.

Our psychological pain is felt on a more sophisticated level than physical pain, so that's why it requires more than the five senses to register it. Psychological pain, because it is elaborated through the thoughts and interpretation of the situation, must be distinguished from physical pain. It is a mental elaboration that occurs primarily in the frontal lobe, which receives all electromagnetic impulses generated by neurotransmitters, chemicals that transmit nerve impulses in the brain.

It is the frontal lobe, that codifies information and translates it into words. This information includes sensations created by thoughts stirred up by our imagination as well as by memories and responses to actual events. If anything, our imagination is more intimately connected to the prompting of our amygdala or heart; this gives rise to our emotions, which are influenced by our glandular system. Since they are mental elaborations motivated by our negative or positive desires, which do not always allow us to give the right interpretation of the facts concerned, they may well become a sick mental fixation difficult to correct.

But in normal conditions, without the strong influence of our ego, the information received and visualized by our frontal lobe stimulates our electromagnetic impulses, generating new thoughts. The more these impulses pulsate, the more new chemical compositions are combined. As a consequence, more creative knowledge arises where stimulation is frequent, as in the universe, where constant pulsation becomes dynamic.

Professor Adrian Dobbs, Nobel Prize winner for neurophysiology, believes that our cerebral cortex consists of 40,000 neurons for each square millimeter and each neuron is connected to a synapse, the point at which nerve impulses pass or are repulsed by each neuron. This can be modified by the waves of one's will. How can the will have influence over the brain's neurons? Professor Dobbs contends that we have to accept the idea of the existence of a psychic energy, which, along with the brain's neurons, creates the mental will. Thankfully, though, we don't have to be slaves to our emotions. By applying our mental willpower, either by rejecting negative thoughts or by converting them into positive ones, we can change our emotions.

If, however, we do want to connect ourselves to the kind of thought process that results in both superior intellect and superior intuition, we have to plumb much deeper, beyond the cortex of the frontal lobe to a place where neither the right nor the left side of the brain has any influence. When we meditate, we are no longer seeing with our eyes, but with our mind's eye. In meditation, we are able to transcend the limits ordinarily imposed by our cortex; we can become connected with infinite space.

Once this connection is made, the energy of the cosmos can amplify the electrical messages flowing to the neurons. The result is that new neural pathways are formed, increasing the innervations of all our brain cells, turning them into more adaptable and more powerful transmitters. By meditating, we are giving our brains the opportunity to become more efficiently wired than before.

Throughout the course of human evolution, we were able to transform sensory information into concepts and meaningful words, expanding our intellectual ability even though we suffered a diminishing of the intensity of our five senses as a consequence. Some animals can hear ten times more precisely than human beings. Insects can detect electromagnetic waves, an ability we have completely lost. Dolphins, known as "geniuses of the sea," are able to perceive vibrations over such vast distances that they can detect the presence of other species many miles away.

Even if we've lost much of our sensory capacity over the ages, in order to adapt to a modern urban society, silent meditation allows us to get back some of it. It's even possible for us to restore our power of vision to match the acuity of our ancestors, so that we can even be capable of distinguishing our own energy merging with that of the universes through electromagnetic waves. At the same time, we will also be able to stimulate our hearing to the point of perceiving sounds we have never heard before.

The most sophisticated computers cannot compete with the power of our brains, which are able to create pathways for new thoughts and codify each new piece of information it receives in order to then store it in its memory bank. The quantity of information kept in the cerebellum and cerebral cortex is vast and densely packed, since it also includes information rejected by the ego. As a result, it is impossible to retrieve most of it.

We can reawaken some of these buried memories through unusually deep hypnosis, but this could be dangerous because our egos may still reject the truth. It would be much better if we tried to retrieve our deepest memories gradually and in full consciousness, until we have the courage to confront the truth that we repressed.

We are fortunate to have such an abundant resource for self-discovery available within us; it is up to us to awaken it silently and slowly, day by day. I think, therefore, that our bodies, in conjunction with our glandular system, have the capacity to retain the memory of every emotion we experience.

I fully understand now what my father meant when he said that if we do not understand our bodily functions, the only things that truly belong to us, we can't synchronize with the rest of the world.

With a deeper and deeper grasp of the workings of our bodies, however, we will be capable of recognizing how the entire universe is based on these same functions. Once such an understanding is achieved, we will be in a better position to integrate ourselves with the universe. By stimulating our neurotransmitters, we will create a new path in our brain, opening us to new horizons and new knowledge, as well as reawakening the incredible power that is in us.

My father often drew an analogy between a body and a car. If a car stops, usually it's because it has run out of gas and needs refilling.

Our body is the same: If our physical and emotional level of energy is low, we have to stop and refill it. It's funny to think how concerned we become the moment we hear our car make strange noises, and yet we hardly pay any attention at all to the messages emanating from our body. We keep pushing on, until we are forced to halt by becoming sick or even dying.

My father encouraged all to respect their own body as a temple, to listen and carefully tend to all its needs. He maintained that we need to conceive of our relations with our body and the universe as an ideal partnership where information is constantly shared in the same way that information is shared between the central nervous system and the peripheral nerve cells. Which is only another way of saying that we must respect the integrity of the universe.

Chapter 30

The Physiology of Manipulation

By following my father's recommendation on understanding our bodily functions in order to free us from any inconveniences, we can consciously belong to ourselves. With this in mind, I kept trying to understand Friar G.'s need for orchestrating my feelings. Whenever he manipulated me, I felt so many different sensations in my throat and thyroid that I decided to pay more attention to these parts of my body. By recognizing my ignorance, I began to learn as much as I could about them. I started studying *Gray's Anatomy,* where I learned about the hypothalamus, which is the principal nerve center of the endocrine system, the command center of the brain. No one can imagine my profound shock at finding the amazing explanations for my harsh behavior.

The nerve cells of the hypothalamus produce stimulating hormones that release pituitary hormones. These, in turn, affect the thyroid. If the pituitary gland becomes inflamed, for instance, it can affect the frontal lobe of the brain and impair vision, making it difficult to distinguish objects.

The rise or fall in hormone stimulation affects our emotional behavior such as fear, anger and sexuality. Many of the symptoms of an overactive thyroid gland—called hyperthyroidism, as well as an under-active thyroid gland, hypothyroidism, have a very drastic effect on our behavior.

Symptoms of hyperthyroidism include uncontrollable rage, anxiety, frequent, urinal incontinence, excessive hunger and thirst, elevated blood pressure, insomnia, tachycardia, overheating, sweating, heat loss and shortness of breath.

On the other hand, hypothyroidism causes dry nails and skin, hair loss, low blood pressure and obesity. It can also provoke sexual dysfunction, diminished memory and emotional reactions, like excessive weeping and laughing, as well as deep depression. Some sufferers will sleep excessively and be incapable of thinking clearly. If the condition persists over a prolonged period, hypothyroidism can lead to coma.

The more I read, the more I understand the uncontrollable weeping and laughing, the awful insomnia, the fear and all the other hitherto unexplainable physical and emotional upheavals I'd been subjected to. It even accounted for the suicidal depression I went through in New York, when I was hoping that I'd at last escaped Friar G. Now I have an explanation for some of the saddest and most embarrassing episodes of my life. Why, for instance, I lost control of my bladder in Cannes or why I was so apt to fly into violent, uncontrollable bursts of rage against my dear husband. Finally, I could see that by seizing one single, essential part of my brain, the hypothalamus, Friar G. had been able to manipulate my body, my metabolism and my emotions.

If I were to make substantial progress in my search, I know that I will have to get beyond the limitations of my intellect. So I closed my eyes and concentrated on the space between them. After a while, to my great surprise, I succeeded in connecting with my mid-brain. An image of the embryo inside the womb flashed in front of my mind's eye. Intuitively, I interpreted the image to mean that the beginning of our functional life originates in the mid-brain. It is in the mid-brain, too, where I believe, our subconscious, unconscious and ego also reside.

As usual, I knew nothing about this part of the brain; I immediately consulted my medical books. What I learned is that the mid-brain is only a part of the limbic system, including the hypothalamus and brain stem which plays a crucial role in the functioning of the autonomic nervous system and operates on a subconscious level: We are not aware that our pupils are dilating or that our arteries are constricting, when we show an emotional response.

The autonomic nervous system involuntarily conserves our body's energy during periods of rest; this is why, even if we are in a coma, our basic biological functions continue to operate independently of the conscious part of our brains. Knowing that our autonomic functions are stimulated at a subconscious level, I could now finally understand how Friar G., without my participation or possibility of resistance, could have hijacked my physiological and emotional functions.

My revelation didn't end here since the autonomic nervous system emanates from the spinal cord. So if the spinal cord is damaged in areas corresponding to specific functional aspects of the esophagus, trachea, heart and kidneys, it can manifest similar symptoms, as those during the paralyzed Paolo's healing process, when Friar G. maliciously transfers his symptoms into my body. Such manifestations occur as a contracting esophagus and a racing heartbeat.

This terrifying experience gave me some insight into what happens when a person suffers a stroke. I worry that I will die of suffocation. Even when I swallow a liquid, I choke and experience terrible pain without any possibility of protecting myself. This reaction is produced by involuntary reflexes. This constriction not only prevents food from being swallowed, but also can curb the expression of our ego as well.

A closer examination of the autonomic nervous system reveals anxiety attacks that can also be produced by stimulation of the autonomic system connected with the seven cervical nerves in the neck. When Friar G. managed to provoke extreme anxiety and longing in me for Gian one night, he caused my cervical nerves to pulsate with such intensity that it scared me. The pulsation increased to such a point that it reached my temporal lobe. I became despondent. I was in such a panic that my right hand shot up automatically and I found myself making a slicing gesture across the base of my throat. Terrified, I tried to concentrate as hard as I could on controlling the pulsation for almost half an hour, until the pressure from the pulsation finally started to ebb. Even so, I still felt a terrible compression inside and behind my left ear.

This experience made me suppose that through this stimulation from the cervical nerves it is possible to try to activate central vertebral nervous system, as well as the autonomic nerve ganglia. The electrical pulsation begins in the cervical vertebral nerves, and then travels through the dorsal vertebrae to the thoracic nerves, ending in the lumbar sacral coccyx. This led me to believe that through the stimulation of the neck, which joins our brain to our body, it is possible to cure many sicknesses and even reactivate brain cells.

Now I can also explain the cause of the incessant, unceasing movement of my head, which made people think that I was crazy. Once again it was an involuntary action, stimulated by Friar G's electrical waves impacting on my cervical nerves. I was compelled to move my head for 24 hours one day, while Friar G. controlled my body. By this pulling of my cervical nerves, all my organs were constantly being stimulated.

The stimulation can also originate from the sacral nerves, since they are in constant contact with the cervical nerves. Walking quickly and alertly is a form of exercise that can duplicate the effect of my autonomic head movements. It may be the best way to reactivate our lumbar areas and, by extension, our brains.

If the universe has any intelligence at all, I think it is the kind of intelligence represented by the limbic system in that its behavior seems to be unconscious, automatic and repetitive, all of which are characteristic of the functions of the primitive brain stem. The repetitiveness is based on all living things, the universe repetitively consuming gas and provoking explosions to creates new stars. Nature is constantly dying and renewing. The four seasons regularly and punctually are repeating themselves. From the beginning of the universe, all life of the animals is a non-exhausted repetition, stimulated by the senses located in the limbic system.

Only human beings, alone among all the species, developed the capacity to give meaning to information received from outside, such as natural phenomena. But that capacity also comes with an obligation;

if we are to grow, we need to stimulate and develop our unique inheritance, namely the frontal brain. Otherwise our existence will be reduced to the level of animals, condemned to perform repetitive actions.

We have the potential to become the only real "Gods" there are by virtue of our creative brains. Only we can give meaning to all phenomena that surround us and name them, even though with all our creative potentiality, we have the tendency to be repetitive. As it is, most of our life is based on daily routines that rarely change, unless a significant event, especially a calamity, intrudes. That's why we must constantly struggle against the tendency toward repetitiveness. By studying our primitive brain, we can understand why this repetitive behavior continues.

In trying to forge a new path to other neurons, electrical impulses meet far more resistance than when they follow a familiar course. The repeated use of the same pathway may be responsible for the formation of habits and the accumulation of memories. This forms a template for the same response the next time it is stimulated. However, if the neuron is never stimulated, as in the case of the optic nerves in the blind or the auditory system in the deaf, it will never develop the electrical stimuli that will allow it to reach the cortical center that controls the senses. But while we may not be blind or deaf, we are still handicapped unless we stimulate our frontal brain and cortex. Otherwise, we can risk reducing our life to a series of repetitive actions and repetitive feelings. And often the feelings that are produced in this way are negative ones like hate, resentment etc. Without the possibility of changing or putting a stop to them, these negative emotions can fester and worsen. They will become unconscious habits, until the energy necessary to stimulate them is exhausted.

The same thing happens when it comes to acquiring new knowledge. If we do not stimulate it continually, our intellect will stagnate. Adding new knowledge to our brain automatically creates a new path and a memory to go with it. This memory creates the potential for repetitive function. To fight our innate tendency for repetition, causing it to turn into an indefatigable repetitive stimulation of our brains, we need to continuously stimulate our minds.

Now I understand why all the great philosophers always taught us that ignorance is an enemy to be feared more than death itself. Ignorance has nothing to do with the degree of education, either; even the best-educated people can sometimes be ignorant. Rather, it is lack of curiosity that makes us stagnant.

I can better understand the terrible behavior I displayed, when I fell under the power of Friar G. For what he did was to reduce my brain to the state of an animal's with all its instinctive tendencies and isolated my intellectual capacity for judgment. He induced in me a repetitive, whining, complaining nature with frequent spells of weeping and feelings of guilt, making despair and depression a part of my everyday life.

Because nothing ever changed for 27 years, I have always wondered how it was possible that Friar G. himself never became bored. But now I see what happened. He wasn't the one who was repeating the same actions; it was the autonomic part of my brain. He only caused the repetitive behavior indirectly, when he stimulated my animalistic instincts.

What amazed me even more was that it wasn't Friar G.'s determination that was causing such tumult in me, but rather the determination of my cells stimulated by his electrical waves that came in contact with mine. This explained his incredible resolve, which always amazed me. Actually, such determination is a part of our animal-brain's ability for repetition. This is true until the new forces interrupt it, creating a new path of new knowledge.

I am almost sure that the greatest part of religious spiritual life is based on the subconscious involuntary nervous system of our animal brain, on monotonous, repetitive animal-like behavior. All possessed spiritual people, including the prophets, have been subjected to constant repetitive action. Only through the manipulation of our subconscious system can such possession be achieved.

I often compared myself to the many simple women I used to see in Rome. They were constantly cleaning house and complaining about their children, husbands and neighbors. They never read a book or showed any interest in the world around them. My supposition is that their brains were probably never stimulated enough to develop the full potential of their conscious frontal lobe. Instead, they were living as if on automatic pilot, their behavior almost entirely governed by the unconscious, primitive brain. I don't mean to exclude men, of course. For there are just as many men whose lives are made up of repetitive actions and who only worry about their cars and their favorite sports teams!

Pity then the children who are raised by such parents and who are never given the chance to be properly educated. They will probably end up motivated by the same autonomic impulses, endlessly repeating patterns they learned from their parents. Some may even take to a life of crime simply in a desperate attempt to create some excitement and escape boredom.

From my experience, I am convinced that our bodies, especially our brains, are our best teachers, and our power. The only solution to the riddle of our lives lies in taking the time to learn how our brain functions and thereby develop a better grasp of our problems. If we are lucky, we will be able to resolve them without the help of psychoanalysis. As we know, hormonal imbalances can occur that may have all sorts of unpredictable consequences.

Studying will develop our conscious brain as much as is humanly possible, especially when you start to realize what kind of power can be unleashed once the autonomous cell system is stimulated. In learning about how this system operates, it may actually be possible for you to dominate the automatic impulses. My father was right, always repeating that if we don't understand how our body functions, then we cannot possibly hope to understand our life.

As I've already stated, I believe that my frequent outbursts and lack of any sense of shame were because my hypothalamus was thrown out of balance. I was forced to surrender control over my actions. Because it exerts such influence over the automatic nervous system, the hypothalamus basically serves as the higher nervous center governing the lower. By stimulating the lower center, Friar G. was able to make it prevail over the higher, controlling center.

One thing that I will never stop trying to prove is that no one, including Friar G., has God-given, supernatural powers, since any control over us has to involve our biological system. We all can develop the same power inside ourselves.

When man doesn't understand powers like those that affected me such telepathy, brainwashing, and possession, all of which are still incomprehensible, he turns to the church for explanation and solace. Just as scientists have finally been able to explain hurricanes, earthquakes and tornadoes, someday man will also discover the sources of telepathy and brainwashing. As long as horrible phenomena like these remain inexplicable, in our impotence we will turn to God to seek justice. But in my case, I actually turned to the source of my obliteration. The result was that all my imploring was answered with a deep silence. I could only think that our prayers have no effect at all because they accomplish nothing.

Think of all the millions of prayers said during World War II by Hitler's victims. It wasn't God who saved Europe from Hitler; it was the Americans. Throughout history, whenever people were threatened with persecution and death, prayers would be offered for salvation. The prayers were never answered.

Martin Scorsese brought this home to me when I viewed the 1997 film "Kundan" about the life of the Dalai Lama. Seeing it left me desolated, especially when I thought about all the prayers that the monks recited day and night, hoping to stave off the invasion of their country by Chinese forces. Despite all the energy they expended in prayer and ritual, they were no match against well-armed Chinese troops. In the end, even the Dalai Lama understood that Tibet's only hope lay in garnering the support of the West and rallying the international community to his country's cause.

In fact, the Tibetans, to attract the world attention to their cause in the name of the Dalai Lama, have been sending prayer flags for freedom which are blue, white, red, green, and yellow, representing the earth and the universe. As a matter of fact, all the stars are of the same color. Tibetan prayer flags are traditionally hung in places, where wind can blow across them, so that this wind sends the prayers along with it to its destination. They were sent to Washington before President Clinton left for China. These prayer flags were hung in such a way to reach President Clinton. The Tibetans understand that only through human beings can they be helped. There is neither God nor saints to listen to our prayers.

Again, the theory of science that claims that God does not know anything about our lives on earth nor about the universe has confirmed itself. God does not even know the origin of tornadoes, earthquake or hurricanes, which is why he cannot stop them. Recently in Italy, an earthquake destroyed a church sacred to Francis of Assisi, killing people inside who were praying. In the U.S., tornadoes have devastated local churches in the south, again taking the lives of those who had sought refuge inside them.

When faithful Muslims from around the world make the Haj or pilgrimage to Mecca, they all too often meet death, instead of salvation. In 1991, well over a thousand people were burned to death in a tunnel on their way to the holy site: seven years later 150 were trampled to death when they were trapped in a crowd. Why could not God protect his own holy places? No one I have ever met has offered me a satisfactory answer. This is yet another example of how our destiny does not lie in God's hands but is entirely our own responsibility.

The other day when I was walking on the street, I began thinking how my father did not come to help me in the name of justice. And in this same way I questioned a long time ago God's silence in the face of my subjugation. And now, I have begun to do the same, this time regarding my parents and friends, but as usual, there is nothing but silence.

Each time I receive confirmation that our prayers do not have any meaning; I can't help but think that it would be far better to put a stop to all religious observances.

Rather than delude ourselves by investing our love in a God that doesn't exist, why do we not start to love one another instead? Why don't we respect ourselves and cherish our relationship with the universe? I believe that only through human beings I can find vindication for my suffering.

All those who believe in the power of God are convinced that through their prayers they are saving the world. As Jesus was to have taken our sins upon himself, so too Friar G., Padre Pio, and the Pentecostals are also convinced that in the future no one will suffer from any serious illnesses, such as heart disease and cancer thanks to their rites and prayers. Likewise, the early Christians looked upon themselves as saviors of the world with a monopoly over the truth, brainwashing themselves along with others.

The leaders of these groups organized prayer meetings, healings, and other more specialized techniques of indoctrination. When people are told that Jesus Christ heals through them, they immediately feel among the chosen and distinguish themselves from the insignificant and common man, saying, "I am better than all of you people; I have a gift and your life is in my hands". They don't realize that there is an incredible power inside of everyone which has yet to be tapped. Each of our strong desires emanates such a powerful energy it can heal as well as kill us, depending on the intensity and perseverance of the intention.

All religions have their own powerful, repetitive word sounds which are demonstrated through the use of different mantras, including "om," "nam myho renge kyo," "om nami pema hum," and "Ave Maria." All of these mantras contain positive energy as well as negative, depending on the meaning that we invest them with. Every meaning has a magnetic force with its own individual sound and each sound has its own power. It is our own power that is manifested when many people recite a mantra at the same time, generating an intense vibration that establishes a deep connection between the participants. This can affect sensitive individuals more than others, as well as others still with uncontrollable hysteria.

But what is most important is that by reciting these mantras, we are able to silence our brains. This silence is essential, since it makes us receptive to our own energy as well as that of the universe. When we inhale, we take in the energy from the universe; when we exhale, we send out our own energy, resulting in a continuous exchange. Through breathing, we are creating a union between our body and our mind, unifying ourselves also with the primary cosmic energy. Breathing is the connection between the conscious and the unconscious; it takes us beyond our intellect. Like an electrical current, it can pass through any matter in a flash.

Case in point: I was referred to a certain Steven, who is said to have the ability to direct and control his energy. His meditation consists of breathing by which he stimulates an incredible power in himself with which he is supposedly able to open our Kundalini. I was hoping that perhaps, through his energy, he would be able to free me from my enslavement. I began going to him every day, hoping that by my perseverance I would be free of Friar G. However, the friar, as usual, countered my inner silence by introducing strangely sexual thoughts about Steven. To interrupt this, I began repeating as a mantra, the words, "I beg freedom from this piece of shit, Jesus," hoping that Friar G. would be gone at least for the sake of his Jesus. But nothing happened.

The same thing occurred when I went to see the Dalai Lama. I was forced to repeat the identical mantra with the difference that I had been repeating it for three days without anything happening. I was not liberated, nor did the Holy Spirit or Jesus come to me, either to help or even punish me. This only confirms that our prayers have no effects. There is no one to even hear them, let alone grant them.

Steven taught us that we have to repeat to ourselves, as a mantra, the words "I can make it, I can do it," the utter contrast of Jesus's teachings was made apparent to me, which is "I cannot make it, I cannot do it." Only through God can one think or speak. Instead, I should say, "Yes! I have to do it, I can do it! I have to succeed by my own will power!"

I began to think that perhaps it was my life's mission to help others avoid such destructive power as submitting our will to that of God, rendering us passive and susceptible to his domination. Ultimately, we are forced to accept the idea of destiny's design that in reality doesn't exist. Instead, we have to fight with our will and with alert participation in our lives, create our own design for a better existence. Our lives are in our hands and in the hands of all humanity.

The last intriguing thing for me was how Friar G. and Padre Pio, as well as others can remain connected with their subjects or victims for such a long time. Often I would experience a pain in my umbilical region that was sometimes so strong that I would even stand in front of the mirror in an attempt to see what was going on. My umbilical area was all red and swollen, and it was painful to the touch. As usual, I immediately consulted my medical books to see what I could learn about the umbilical area. I also consulted some doctors. They contended that once our umbilical cord is cut, it ceases to have any function. I insisted, on the contrary, that the umbilical cord still has a role to play in our adult bodies. When I tried to explain to one doctor the reason for my interest, he told me I was crazy. Nonetheless, I believed I was on to something. After all, the umbilical cord is our first connection to life. It was through this cord that we are able to breath and take in food and oxygen. How was it possible that after performing such essential functions, the umbilical region has nothing more to do with our bodies?

Finally, my dilemma was resolved: The blood from the umbilical cord once discarded as medical waste now was named by Harvard University as one of the most important medical discoveries in the last decade. The research has revealed that the blood of the umbilical cord contains special cells called "stem cells," which divide to make new blood and immune cells. The cord blood is a rich source of stem and progenitor cells that are present in bone marrow. The cord blood stem cells guaranteed a match for the newborn and the stored cells can cure every disease during his life. The cord blood stem cells are effective for treating a number of diseases, such as leukemia lymphoma, anemia and blood disorders, infectious diseases, including Aids, as well as rejuvenating the marrow-producing system. Well, I have to admit I was very proud and happy because my supposition was again confirmed.

As has happened before, my belief in magnetic forces which have often led me to solutions to my dilemmas brought me to a story on CNN News about an international team of scientists working on an experiment called the muon g-2, the largest super-conducting magnet to create a very intense source of an infinitesimally small subatomic particle called the neutrino. The elusive neutrinos come from nuclear reactions inside stars or when cosmic rays collide with our atmosphere. Millions of them pass through the Earth every day. The mass of an individual neutrino is thought to be perhaps a billion times less than an electron, the particle with the smallest known mass. Being almost without mass, they have no obstacles and can pass anywhere.

I immediately visualize this super-conducting magnet capable also passing through the skin. In the latest discovery, it was found that the skin contains stem cells that are able to develop and differentiate into a variety of specialized cells, including neurons, smooth muscle cells and fat cells.

Consequently, this discovery has enabled me to speculate on how Friar G. could transfer to my body the symptoms of paralysis, not only through my umbilical cord but also through the skin and subject me to it for such a long time. Our cells are the only connectors with both our inner as well as our outer life. And since they are transmitters and receptors alike, they can also be transmitters and receptors of our thoughts and our will, as well as various diseases from far away, all through the agency of a super-conducting magnet. Since our cells have the capacity to migrate to the damaged areas in order to regenerate the sick cells and the ability for repetitive process, it follows that until the cells are regenerated from whatever was ailing them, they will not abandon us. Thus we are left with only two possibilities: either we die or we get cured.

No doubt, thanks to our scientists and their constant discoveries, I have gained more understanding about Friar G.'s design in trying to regenerate the sick cells of paralysis transferred to me through constant stimulation of my cells. I believe that with the incredible power of our will, we indeed can connect ourselves with the other person on a deeper level and with the help of our receptive cells, all kinds of illnesses independent of our will can be transmitted to others.

Continuing the idea of the umbilical cord as a possible conductor, it reminds me of an occasion when I would inadvertently run into an Italian woman, who believed she was a guru. She tried to explain to me how difficult and painful it was for gurus to carry out their mission because they are bonding themselves with persons they choose to be their disciples through the umbilical region. After this occurs, she went on, it becomes very difficult and painful to cut that connection. They become like a mother. They can bond with 20 or more persons simultaneously. When I first heard this, I did not pay much attention to what she said, probably because I didn't understand at the time what she was talking about. And I also thought that she might be a little crazy, too.

Very often it turns out that the truth was deducted from our life experience or taken from our intuitive capacities, which later on were confirmed by scientists. So the approach of Yogis also should be taken into consideration, not as a supernatural belief but as a consequence of their meditative power that concentrates on their inner being and often produces rational deductions. Curiously, they focused also on the region of the umbilical cord. In fact, Yogis consider this region as one of six Chakras, the most powerful called the Manipura, which is at the center of the body. It is a central site for the accumulation of energy.

If one knows how to open these Chakras, one can escape the tyranny of a vegetative life and never get sick. It will also give one the capacity to control all bodily functions. This led me to believe that by opening the Chakras, we can reactivate the function of the umbilical cord by means of the anomalous magnetic movement of the neutrinos that are based on the electromagnetic force, and initiated through the power of the brain.

We already know that our cells make very good transmitters and receptors; we can send our thoughts and wills to influence people far away. Many international scientists have studied this phenomenon, which has been discussed in *Parapsychology* by Trento Procaccianti Editori. All have confirmed the existence of psychic energy, manifesting itself through the psycho-magnetic field. They have shown that telepathic clairvoyance is based in part on the capacity to receive electronic impulses sent by electromagnetic mental waves. Telepathy actually relies on magnetic energy and is established by the rapport between the transmitter and the subject, using the power of suggestion at a distance, thought transference, and the use of hypnosis.

From the readings I have done, I have learned that the electric current and the electrochemical energy transmitted by the brain through cerebral waves, together with psychic waves, can modify the subject's reaction both electrochemically and physically. The magnetic energy transmitted from one person to another is so strong that it can cause the deformation of the personality and produce physiological modification, as well. As a matter of fact, the power of thought that emits magnetic radiation is so strong that it can actually be photographed. This psychic technique, known as psychotronics, is utilized by all sciences, as well as by religious groups and individuals, such as Friar G.

The power that telepathy, and other psychic phenomena, represent is so extraordinary that there have even been attempts to develop them to wage psychic warfare. The Russians were investing millions of dollars and recruiting some of their best scientists and psychics to find out whether it was possible one day to control the world telepathically. Because so little is known about how telepathy works, they began to do some intriguing experiments.

They conducted an experiment with the Russian psychic, Ivanova, in which she was put into the complete isolation of a Faraday cage, and submerged under water, leaving her impervious to electromagnetic waves. Nonetheless, Ivanova was still able to communicate telepathically, leading researchers to conclude that communication must exist on a level that operates on different principles, other than ordinary physics. This type of perception has its own laws, and its own mental space and time. These mind-waves can be considered the equivalent of the dematerialized neutrino, the neutral current or fast electron and if sent, travel faster than the speed of light. It becomes a special type of mental space and is held by different laws, as they do not belong to the laws of gravity.

Experiments in this field are continuing, and the prospect that these powers will be used to achieve world domination cannot be ruled out. Of course, this dream is not a monopoly held by the Russians; many countries dream of accessing these telepathic powers and are diligently experimenting with supernatural phenomena for their own use. We can only hope that it will be for peaceful purposes, for the world must be assured that no tyrannical government is capable of practicing this power of hypnotic domination. The only way to prevent this from happening is to exercise our own individual will and resist falling prey to any religious or political ideology.

Chapter 31

Destiny Does Not Exist and God Does Not Design Our Future

By accepting the concept of anti-matter and tachyons along with the neutrino, the super-conducting magnet, we also accept the contradiction of the theory of relativity since all of these travel faster than the speed of light. And so it would be easier to accept the idea that we are creating a future, which confirms that destiny does not exist and that God does not design our future.

This future that we create is based on a special type of mental space called probability, which travels in a different dimension of energy-time. All scientific research and artistic creation begin from the perception of the waves of probability. They start from our faculty for imagination and fantasy where the potentiality for the actualization of the future resides. All this is activated in the imaginary mass which has special psychic particles with amazing narcotic-like faculties. This imaginary mass has the power to act on the person's neurons, particularly the receptive neurons which have the ability to perceive the transmitted waves. The waves sent by imaginary mass and which are perceived by the probability waves, anticipate future events, predetermining and conditioning the seeds of chance. Some individuals seem to be able to perceive the future by precognition or intuition.

For instance, a struggling fiction writer, Morgan Robertson, wrote a novel at the turn of the century in which a magnificent ship called the Titan sets sail from England on its maiden voyage, with some of the wealthiest people in the world on board, and then, in the North

Atlantic, strikes an iceberg and sinks. The author even predicted the length and tonnage of the vessel with uncanny accuracy. This was a decade before the Titanic was even built!

Such examples are almost commonplace. Many people seem to be able to sense the future in much the same manner. It is believed that the precognitive experience is the ability to perceive the waves of probability in such a way that the observer can anticipate a future event. We create a new future from the imaginary waves, which will turn into reality. But for this to happen, the dynamic force of our brain, along with metaphysical persistence, must go deeper and deeper on the same path.

This initial energy will one day be put into action. An example of this is the astronauts who, starting from imaginary mass by their extremely patient research and passionate perseverance, designed a new future for all humanity. The probability waves are accomplishing a new life in space, and science is now ready to clone human beings, thereby defying death. This future, undoubtedly, was not designed by any God, but by human effort.

Human beings have a unique biogravitational field that allows energy to pass freely through liquids, solids and gases. The brain is capable of transmitting thoughts to other individuals and through the power of concentration can even move objects. I have seen this phenomenon demonstrated, when my friend, Uri Geller, paid me a visit while I was living in Rome. He asked me whether I'd mind if he removed the stone from the ring I was wearing. I was so curious to see whether he could do it, so I said yes. To my astonishment, he actually succeeded in extracting the stone from its setting by fixing his gaze on the ring. He never moved from his place all the while.

He was also able to bend forks and move dishes around telekinetically. Once, when I got a busy signal, he told me not to worry and by concentrating his energy, broke the connection at the other end, freeing up the line. Geller's demonstrations showed me that there is no electric or physical barrier that can block the electromagnetic waves emitted by a human brain. With this same power, we can design a new path for our future, just as we create a new path and direction, which again will turn to a repetitive action and it would remain as such forever until we will to change it.

In this world as well as in the universe, nothing remains autonomous; all bodies are constantly emitting electromagnetic pulsation, establishing between themselves and their particles a union of continuous interaction. In the same way our psychosomatic energy radiates in the universe, and we conversely absorb the energy that is radiated from the stars as the stars absorb energy from the planets and vice versa.

All forms of life are connected and cannot exist without each other, just as the gravitation pulls one object to another creating a vibration. Each atom, too, has its own vibration, which produces sound, electrical, magnetic, thermal, acoustic and seismic forces. Gravitational attraction holds all of these forces together in perfect universal harmony.

Through the power of our faculty for imagination, we design our future. And being aware that nothing can block the electromagnetic waves of our transmitted thoughts, the energy can pass free without any obstacles. Therefore, I am led to imagine that after our death, the energy of our thought can survive. Still, in my imagination about this possibility, I have an obstacle which is the contradictory theory of science.

The sciences theorize that nothing survives our body after death; our bodies are transformed into different chemical substances, good mostly as fertilizer, and our energy fades into nothingness. As far as the end of time is concerned, scientists envision the following; they deduced that the initial energy provided by the Big Bang was causing the universe to expand indefinitely. They know that the faster a galaxy is moving, the redder it will appear. It is almost certain that gravity will never be able to contract the universe therefore galaxies will fly farther and farther apart, and then galaxies themselves will dissipate. All mass will be torn apart, until even protons decay.

After protons, the only objects left in the universe will be black holes, and even they will evaporate. The evaporation of black holes is estimated to occur 10,000 trillion trillion trillion years from today. After that, the universe will be cold and empty, consisting only of wandering protons, neutrinos, electrons, and positrons. And from there, there will be nothing else. The universe truly never ends, but it merely becomes infinitely large and infinitely empty.

But because I believe in the genius of humankind and since this is estimated to happen in trillions and trillions of years from today, humanity by that time would have acquired an enormously extended knowledge through the process of higher evolution. And perhaps we may very well be living on some other planet with far more perfect harmony.

However, going purely by my intuition, I would try to keep advocating and proving my belief, even though not supported by the scientific view that the energy of our will and our memories will remain in the universe after our death. My belief, my intuition is confirmed by the existence of anti-matter, such as photons, neutrinos, and electrons surpassing the speed of light. Moreover, it is also known that matter can change its form and turn to energy, which is what happens in an atomic explosion—just as energy can turn into matter. That is why there is good reason to believe that even when we die, it is possible that the energy of our memories will be preserved.

In *Space and Eternal Life,* B. Brown, a neurophysiologist specializing in psychosomatic medicine, claims that the mind transcends the brain and survives after the death of the brain; the "mind" manifests itself as an entity distinct from the physical structure of the brain. Aristotle calls the "mind" pure intellect, superior to rational thought.

I believe that the whole universe from the very beginning is filled with radioactive substances, positive or negative, consisting of our thoughts, since our species appeared on the earth. Just as all living forms emanate their own radiation and vibrations, so do human beings fill universal space with the energy of their thoughts, feelings, will and wisdom, creating their own vibrations and sounds. All this energy is collected in the universe, fusing our knowledge with the natural knowledge of the universe

Our present, mature consciousness is derived from a cosmic consciousness, which is a result of the energy accumulated by billions of lives that have lived since the beginning of time with our struggle to evolve, and has become a part of human knowledge, affecting our mental evolution. Likewise, our DNA is derived primarily from the cosmos, as well as from our parents. As the stars are our parents, they are related to us in all-pervasive universal waves, which undergo transitions and transformations as a pattern of eternal change. All things are associated through opposites and arise from things that are related.

I also believe that even if our creative thoughts were never put into words, their strong preponderance of purpose would be so transfixing that they would remain in the universe in the form of potential energy, to which one day we could give meaning. These unpronounced words could be the seed for the probability waves of the future. Eventually, someone will perceive this thought form by reflection and develop it into a concept.

Our thoughts have the unlimited reach of a telecommunication system, and the magnetism they emit will attract other thoughts of perfectly equal energy and level. This is why our collective memory and the unlimited knowledge present in the universe are as accessible as a collection of books in the largest imaginable library. Here we can find the energy of more enlightened beings, and if in our lifetime we are able to develop our awareness fully, after death we will have a better chance to become part of this universal knowledge ourselves.

In attempting to attain the knowledge of knowledge, we first need to fuse with the universe; once the body and mind are in harmony, we will be able to mirror and achieve the same precarious equilibrium of density that is to be found in the balance of gravitational forces. By reaching this state of balance, we will attract the same potential thought and energy that have remained unexpressed in space, creating a new potential for the future. Similarly, this occurs in sexual reproduction, when two cells must find each other in order to determine an equilibrium in which they are right for each other. Those people who are in a position to intercept these energies can make them manifest in this world and will be called "genius." Anyone who is able to establish this equilibrium has the capacity to become a genius because he or she can catch the energy of the thought already in existence, but not yet developed.

A good example is the philosopher, Heraclitus, who lived in 504 B. C. His theory of perpetual transformation, of the constant becoming, was the first metaphysical speculation in recorded history. It was only in 367 B. C. that Aristotle, with his deep, probing intelligence, fulfilled Heraclitus's theory of continuous transformation by proposing that everything potential must become action. Aristotle defined metaphysics as the study of the intellect through logical penetration of the essence of being, and the discovery of the original causes of reality in constant motion. Centuries later, the Big Bang theory confirmed through metaphysical speculation that the continuous transformation of elements, like helium and hydrogen into carbon, had given origin to the known universe.

By drawing on the universal intelligence, human beings of exceptional perspicacity can advance evolution. Certain ideas are out there, so to speak, and they generate magnetism, which then attracts individuals who 'discover' them, that is, pull them out of the ether. But the time has to be ripe. Which may help to explain why both Alfred Russell Wallace and Charles Darwin arrived at the theory of evolution virtually simultaneously.

Each person who has such a perception in catching knowledge from the universe would incarnate this energy, which does not belong exclusively to the person that initiated it, but rather has become a part of human knowledge. This for me is the only acceptable form of incarnation that I can perceive. I do not believe in reincarnation as

Buddhism teaches; for example, the concept commonly known as reincarnation includes many past lives of the same person demonstrating knowledge through his or her experiences from one life to the next. I don't believe that the person who has created an idea not yet pronounced or completed after death goes back to the same origin of thought waves even if not identical in her physical reincarnation. I believe this knowledge will become a part of the cosmic human library and whoever has the capacity to capture the seed will develop it as his own.

When I considered Shakespeare, Mozart, Beethoven, three geniuses who succeeded in attaining the maximum of their artistic gifts, I could only conclude that the essence of their energy must have begun a long time ago and then was expressed in minor degrees by other artists without reaching the highest level. Based on the same principle of gravitational attraction, it follows that a genius like Mozart was already born with the predisposition to attract or be attracted to the exact same level of musical energy already existing in the universe, waiting to be brought to completion.

Of course, only by emptying our mind fully through deep silence might we be able to catch an energy not yet completed and have the honor to make it meaningful. Aristotle presumed that every living intelligence is born with a predisposition for the contemplation of the truth, and in order to reach its full potentiality, the intellect must become free of any kind of "forms." For instance, if a sound is too loud, it will prevent us from hearing a softer sound. It follows that if the intellect is able to fully grasp a very complex subject, it will find it easier to understand simpler ones.

The seeds of great ideas take a long time and many generations of thinkers to mature and come to fruition. Geniuses often consume the entire body of knowledge about the unique talent they inherited from their parents. As a consequence, their own children are probably left depleted of this potential and will have to strive to intercept a new knowledge from the universe that has already been initiated.

Much in the same way as the wheel of life is characterized by a continuous give-and-take, it may require generations before this potentiality is again developed to its optimal degree, confirming the famous "maximum and minimum" of Heraclitus and Aristotle, which states that the same form, without changing, continually changes in degrees.

I have been compelled to meditate further on the meaning of my experiences not only through intuition, but also by means of my dreams. I have already mentioned a dream about my death, in which I was being sucked up into a vortex, where I was surrounded by immeasurable different shades of emotion. I came to realize that, after our death, we are all pulled by a magnetism corresponding equally to the same state of emotion. For example, if we die in a lower intellectual/emotional state, we will be connected to that state.

Even though all elements are in a continuous evolutionary transformation, it can happen that after our death, our energy could be subjected to a transformation through liberation from one state to another. It can occur in the same way as, for instance, hydrogen and oxygen react together to produce water. This is an example of a transformation that can occur in an unconscious process, which would ordinarily take billions of years; instead, when it occurs in conscious life, especially in the higher level of consciousness, it can be actuated during one lifetime, instead of billions of years and we can call this evolution.

My view, though, is since there is only one energy, but in many different forms, it cannot be divided or cut off. It is my conviction that each element of the universe has its own intelligence and this intelligence is not conscious, unlike in human beings. Only human beings can have conscious thought and only human beings can give meaning to everything. And if the unconscious life survives in its repetitiveness, all the more reason that the conscious energy of our thoughts should survive; in particular, when reaching the same balance of the same energy.

The only conscious living intelligence is humanity, which, nevertheless, is held together with cosmic intelligence by a gravitational intelligence. The energy that remains in the universe after the end of each human life, like that of Jesus, if not captured and materialized, cannot be put into action again. Only a living person can channel its potentiality, giving it meaning and expression. So no matter how long and hard we pray to God, Jesus and all the saints, we will never receive any answer because this energy freed from matter cannot intervene in our worldly affairs.

It would only be expressed through those persons who capture and use this energy. Whether they use it in the right or wrong way depends on their degree of knowledge and maturity. Only we can create our future. Our energy can be used to influence others either positively or negatively, as it happened to me in an absolutely nefarious way. That is why we have to respect ourselves, as well as our fellow human beings, because our destiny can be helped only through positive human interaction.

I do not know if a figure like Padre Pio was able to produce stigmata in his attempt to incarnate Jesus by connecting himself with the universal energy or whether it was an effect of the hysteria, as the doctors claimed. What I do know is that the astounding energy of our willpower can make us transform and even transcend our bodies. Some species of fish, for example, in their will to survive, are instantly able to make themselves blow up and harden like a ball, so that they'll be spit out if they're swallowed by a bigger fish. It is not surprising, then, that if we set our mind to it, we can also cause any transformation we want in our bodies.

I still continue my search for a more scientific corroboration as I still find myself in conflict with the basic principle of science that affirms that there is no life after death. This keeps me in constant doubt as to the validity of my ideas, regarding the persistence of our thoughts after death. While I was grappling with these issues, I received from a friend a copy of *The Tibetan Book of the Dead* (Oxford

Press, 1957), edited by W. Y. Evans-Wentz. After reading it, I became convinced that there was some truth to my dream, that our energy is attracted magnetically to thoughts and that our ideas are a part of universal knowledge.

What most amazed me about the book was how it came to so many of the same conclusions that I have reached about our minds surviving our corporal death, and that they were similar to those the ancient Tibetans had reached after centuries of dedication and contemplation. And I, through my intuition alone and without the benefit of previous education, came to a common point with the Tibetan thought. This confirms my belief that we are able to catch knowledge from the world around us through our own proper disposition and perception, independently of our education.

According to *The Tibetan Book of the Dead*, after we die, the energy of our consciousness continues to transform itself by means of a very slow process. Human energies that have accumulated over the past occupy their own level. Energy produced by our consciousness will become attracted to the particular level that is appropriate to it, while at the same time it will be repulsed by levels that are either higher or lower. "Since thoughts have not a material body of flesh and blood, whatever may come, sounds, lights, or rays, are all three, unable to harm thee-thou. It is quite sufficient for thee to know that these apparitions are thine own thought forms."

Planets surrounded by moons, stars, and clouds radiate diverse levels of energy and radiate different colors of varying hues. According to the Buddhist belief, we have nine consciences represented by our astral colors in thousands of gradations. After death, we have to pass through all of them depending on the level of our ego's freedom. The ninth light, the last one, belongs to the most brilliant color symbolizing the highest level of consciousness, whereas the dullest hues symbolize the lowest. Bright green, for instance, represents All Performing Wisdom, whereas dull green represents jealousy, envy and dishonesty. Bright red represents liberation from attachment, whereas dull red is characterized by hunger and passion. If our conscious energy is attracted to lower levels, we will never reach a level of pure intellect characterized by the pure light of love. This process of transformation, which is similar to the attraction of gravitational force, continues until energy is absorbed by the highest level of consciousness, pure intellect.

As long as the universe exists in dynamic movement, the highest level of consciousness will continue to evolve. Energy moves in a continuous stream of vibrations produced by the radiation of thousands of thoughts, which produce sounds in which each vibration emits colors. At first, all the heavens will appear deep blue, but then gradually will switch to luminous yellow, representing wisdom and equality; then will change to bright red. Finally, we will reach a state marked by the glorious white light of pure knowledge and pure love.

Millions of years may have to pass, though, before our conscious energy reaches this, the highest and most perfect level. This is why it is so important to free our consciousness from as many desires as we can during our lifetimes. If we allow our consciousness to grow while we are alive, we will be better able to receive pure, intuitive, intellectual knowledge. This means that once we die, our energy will be attracted to a higher level of light. Intellect, which is unconstrained by any mental limitations or obstructions and is aware of its own consciousness, is the purest form of energy.

Naked consciousness recognizes itself as clear light and remains permanently united with the pure intellect of the universe. Tibetan prayer flags, reflecting the colors of the earth as well as those of the universe, mirror also the dominant colors that appeared after the Big Bang, when gas expanded and cooled, releasing a sea of orange light in the entire universe. This orange light has now shifted to a deep red color, indicating that it comes from far away, and it appears as a microwave background radiation of twenty billion light-years. Blue denotes a very young star. Many colors are obscured by nebula gas recognized as clouds. They are so dense that they do not permit the colors of the stars to be seen. This leads me to the analogy of our existence being so obscured by our ego that we are not able to see our own colors.

Scientists have corroborated the ideas expressed in *The Tibetan Book of the Dead* about the relationship of color and energy. The color emitted by energy is called the spectrum. Each substance in nature has a spectrum; it emits a certain wavelength of light and electromagnetism. Light can be regarded in two ways, either as a wave traveling through space or as a stream of particles called photons. Light waves are waves of electrical energy combined with magnetic energy that travel through space together. They are always the same, even though scientists refer to them by different names, such as electromagnetic spectrum, radio waves or ultraviolet, X-rays or gravity waves. All are characterized by their ability to pass through objects

Each spectrum is unique to a particular substance; in this respect it is like a fingerprint. From analyzing the spectra, we can learn an incredible number of things about an object. For instance, by studying the spectra of stars it is possible to determine how far away it is, its size, age, temperature, chemical composition, magnetic fields, its rate of spin, and the speed with which it is hurtling toward earth or away from it.

Every living thing has its own spectrum. In the same way human beings reflect their emotions through colors. These colors reflect the state of our consciousness. If we all have our own spectrum, our own individual light and electromagnetic waves that we emit, then it may become true that these waves establish the vehicle, which would connect our memories with the universal memory. Since it is true that our spectrum signals our identity while we are alive, we can say that the same spectrum survives after our death, holding our memories and embodying us with the light and energy of the universe's spectra. This supports my belief about the repository of all human memories existing after death.

Great men such as Buddha, Socrates and Aristotle declared that it is not possible to separate knowledge from the idea of knowledge, which is the definition of the pure intellect, just as it is not possible to separate love from the idea of love or sweetness from the idea of sweetness. Knowledge of knowledge can come about only in that consciousness, which has a perfectly evolved intellect. Once that consciousness has attained such a high state, there is no possibility, nor is there any reason, to return to a lower one, for the process of transformation is now complete. Pure intellects recognize others of pure intellect, symbolized by the clear white light. But if it is not recognized by this clear light, then it can be assumed that it is being drawn to the secondary, clear light which exists on a lower level.

In our moments of silence while concentrating, we inhale and exhale harmoniously, we release our energy, fusing it with the energy radiating from the universe. Breathing is not only the means by which we sustain our life; it is also a way of generating and acquiring energy. Nothing perishes, but everything is in continuous transformation, just like our ego, with all its potential. Our bodies constantly radiate electromagnetic forces, which are collected and stored in universal memory. There is only one energy and it cannot be divided, only transformed.

This makes it so difficult to understand how Jesus could exorcise devils from people, since energy is indivisible and can only be transformed. We are the only ones who can transform and redirect our ego energy in different directions, since it is only our brain's will power that is able to transform good into evil.

If we learn not to be so absorbed in our material desires or in biological impulses and psychological desires, then our ego can be freed to release life-affirming energy. But since our ego functions at a lower level, it can become very powerful when it is filled with desires and motivated by a strong will. The intensity with which the ego follows its goals can cause it to carry out unusual forms of life cannibalism.

Our life is deeply affected by magnetic forces and its attraction. The magnetizing forces are mutually attracted, one force can be transformed into another, united by electromagnetism. The same phenomenon can occur between two people, creating cause and effect. In the same way, electricity affects magnetism and magnetism creates electricity. This energy can penetrate a different matter with distinct attraction: positive/ positive; negative/ negative; positive/ negative. Usually matter seeks similar matter to form a nucleus, just as in our lives we are frequently drawn to others according to our needs. Often electrons borrow temporary energy from the quantum vacuum (energy-filled space) to create a unit of energy. Then this energy will return to space.

We also can experience the same positive exchange in our lifetime, when we borrow the energy of another person temporarily and then return it to him. Unfortunately, the opposite happens with strong egos, which are driven by the desire to possess others. It is even worse in the case of any physical debilitation. If our cells are not balanced, we have an unconscious need to replace them to heal the body; in such cases, our magnetism will attract us to similar forces with the cannibalistic instincts.

This magnetism explains why we are so often immediately pulled to those who appear to be just like us. It seems easier to communicate with similar personalities who understand us intuitively. We all prefer to stay with what is familiar to us, even if it turns out to be destructive to our lives, just to avoid experimenting with the new.

Often, however, this attraction awakens the stronger person's cannibalistic instincts, leading to the annihilation of the weaker. What in the beginning seemed easy and spontaneous, brings a lot of pain in the end. This magnetic attraction affects every aspect of our being—chemical, biological, intellectual and emotional. This attraction is even mistaken for passionate love, when in reality it is our cells' strong will driving us to fulfill their needs.

This unconscious consumption of cells is stimulated by our ego, which desires the possession of the spirit or body of another. During the process of fusion, the weaker can lose much energy and can die.

Similarly, when the mass of stars becomes infinitely compressed and gravity becomes very strong, it can result in a black hole. But when we are truly free of our will for dominating others, we find love and respect for them and for ourselves.

Often, married people who still love each other, end up separating or divorcing without understanding the reason why. What actually happens is that the weaker partner in a long relationship begins to feel cannibalized and must escape in order to survive, if he or she still has enough strength. This happened to a couple I knew. Without knowing exactly why, the wife felt as if she was being drained of all energy by her husband. It was her survival instinct that forced her to escape. Her husband was shocked by her decision to leave him. In his unawareness, he thought he loved her, but it was his unconscious, egotistical need to survive at her expense that was playing a big part in this relationship.

Many years later, in fact, he discovered that he had developed a benign tumor in his throat. From the biological point of view, it was a basic matter of his cells "devouring" his wife's, in his unconscious need to replace them at the onset of his sickness. However, when she left him, his powerful ego drove him to become destructive and hateful towards her. He began to act terribly, making her life miserable for many years by refusing to support her financially and even kidnapping their daughter. He could not understand why she had left him; after all, hadn't he given her everything she wanted? What made it more difficult for him, of course, was that his wife didn't quite know how to explain her decision. The truth is that what is invisible remains impossible to explain even when it exists.

Therefore, we should not be shocked nor should we deny our cannibalistic instincts if we realize that in our universe, cannibalism has been openly practiced without any shame and with impunity. When I read about the existence of the cannibalistic instinct in the universe, I was terribly shocked and surprised but also relieved. It gave me comfort knowing that people would much easier accept the truth that our cells are authentic cannibals and I avoid the accusation of having an abnormal approach to life. Let us not forget that we are children of the stars.

In *1001 Things Everyone Should Know About The Universe,* William A. Gutsh, Jr., Ph. D., says, "We can explain why some elliptical galaxies are extremely large and massive. They are cannibals and they eat their neighbors. It seems that two stars are gradually drawing closer to each other because they are losing energy. In this process the neutron star continues to draw matter from its companion until finally it crashes down on to the star's surface, exploding in a brilliant burst of x-rays. In time, it was realized that the pulsars in the binary system were indeed old, but were managing to masquerade as youngsters by slowly eating up their close companions. Simply put, matter from the companion star continued to accumulate on the pulsar; it not only added mass to the pulsar, but also added to the pulsar's rate of spin, thus allowing it to dance faster than its single contemporaries. It will likely continue to do so, until there's little if anything left. What price deception? Some stars have no shame."

During the time I used to go to Friar G.'s church, I met a family in which the father was always complaining about how tired he was, how he no longer had the strength to support his wife or children. He was constantly urging his two daughters to study harder and graduate as soon as possible, because he had no energy left. The two poor daughters were so oppressed by his complaints that they ended up in a mental hospital, in a deep depression. The father was not only mentally abusing them, but I suspect, depleting them of all their psychological and physical energy, until they got sick. In fact, every form of human intercourse involving an ego that derives its strength from desire contains a certain degree of vampirism.

Even in matters of health, the church had a power to shame us when we contracted natural diseases. We were already morally dependent; then we ended up sexually frustrated, and as if this was not enough, the church even made us believe that our sicknesses were a testimony to our diabolic impurity. Thankfully, the younger generation today is aware of the enormous medical progress we have made and are more apt to have a yearly check-up and take advantage of the fact that genetic defects can be detected in advance. Eventually, we will be able to stop using others to sustain our own energy and instead try to replace our own dead cells. We will stop believing that sickness and deformation originate from evil spirits.

Chapter 32

Is This The Meaning Of Real Love?

I doubt that Jesus realized how many people He might have psychically injured by accusing them of being possessed by devils or how many would be injured and humiliated by the church that his followers founded. Even after two thousand years of Roman Catholic propaganda, it is hard to accept the idea that Jesus is "love" or that he is meant to remind us of a loving God. We are to assume that real love is only demonstrated by donating our life to others, by following the example of Jesus who sacrificed His life for us. This love has always been conditional to our obedience and filled with false promises, like miracles.

I feel deep compassion for all the possessed: the prophets, the apostles, the gurus, even Jesus Himself. After living for so long with my terrible reality, I realize it is the worst, the most cruel and barbaric experience that anyone can have. I, too, now fully understand what it is like to become a vehicle for someone's power. This most extreme form of subjugation is meant solely to satisfy the possessor's own ambitions, which only confirms how human beings can hate each other. Could this be the result of the history of religion, which teaches us to love and to serve God as the Supreme Being while at the same time it exhort us to dishonor and diminish ourselves?

Leaders like Friar G. can command and move their victims to execute their will and fulfill their orders. However, as transmitters, they can profess their innocence, pretend that they had nothing to do with their followers' actions, and who would be the wiser? When power ends up in the hands of barbaric, ignorant people, they can cannibalize and rob others of their spirit through brainwashing, and no one can stop them.

Religious teachers and gurus should encourage a love of knowledge in their followers, instead of brainwashing them and making them emissaries of their beliefs and sending them around the word to kill people in the name of God and Jesus. What is worse is that these self-appointed oracles are so eager to see their predictions materialize that they do not hesitate to use their followers to provoke some actual disaster. If an apocalypse doesn't happen spontaneously, they will create one of their own. We have to worry about fanatical groups because they will stop at nothing in the name of God or some ideology to demonstrate their power, exhibiting no respect for human life.

In our ignorance we do not realize that each person who was murdered had the potential to become a real "God." Unfortunately, we are still cannibalizing each other, making a jungle out of modern society. Like scared animals, we attack even before being approached. If someone is nice to us, we immediately go on alert so as not to leave ourselves open to being taken advantage of. Spontaneous loving communication between people is becoming more and more rare.

We arrive at such a point that when our life is saved by doctors, the patients, instead of being grateful to them, prefer to express gratitude to God. Our ego doesn't allow us to have an obligation to a human being. Therefore, in referring to a "miracle" it is easier to disrespectfully, ungratefully ignore the care and professional service that the doctors have given to us. We do not feel mutual respect and we prefer to shame and humiliate each other by always looking for the negative side instead of the positive.

The case of Dr. Kevorkian, as usual, is understood only from a negative point of view, ending almost as though we were living during the time of the Inquisition. The courageous Dr. Kevorkian tried to give dignity to our death, and to alleviate our inevitable struggle in our unconscious state, which would only reduce us to an animal condition. He tried to help us by giving the end to humiliation. Dr.

Kevorkian ended up in prison. People are demanding this compassion, but, of course, it is against the morality of the church. (Similarly, since the church is opposed to birth control and abortion, does it help to support families financially and morally to survive with dignity with another child, adding to their other children?)

We create our destiny; we must become aware of it and take responsibility for our lives. Humanity was put on this earth to be happy, not to suffer. We should allow our real vocation to grow in harmony with the natural knowledge that is already inside us and try to give meaning to our experience. In this manner, we can discover love for ourselves and consciously recognize our real vocation that was given to us from our parents' DNA, as well as from our first progenitor, the universe. This DNA has to be recognized and then developed to the utmost, giving us freedom from the many different images we assume during our lifetime to finally *become* ourselves.

Ignorance causes us to become slaves of superstition and impels us to seek out supernatural powers, or those who claim supernatural powers, to protect us. Our greatest mission should be to erase ignorance; therefore, good teachers are the future of the world; humanity is truly in their hands. For this reason, I believe teachers should be the most respected members of our society. On the other hand, as individuals, they have the responsibility to develop real knowledge within themselves. By opening up to new experiences, they can free themselves from the resentments, confusion and stagnant concepts that arise out of attachment to the ego.

The teachers should be untouchable and not subject to any outside political or religious influences that may affect their mission, as this is too important for the future of any country. Whoever decides to become a teacher embraces the highest vocation that can be chosen. It is equivalent to a doctor's responsibility and code of ethics. To be a teacher requires love and respect for oneself, as a transmitter of knowledge in full conscience. As Socrates says, the worst enemy of human beings is ignorance; it brings only unhappiness

If we love children as much as we say we do, we would bring them up to be happy and free of hangups and scars. Instead, society, religious groups and politicians feel free to use them for any noble cause that they can dream up. Seekers of good image, such as politicians or priests, like to be seen in public holding a small child in order to represent their *own* purity and not the child's.

Parents, too, often fail their children, although they insist they do everything in their best interests. Many parents are still searching for their own identities and are often afflicted with terrible complexes passed on to them by their own parents, who, in turn, were intimidated by religious teachings, the church or some other outside political influence, As a result, these parents aren't able to take care of themselves, to think for themselves, to make important life decisions, let alone care for children. In life, there is the law of cause and effect; if we do not respect and love ourselves, how can we then love our children? A lack of love in one case causes a lack of love in the other. That's why angry children are prone to tell their parents, "I didn't ask to be born!"

Recently, television showed the shocking story of a 14-year-old boy, who killed his mother. As if killing his mother was not enough, the boy went to school and opened fire on his classmates. When questioned as to what caused him to commit such a terrible crime, he started to cry saying that his mother had always been screaming at him and always criticizing him, telling him he was a good-for-nothing. In fact, he felt that she hated him.

Unfortunately, this is not the first case of a troubled youngster massacring his fellow students at school. Recently, similar cases have been rising at an alarming rate across the country. In another instance, a young boy who had isolated himself from his parents by listening to loud music that consisted of lyrics such as "Kill them, kill them, kill all of them," went to school one day and started shooting randomly at students. His parents later admitted that they had ignored his antisocial behavior: in fact, they raised no objection to his choice of violent music.

In response to this increasing violence, a special commission was set up to research the social environment in which such children are raised. It was concluded that there is often a big barrier between parents and children, which doesn't make for easy dialogue. The lack of communication between parents and children is recognized as a growing problem. Most important, they have not learned the art of listening to others, and especially their children. Often the parents are afraid to talk to their own children as they are so paranoid that they don't have the courage to open up any kind of discussion. They would prefer to please their children and keep the peace, even if it means giving them weapons for their birthdays or whatever else the children think they should have, regardless of the consequences.

The breakdown of communication also manifests itself in parents failing to read certain signs. Even as children may fail to express themselves verbally, they still unconsciously communicate their psychological states. It could be inappropriate sexual behavior, or indifference, if not actual cruelty to animals, or even in the way they decorate their rooms. A room painted completely in black, or decorated with violent images, or filled with knives and small arms could be an indication of an aggressive tendency not only toward their parents, but the entire society. Combined with parental indifference, any or all of these factors could add up to fatal consequences for everyone.

Children are very clever; they're like animals in that they have a strong survival instinct and we, as parents, are all powerful. But because kids are clever, they can pretend to love us. Don't be fooled, though. Sooner or later they will turn against us, because they have too many scars inside. One of the fundamental reasons why parents fail their children is because, unaware of their own true feelings, they are blind to the feelings of their progeny and discount them. I think we need to bring our deepest feelings to light in order to be free of them.

Maybe we should do what they do what I have heard they do in Japan. There they dig a hole in the ground and symbolically bury their feelings. Nowadays it isn't easy to find a piece of land big enough for this purpose, just as it isn't easy to find a place where we can be free to scream. We can, however, create a ritual for ourselves by finding an object like a box or a stone, so that it can become the receptacle for our confessions. It's the same purpose that churches have served all these centuries, but with one notable exception: We won't require the intervention of any priest or holy man whose purpose is just to humiliate us by submitting us to what he believes to be an infallible God. Moreover, freedom from a pathologically sick priest would enable us to divulge all of our secrets and gain liberty from our frustrations.

Contemplation still remains the best way for liberation. Wouldn't it be nice if we dedicated half-an-hour a day to sit together with our children and reflect in silence? Afterwards, perhaps there could be a discussion in which we each expressed our self-disapproval, not to humiliate ourselves but to grow stronger and more knowledgeable. Nor should we try to please our parents by disregarding our personal convictions, but instead, develop mutual understanding to improve our relationships with each other.

Parents should temper their position of authority, especially as children grow older, and by remaining humble, ensure that they become their adult children's best friends, and not their bosses. At any rate, it would be proper to allow them a wide range of freedom from too many opinions, rules and suggestions by giving them the chance to develop their own point of view and develop their sense of responsibility. This would help avoid much frustration and the sense of injustice from not being told the truth. It would help prevent drug and alcohol abuse, as well as suicidal tendencies. Wouldn't this be better than simply going to church and having one's children led away from the love of truth?

Children want the truth; they do not want to be cheated, told lies, or be taken for granted. They believe whatever is said to them, and when they discover that they have been lied to, they feel a disappointment that causes a deep delusion and insecurity. What security about the nature of truth can be offered to children by a church which affirms that Jesus came from the Holy Spirit? All too often, their honest questions are fobbed off with half-truths or with the dictum that "that is the way it is; you must believe it." The church has, over the centuries, lost serious credibility for many human beings and has disappointed innocent believers like children. Whatever is based on non-truth cannot be eternal.

In the name of this same love for truth, it is not moral to baptize infants in an unconscious state, since this confirms their future in an imaginary, immortal and eternal life, which can only arouse fear and awe. It is selling the existence of the child for the rest of his life without giving him the right of choice, as also imposing a religious creed on the young person before he or she is able to evaluate and give consent to it. Children should grow up in freedom from ideological or religious brainwashing. They should only be encouraged, whenever possible, to grow in moral awareness and stature, as well as understand the consequences.

Therefore, freedom from religious control, as well as from jingoistic government is necessary for our freedom to enjoy life. The separation of church and state is necessary; clerical authorities should not be permitted to legislate their own parochial views, whether moral, philosophical, political, educational or social, particularly in public schools.

And we adults should be free from taxation to support religious institutions and have a say on whether or not we should contribute to those religious organizations. It is stated in the First Amendment that neither a state nor the Federal Government can set up a church. No tax in any amount, large or small, can be levied to support any religious activities or institutions, whatever they may be called, or whatever form they may adopt to teach or practice religion. Neither a state nor the Federal Government can, openly or secretly, participate in the affairs of any religious organizations or groups and vice versa. Therefore, the church should not be exempt from taxation as the Vatican was during their heyday, the years of the Fascist regime. The uncanny ability of the church to collect money from people and then not account for it in any way is indeed incredible.

One case in point that was reported by the news media involves Thomas Gradilone, the former pastor of Our Lady Queen of Martyrs Church in Queens. He will not be charged with secretly spending $1.8 million in church funds. Despite the disturbing pattern of financial misdeeds, Queens District Attorney Richard Brown said Gradilone cannot be charged because of the wide leeway given to pastors when handling church funds without any accountability.

The typical secrecy practiced by the Catholic Church is especially applied in avoiding scandals involving its pedophile priests. According to several New York Times articles during the month of March 2002, the church has settled about 50 secret lawsuits for a total of $10 million. And this was just one archdiocese, while others still are following in these same footsteps by secretly covering up settlements involving hush money. One of the largest awards ever given by a civil court, $120 million in a concealed sex abuse case, was made two years ago in Dallas was not revealed until 2002. Let's not forget to mention the multimillion-dollar settlement that the Diocese of Bridgeport paid out in a case brought against six priests along with Cardinal Egan.

Yet another recent settlement, this time $100 million is to be covered by a $300 million fund raising campaign that archdiocese of Boston has raised. All together the church's legal liability in sex abuse is estimated at $ 1 billion.

Finally we are able to learn how much money each archdiocese is generating and where the money goes. Wouldn't it be more moral and useful to sustain the research of scientist with donations, than to support the political and moral ambiguity of the Catholic Church? Maintaining the Vatican's secrets since there are many is a very expensive proposition.

There is no doubt that Catholicism is a most powerfully organized structure having its own state, the Vatican, consequently making it by far the most influential religious-political organization. This prompts me to give an explanation as to why I often oppose Christianity, and in particular, Roman Catholicism. The Vatican's political power gives all the more reason to see it as the basis for much of the worst deception and dishonesty that have ever been invented. There is only one truth and anything that is not intrinsically truthful needs constant affirmation, and since theological truths cannot always be proven, they are violently imposed.

And where can we find the truth if we are still being guided by the Old Testament, which is a product of human imagination and motivated by vindictive inclination, which spreads the fear of the last judgment, while humiliation and polygamy appear to be normal, and up to the present day, still serves other religions as a basis of divine truth? Judaism is primarily based on this ambiguous truth of the Old Testament, which allows Jews to disrespect and subject women under a religious authority that allows a Rabbi to deny a woman's rights. And Jesus, by affirming the same obscure truths, does not discard anything from the Old Testament, but rather fulfills the New Testament by threatening us with an imaginary legion of devils solely to keep humiliating humanity.

Islam, instead, has taken into consideration all religions, particularly the Old Testament, which is the basis of Judaism, and the New Testament, without even excluding the Greek philosophers so deliberately criticized by Jesus. As a response to the experience of other religions that tried to monopolize God, Islam, so as not to contradict anyone but to show itself in accordance with all religions in a positive light, avoids presenting a straight historical narrative as it is found in the scriptures, as well as using directly the name of God. Instead, Islam uses the word Him. There is no God but He, The Living the Everlasting; To Him belongs all that is the heavens and the earth.

This prevents Islam from discarding science since Islam doesn't need to defend the idea of instant creation and the legacy of Jesus as God. Islam doesn't discard anything; instead, it concentrates on mathematics, geometry, astronomy, without excluding the use of

Aristotelian logic. Since Muslims do not eliminate the pragmatic vision of science but rather try to adapt it to support Islamic dogma, this might explain the popularity of Islam.

But as a result, the Koran has strictly become a severe codification of God's laws, that, together with the punishment imposed by the last Judgment and promises of eternal reward, obligates Muslims to a very stringent adherence to policy on how to live. All in all, it is merely a legal system, consisting of many rules having the scientific approach as its basis along with a complete intolerance to all religions other than Islam.

Instead, Jesus's fulfillment of the New Testament consisted of continuously affirming a new and erroneous concept, that eternal life is the only life that has God's promised reward. Why is he doing this instead of teaching us to respect the life right here? My explanation would be: Jesus's mission was to pose himself as God and ask others to believe this. He is not able to prevent natural disasters, nor can He give any explanation about them. And since he can't stop death from occurring, the best solution is for a promise of future life. He found a new way to distract people from their lives on earth by giving them the hope and dream of life's eternal rewards. And to make this distraction more effective, he followed the old methodology of humiliation from the Old Testament in which we were accused of being unclean and full of sins. Jesus, instead, is fulfilling us with invented devils.

Jesus, by urging us to ignore our lives and to dream about death as the only source of true happiness, wouldn't we today be calling Him an evil spirit? I wonder how we would consider today the action of early Christians, when they wanted to spread Christianity all over the world and strongly imposed their belief that Jesus was God? Therefore, their provocative terrorist actions against Romans, philosophers, scientists and intelligentsia cost thousands of lives. Again, during the barbarian Inquisition, 7 to 9 million women were burned or hanged and accused of being devils and witches.

The witch hunt from the 15th to 18th centuries was the most

satanic event of European history. And the persecution of Jews could be equally considered another satanic event began because the Jews refused to accept Jesus as God. The long history of the persecution of Jews by the Christians reached the lowest point with Hitler and its unjust consequence continues to the present day without any end in sight. If these violent and brutal impositions of the first Christians were happening today, wouldn't we be calling them terrorists and declare a war against these fanatic and possessed preachers?

Similarly, Muslim fanatics today seek to aggressively re-impose their beliefs throughout the world with terrorist acts to attract its attention by imitating the example of persecution set by Christians and their intolerance of the opposition which they sought to eliminate. Muslims also sought to eliminate non-Muslims by converting or killing them as infidels and blasphemers of the almighty Allah. Islamic indoctrination centers install terrorist cells, particularly in prisons and among the unemployed and disfranchised much in the same way as the first Christians proselytized among the illiterate and poor to spread their blind fanaticism around the world. Muslims are also converting many to a radical Islam, while extending farther and farther into Europe. Pragmatism notwithstanding, Muslims do not forgo the practice of humiliation, especially when women are concerned, and to spread the fear of the last judgment, they also keep promising future reward as Jesus did. So the poor illiterate, who has been suffering and starving all his life, is promised high compensation from God for killing people who refuse to recognize Allah as their God. God, it would seem, was invented, among other things, to command and control the poor and illiterate.

As the poor and illiterate have always been in great abundance in all places and at all times, it has always been easy to fish among them for followers. Since the young and hungry are susceptible, religious fanatics brainwash them to spread violence and terror against people of opposite beliefs. According to William Edelen"s research, it seems that the founding fathers of America would agree that such an appropriation of a person is a violation of human rights. He reveals that such figures, as Jefferson, James Madison, Benjamin Franklin and Thomas Paine, were deists highly critical of Christianity and other revealed religions. Paine (whose pamphlet *Common Sense* was the spark-plug of the American Revolution) claimed that "the most detestable wickedness, and the most horrid cruelties, and the greatest miseries that have afflicted the human race have had their origin in this thing called revelation, or revealed religion." And Jefferson followed suit with his observation that the God of the Old Testament "is a being of terrific character: cruel, vindictive, capricious, and unjust." Paine, Jefferson and other deists lamented the intolerance and persecution that were common features in the history of Christianity, Islam and other revealed religions. In their view, people who believe they have an infallible lock on divine revelation will often feel justified in using violence and terror against dissenters and unbelievers.

Christians today consider themselves to be good, pure, and innocent promoters of love, even though Jesus's love is full of contradictions, ominous threats and conditions, "Whoever loves father or mother, son or daughter more than Me is not worthy of Me. Whoever remains in Me and I in him will bear much fruit, because without Me you can do nothing. Anyone who does not remain in Me will be thrown out like a branch and wither; people will gather them and throw them into a fire and they will be burned."

These cruel threats are completely contradictory to the idea of a loving God, although Jesus had learned about unconditional love from Buddha, Confucius and Tantric Yoga. Yet, Christians, to promote Jesus as the one and only promoter of love, have degraded and slashed the real meaning of unconditional love that was taught by Buddha Confucius and Socrates, a love that should rightly predominate the world.

The truth of a God that has a thousand masks is based on shameful untruthfulness and on unmitigated political corruption. Therefore, it is constantly contradicting itself such as the instant creation of the world by God, the affirmation that Jesus is God since he came from the Holy Spirit, his questionable resurrection, and a pure world created by God that ended up with unclean humanity. But not to worry, for all we have to do today is just to buy a CD-Rom complete with indulgences appropriate for all kinds of sins, obviating the need to go to church. Since indulgences are based only on money and political corruption together with the latest technological advances, perhaps the crucifixion of Jesus wasn't needed.

And not forgetting the Angel Gabriel, who declared Jesus to be the only Messiah through whom God becomes visible and who died for our sins. Centuries later the same Angel Gabriel declared Muhammad to be the last prophet. Where then should we put Jesus after this more recent election of the Angel Gabriel?

If the Angels and the Holy Spirit existed together with God, they certainly would be more consistent and not contradict themselves as they so often do in their declarations. The inevitable conclusion is that they are indeed non-existent, and so we truly can't be possessed by them or other supernatural entities. Thus, the only possession that can be achieved is from one person to another.

The possessor is one who has developed his or her inner power or has already been possessed by a stronger subject. As far as the word possession implies, given that it has negative connotations, it could never be based on honest principles, even those having the purest of ideological or religious intentions. A possession usually occurs when a very preponderant ideological or religious influence is exercised over a subject with the eventual goal of overtaking and dominating the world by brainwashing the masses. This would contradict the concept of human rights and democratic freedoms.

There is however another type of possession, one in which we can be subjected to our own possession. As possession implies feelings, passions and blind beliefs, it follows that such a case can occur only through illusionary religions or political ideologies. After this strong belief has been instilled in us, the process of possession is actualized and when reinforced with a strong imaginative ability, can succeed in overpowering us to such a degree that we end up possessing ourselves. Our own irrational imagination, by possessing ourselves, can lead to a split personality

Such was the case of the prophet, Mohammed, who had such a powerful imaginative capacity, which had him obsess over the narrative facts of the Bible, that in the end he possessed himself with the conviction that he had been called to be a prophet in the tradition of the great Jewish prophets and of Jesus. He was given over to such an extreme possession that he envisioned the Angel Gabriel appearing to him and confirming him as the last prophet to proclaim the existence of the one, true God.

As an upshot of his powerfully imaginative capacity, Mohammed reported the revelation given to him by Angel Gabriel to the Guardians of the Meccan gods that "Allah was the only God in town." But due to a bad celestial transmission or a message not spoken loudly enough by the Angel Gabriel, Mohammed missed an important part of the message: That the Kaa'ba at that time was pagan and there were already three favorite goddess of Mecca—al-Lat, al-Uzzah and al-Manat. Shouldn't Mohammed already have known this? The poor reception of the celestial message from Gabriel, prompted Mohammed to flee Mecca. This all-important revelation was expunged from the Koran by the claim that the revelation given to Mohammed had come from Satan and not from Allah. Thus began the legend of the "Satanic Verses." It seems that Satan is the culprit of all bad celestial receptions not only in the history of all Christian contradictions, but also in that of Islam.

Similarly, Padre Pio, after having heard the story about Saint Francis, was so taken with it that through his very powerful will and imagination, he possessed himself so thoroughly and completely that he was able to stimulate the stigmata on his hands. In both cases, the condition of split personality should be taken into consideration since Mohammed was epileptic and Padre Pio schizophrenic.

Today, insofar as Jesus is concerned with his obsession for seeing devils every where, the judgment would be made that he is either schizophrenic or possessed by someone else. And taking into consideration the factors of his being possessed along with his inclination to schizophrenia and his strong visual imagination, we must conclude that Jesus was also possessing himself in the conviction of being God who came for world salvation.

At this point, someone might ask me which category my possession belongs to. Unfortunately, since I have never had any creative imagination nor could I ever visualize even the most mundane events from my daily life, I have been rather unfocused with an inability for concentration, leading me to believe that I lack the potential for becoming a genius. Since I did not have a split personality, nor did I have any visions, nor did I hear any voices; my brain was completely devoid of all mental activities, therefore, I could only be possessed. I was reduced to a catalytic, unconscious life like a puppet, maneuvered by someone else. This is what happens to a possessed person without a predisposition to any kind of schizophrenia, spilt personality or a strong imaginary capacity.

Since it is so easy to possess unfocused and unwary subjects, the only way to fight spiritual terrorism is to root out all religions, which are the source and sustenance of the worst fanatics. Moreover, when they carry with them a deeply seated frustration along with a vindictive motivation in the name of God, they thrust it out to maliciously possess others in order to manipulate and subject them to their will. All told, it is the abominable fountain of discrimination and human humiliation.

This phenomenon is increasing more and more; as a matter of fact, the media are constantly reporting on how in the Arabic world, fundamentalist indoctrination is still being practiced in schools that follow the Taliban's extremist Islam in which loyalty among Arabs is emphasized but hate towards Christians and Jews is extolled. If Arabs are found to be fraternizing with Christians or Jews, they are liable to severe punishment or even imprisonment. Parallel to this, Jesus admonished that "whoever does not remain in me will be thrown into a fire and will be burned."

The latest events of Bush's war against evil has remarkably increased the hostile feelings between antagonistic religions. Bin Laden states, "There is no way to forget the hostility between us and the infidels. It is ideological, so Muslims have to ally themselves with Muslims." Muslims and Christians recently have been massacring and torturing each other. The New York Times reported that a Muslim boy in Indonesia, when recalling the recent destruction of eight Christian villages, proudly declared that it was done to restore Muslim dignity.

Indonesia, a largely Muslim nation of 210 million in which militant Islam has made strong inroads against non-Muslims, has become a more dangerous place than ever. There is a potential for Muslim extremists and terrorists from not only neighboring countries, such as Malaysia and the Philippines, but also from the Arab world to link up with Indonesian Muslim groups. They are, more often than not, organized by clerics who cooperate with militant groups on their own terms.

All these countries are predominated by poor, unemployed populations, having large numbers of uneducated young men ripe for brainwashing and thus ready to die for their faith by dressing in white robes for a holy death. One of the ways of expressing the hatred that is instilled in these extremists is the burning of Christian houses with signs that read, "God has no son," "Jesus could not help you" and "Death to all Christians." The conflict is so radical that it has turned into much the same hatred that has plagued the Palestinians and Israel, as well as the Protestants and Catholics in Northern Ireland.

The power of religion is rapidly increasing. Pakistan alone has at least 33 religious parties, which are important in terms of their ability to mobilize students in educational institutions and to manifest their strength in the street among the people in the villages and everywhere else. These parties would never mobilize in the name of politics, but in the name of religion they can mobilize anyone at anytime even the armed forces.

There are 225,000 mosques in the country and from each pulpit when the call goes up and a voice proclaims a jihad, a holy war is announced. As we can see, no political party has such a wide infrastructure, but as religious parties, if and when the attack comes, they will sink their differences and take their supporters and their armed activists out onto the streets.

The group, Jamaat ul-Fuqrah, which claims to have kidnapped and killed journalist Daniel Pearl and whose leader is Sheikh Gilani, is believed to have a large number of followers, not only in Pakistan, but also in the United States. Jamaat ul-Fuqra is an Islamic sect that seeks to purify Islam through violence. Their members have attacked a variety of targets that they view as enemies of Islam, such as heretics and Hindus. They are also implicated in attacks during the 1980's, including various assassinations and fire bombings across the United States. Jamaat ul-Fuqra has most of its cells located in North America and the Caribbean. This is but one example, regarding religious power not only in Pakistan, but all over the Muslim world, where it is rapidly extending.

It was also reported in the New York Times that since "the Bible-minded Bush" has threatened the world with a global crusade, against evil, the Muslim world has developed a great hatred against America. The Charismatic religious leaders of Islam are arousing anti-American and anti-Jewish sentiment, in which even women and children are screaming in the streets, "I will kill all Americans," while using the worse curses against them. This saddens me a lot because I love America very much and Americans don't deserve such hatred.

The consequence of all this renewed hatred is that young Saudis grow up in such adversity that they are linked to violent Islamic fundamentalism. All Saudis Arabs and Muslims, prompted by the bombing of Afghanistan, are showing pictures of thousands of civilian and child victims being buried with such captions as "Look at the blood shed by the murderer Bush." This new call for revenge is generated in an atmosphere that is conducive to terrorism and extremism, having a virulently anti-American sentiment. All throughout this war, we have seen the authority of nations disappear and instead revert to tribalism with its own religions competing against each other and promoting hatred rather than freedom and tolerance

The article shows surprise at the high marks of admiration that Bush is receiving from Americans for his handling of the war on terror. Bush, by grouping various nations under the same category of terrorism, is creating an "evil empire." The old Christian strategy of terror that attempts to spread insecurity amongst the population always succeeds in being pervasive. Bush continues to threaten America with the promise that his crusade will not end soon, thus only nurturing fear, resentment and anger and leading eventually to discrimination among all peoples and to terrorism as it own frustration.

Osama bin Laden, according to his last tape, says; "This is a matter of religion and creed and not what Bush maintains, that it is a war against terrorism." Bush, being a fundamentalist Christian, refuses to admit that this war is actually a holy war but instead prefers to ambiguously call it a war against evil.

It is not enough to fight terrorism by bombarding the Taliban and holding its prisoners with masks in Cuba. Most of them are so ignorant and hungry that they are unaware of the meaning of the word, "fundamentalism" and its consequences. Since this is a holy war, all religions should be controlled and their followers should be taught the violent history of all religions and its consequences, rather than blind creed and erroneous preaching. Their feudalistic basis claims to have God on their side for the reason of taking over the world by brainwashing and possessing the poor and uneducated people, who, in consequence, developed personalities that are distorted to the point that they are not able any more to distinguish who they really are.

Bush, far from controlling religious groups as a fount of evil and terrorism, instead, goes so far as to violate the separation between Church and state by his support of all religious charities with federal money. In addition, he states that it is wrong to disqualify religious groups from receiving federal money or to believe that giving money to such groups is illegal. By supporting Christians with federal money, he automatically guarantees the same rights to all religions and sects, consequently giving them more power and legality for possessing young people and separating them from their families. This support of government to all religions sustains the superstitions that are already deeply ingrained in us. This includes fundamentalist Christian sects that believe in faith healing, such as "Body Healing" and many others that disdain medical care. Their followers are prohibited from approaching doctors. The parents are so brainwashed and so possessed by the sects that their own faith allows them to put to death their children by not providing medical care or not enough food. All this is committed in the name of God's will, which undoubtedly has great things in store for them.

Without recalling the history of infamous religious fanatics, who provoked the death of many of their disciples, such as Jim Jones and David Koresh, who later was vindicated by Timothy McVeight by his bombing of the Federal Building in Oklahoma City—and not mentioning the disciples of a Japanese cult, who were reduced to dummies and forced to plant containers of Sarin, an extremely toxic gas, in five subway cars in Tokyo—it is enough to say that Bush encourages an environment of fanaticism that regenerates itself by creating more and more such sects.

If Bush is fighting against evil, how then can he give support to the sources of evil and the founts of mental manipulation, which lead to blind ignorance by allowing religious clerics to hold the reins of power over the population in order to brainwash it with the heretical indoctrination and the principles of terrorism.

As Socrates said, evil is a consequence of ignorance, which can not be eliminated by violence. The Socratic method teaches us to search for truth by the constant questioning of rules, as well as by cross- and self-examination. If all brainwashed fanatics were to submit to the Socratic principle of constantly questioning their heretical beliefs, they would slowly come to understand what is wrong and what is right, thus beginning a healing process. A person can only heal by understanding wrong from right and by doing so, will change the direction of his thoughts. There is no other way to change severely brainwashed believers.

Sometimes I am disposed to think that maybe Friar G., after innocently giving up his life for the idealistically pure and incorruptibly honest God, then awakening from being brainwashed, found himself instead confronted with an untruthful God full of trickery. I believe that he has to have been under shock for a long time. And as if this were not enough, he must have also realized that God was invented as merely a wielder of political power. Moreover, not being able to achieve his own personal glory, he might have felt cheated by God's unfulfilled promise of miracles and unlimited power. So he stopped promoting the idea of an honest and trustful God and openly exposed the reality of an invented God by the way I was treated.

This led me to understand historic significant events of the untruthfulness and dishonesty that are hidden behind God and Jesus. This should help us to open our eyes and to start taking seriously the only proven truth of scientists, whose intent is not to fool us but improve our life and to prevent future disasters. Why not support scientific research instead of the charities, which are a source of dishonesty and where no one knows how the money ends up? The Bush administration is limiting support for scientific research; being only concerned for developing the technology of new nuclear weapons for warfare. As usual, the powers-that-be are hiding themselves behind the false morality of the church and prefer to go against the research for new stem cells, which could prevent many illnesses, and consequently, deaths. Loss of life does not seem to bother them.

I hope that Bush with his dictatorial attitude, guided by his extreme fanaticism to Christianity, will not persecute me, as it happened with the famous writer, Salman Rushdie, who is still being hunted by Muslims.

Bush, in his credo, believes himself to be on the right side of God. Therefore, in his passion, almost Jesus-like, he is threatening us that if we are not on his side, we will be considered to be on the side of terrorists, and hence traitors of America.

Dear readers, why don't we stand up finally and fight for our lives and for our happiness, instead of being subjugated by false moralities of some narrow-minded leaders?

I believe that all churches should be transformed into places of commemoration where we could honor our ancestors and the ancestors of others, especially those who died without any fame or wealth. We could meditate over the life of each individual, regardless of whether his actions were good or bad, and learn from his example in an objective way, rather than regarding him as a character in a soap opera. I hope through this practice, people will learn how to lead better lives. It isn't sainthood they aspire to, but awareness that they have much to contribute to the universe. There are so many people who die without ever being acknowledged: lonely people without family or friends. Why not dedicate a place and some of our thoughts to them?

And if some of them had the inclination to write their memoirs, it would provide the perfect environment in which to read them. It is so sad to die incognito, and it would be a consolation for many people to know that something of their lives would be left behind to guide the rest of us. Too many people try to do bizarre things just to be noticed and escape the terrible anonymity of modern life. We have museums and archeological sites, where we preserve ancient artifacts and enshrine the memory of pharaohs and kings, cataloguing every single detail of their lives, and yet we never pay homage to the ordinary people, who might have created these artifacts and lived their lives in obscurity.

Perhaps we should learn to honor these ordinary people in place of worshipping a panoply of saints in the name of God. In many cultures, like the Chinese and the Japanese, as well as the Native Americans, great respect is always accorded the dead, or more accurately, the ancestors. By doing the same, we can learn from the experiences of those who have gone before, and thereby add a new dimension to our own lives. We will come away with a better understanding of what terrible damage can be done if we act under the sway of wrong impulses.

By revering the departed, we will encourage people to live more honorably, because they will know that they will not be forgotten after death. It's even conceivable that racial and social disparity will diminish, and dignity will be bestowed on every single life. After all, we owe recognition to all living creatures for their contribution to the universe; without these ordinary little lives, our understanding of life wouldn't be as mature nor would our evolution be advanced as it is now.

Let us start to transform the altar of the non-existing God and replace him with humanity and the story of its existence, even if it is not always an honorable story. It will, nevertheless, serve to instruct us. I have visualized an empty church with walls full of tiny windows and when each is lit, a small urn with our ashes appears with our own memoir. Anyone wanting some relief from his loneliness or just wishing to honor the memory of an unknown can feel free to visit the site and read a story which might be similar to his own.

Recently, in the news, there was the story of a church bombing in Louisiana. This was not an isolated case, as such crimes have been occurring with increasing frequency. There have been other cases of churches being destroyed by fire; it was later discovered the arsonists were children. I can certainly understand why such acts of violence happen. People are finally beginning to realize how all religions have been deceiving humanity throughout its history, filling us with ideas about the final judgment and impossibly perfect saints or devils, which create fear in humanity. The results? Humiliation, fear and paranoia, solely for the purpose of holding on to power by their false claim of the existence of miracles and a perfect but cruelly vindictive God.

Chapter 33

Why Do We Need A God?

Why can't humanity live without the idea of God? Why do we want to enslave ourselves, why don't we recognize the power and potency of our minds? Religion doesn't make man great, but man makes religion great. The truth doesn't make man great, but man makes the truth great. God doesn't make man, but man makes God. Only man can give a sense to life by recognizing his own potential and finding his own truth, which may turn out to be the universal truth.

I remember sitting in a church in Rome with a friend of mine who was a nun. Suddenly, she turned toward me and pointing at the altar, said, "You know, Maria, one day instead of Jesus, there will be a real man on the altar." I do not know if she read this in the Scriptures, or if she'd come to this conclusion on her own. In any case, they were inspiring words. What she said then is even truer today. We have come to the beginning of a new era, when the fantasy about Jesus and God may finally be put to an end. This spiritual fairy tale only deprives us of our freedom of choice and our sense of responsibility.

From my own experience, I learned that we are misguided when we say that we want to offer our lives out of generosity. What we are really doing is searching for ourselves. Before acting on the impulse to make unsolicited donations to some church or undertaking any mission that provides no spiritual return to us, we should understand our true motivations. If we fail to do this, we will begin to feel abused. Sooner or later, our existences will demand that we find the true meaning of our lives, instead of trying to satisfy our need for love by offering it to Jesus, God or other people. What I once thought to be generosity turned out to be self-sacrifice.

There is no more perfect example of excessive generosity than the sun. For five billion years, the sun has continued to radiate energy and give life to our planet, but eventually it will exhaust its supply of fuel, and some five billion years hence, it is expected to burn out and die. Like the sun, we, too, will die if we keep unconsciously giving our life to others without ever getting anything in return. Once the sun is a mere cinder spinning in space, solutions to even such distant problems will come not from God, but from a highly developed human being.

Through my experience, I have reached the conclusion that religious vocation could be only an illusion. How can such a life-denying vocation really exist? But for those of us who have indeed followed one and have later discovered that God is also a part of the illusion, we may ask ourselves, for whom was this sacrifice made? In this instance, a terrible delusion and emptiness would fill our beings and this is what has happened in my life. And now when I face this reality, I understand that it was only for the political power of the church.

The various Pentecostal groups have only reinforced my conviction that religion can be dangerous. Fanatically imitating the early Christians, they speak in tongues and use faith healing. I remember a Protestant pastor, who used to heal by invoking Jesus while shouting at the afflicted person, "Stand up and walk, you are healed!" Meantime, the pastor was regularly going to the hospital for heart treatments, as well as to receive medication that would protect his fragile heart during his stormy healing sessions. He worried that if one day he were to collapse in front of the whole congregation, what would the people say!

Faith healers and their followers alike think that if life still goes on, it is because of their prayers. They walk the streets with the pretense that we owe them our lives due to their obsessive self-sacrifice, which can turn into such deep resentment that in the end, they would kill us all. When they invoke the Holy Spirit, which supposedly comes to them, they believe they are capable of uttering prophecies that threaten the end of the world. What these groups really seek, however, is not enlightenment, but power and energy.

I remember going from one group to another, searching for the power of the Holy Spirit. For me it was like a drug; I was constantly worrying about losing it, always searching for more. The followers of these groups cannot exist without their congregations; they are like slaves without their masters. I recall a nice young man of about 20, who, one day, arrived at our congregational meeting, crying desperately because he had shaken hands with someone he'd met in the street. He insisted that this person was the devil incarnate, who had robbed him of all his energy! In reality, this kind of belief robs people of their humanity. The dancing and singing that went on in these Pentecostal rituals induced in us a false euphoria. Far from bringing us closer to the truth, they took us farther away from it by filling our consciousnesses with illusions, superstitions and belief in supernatural phenomena.

The need to find freedom and truth is found only in our self. No institution or group can fulfill that need for us. Priests and nuns, for instance, in the Roman Catholic tradition, offer their celibacy or their virginity, as well as their lives to the church, but their renunciation deprives them of all humanity. In the end, they become filled with doubt as to whether this sacrifice was truly necessary, causing them to lose sight of their mission. Those who have the courage to face these issues eventually question the reason for such a fanatic commitment, since they realize that a life deprived of love makes them bitter and sullen. At first, they hate themselves, but eventually this self-hatred turns into a hatred for others. Even more, it can lead to severe sexual and psychological abuse of parishioners, including young people, a growing problem within the Roman Catholic Church.

While I was living in Italy, for instance, I met many Indian and African women who became nuns just to escape hunger. Their families had sent them to a convent under the false pretense that they had a calling. I knew about their plight from firsthand experience.

One young ex-sister worked for me as a domestic for a while, but then the police came for her, because she had been denounced by the mother superior of her convent for running away.

It seems that the church is creating a new class of slaves in the form of priests and nuns, who enter the church out of personal need and weakness, and not because they are drawn to any religious vocation. However, once they recover from their "incubation" period, when they understand the true reasons for enlisting in the service of the church, they feel a strong need for a "normal" life. Like everybody else, they require physical and emotional love for family and material comfort. But then they realize that the prospect of ever attaining any of these things has been taken away from them. This realization can make them very vindictive.

Friar G. was able to take possession of me because at the beginning of my ordeal I was both generous and immature; it was my generosity that impelled me to search for a way of dedicating my life to others, like many of those who enter the priesthood or become nuns. After the abuse I suffered under Friar G.'s spell, though, I found myself becoming bitter and morose. I was just like anyone else who, deliberately or not, renounces his life and puts himself in the position of a victim. As a result, I no longer cared about the misfortunes of others; I felt consumed and resentful because I was deprived of love for so many years.

Whatever relevance the concept of God ever had was appropriated and then perverted by the power-hungry of the world. The best way for the church to keep its power was using the false promises of miracles and spreading the fear of punishment. This not only bound people to the church, but also had the "unintended" effect of robbing the population of its money and keeping it from reaching its potential as human beings in full dignity. At the Church of San Francesco of Assisi, reliquaries containing bits of the saint's robe are still being hawked after seven centuries. Friar G. is no less a profiteer; he cheats and robs while still showing the stigmata on his hands.

Recently, I was introduced to a young woman named Daniela, who pretended to be a writer. She told me of being stabbed in the stomach on the West side of New York's Central Park by three young men. After being admitted into a hospital, she remained in a coma for three months, when she supposedly recovered from unconsciousness after having a vision of God. Since then, she believes to have received the gift of healing. With this tall tale, she frequents churches all over, for example, St. Patrick's in New York or St. Peter's in Rome, where she tries to create a positive image of her deep devotion to God by spending her days in church.

In the meantime, Daniela searches out rich people and offers them her services as a healer or as a marriage fixer. While visiting me at my home, I happened to overhear her on the phone ask for a fee of ten thousand dollars for her service. To give herself more credibility, she mentioned to me that she offers her healing power to St. Patrick's, which, in turn, allows her access to the registry of the church, where she is able to obtain information on every parishioner.

This came as surprise as it proves to me that St. Patrick's as well, in order to sustain the existence of miracles, is in complicity with her to support such a spurious story. People trust her, since they consider her to be a woman of the church, without realizing that the worse swindlers can in fact be found in holy sanctuaries.

Daniela is only 26 years old, and instead of going to work and studying, she has found a fast way to make quick money and to insinuate herself into moneyed society, which, also for reasons of superstition, succumbs to her influence. What I concluded after learning about her is that again people who claim to have visions of God are completely lacking all sense of truth.

The Church was built on the power of the shaman or the priest-magician, a tradition that extends back to ancient Egypt. Therefore, the Church has always denounced magicians, fortune tellers and voodoo practitioners, as they were in competition with the Church's own priest-magicians. This helps to explain the burning of thousands of women as witches. Whatever competes with this man-created God has to be humiliated or eliminated. The Church chose to humiliate people by erasing the advancements brought by knowledge, burning entire libraries and killing enlightened people, who contradicted its vision of God.

Today, fortune tellers and healers are no longer put on the stake and burned; instead, they are rather in close collusion with the church. For example, the queen of voodoo, Marie Laveau from New Orleans, was approved by the priest of the local church to encourage the followers to attend mass. Her profession as a hairdresser allowed her to be introduced, through her clients, to all gossip in town. She also developed a chain of household information in the most prominent homes. Being informed so well about everyone, she succeeded to have power over the police, perhaps by blackmailing them.

After her death in 1881, her daughter, Marie II, and other members of the family followed the tradition as healers and exercised incredible power over the people. Each one of the fortunetellers and healers would try to justify the need for a lot of money, claiming that they had to burn hundreds of candles during the many hours of prayer in church necessary for creating miracles.

In March 2002, once again the church, this time in the United States, has shamelessly brought to attention a new priest, claiming to have the stigmata, healing powers and, as if this were not enough, the ability to levitate. He has instructed us on a totally new and innovative concept, which is to give little attention to material things, i.e., give all our worldly goods of possession to the church. Great multitudes have rushed to see him, worrying officials that the church would collapse. Yet again, people have chosen superstition over scientific progress.

Would that the church would recognize the greatness of humanity, instead of encouraging belief in the supernatural! Unlike science and medicine, which actually do achieve authentic "miracles" by finding new cures for those who were once incurable, the church still chooses the supernatural over the easily verifiable truth.

I began to feel shame about my own weakness that allowed a church-created shaman to dishonor my life in such a shameful way. I decided to stop this dishonorable and evil manipulation of my body by Friar G., particularly after having learned about our biological system and the incredible power of our creative mind, which generates energy and transmits it to the universe.

With the conscious acceptance that we are alone here in this world and only we can give justice to ourselves, we have all the more reason to be unified in fighting evil-energy together, even if it's only one person, such as Hitler. Similarly, there are religious organizations with the Vatican as the most powerful, who want to dominate the world by creating incredible energy among their followers through threats, which in turn, can be transformed into admiration back towards them. All together, they create an incredible energy that can be destroyed only by the unified opposite energy, as was the case with Hitler, and today unified human rights have been able to make the necessary opposition against the secret handling of sex abuses by the Vatican. I hope that in the future, the same unified front will question the ambiguous ways in which donations are spent without accountability.

The power of the unified energy for truth is prevailing against the offensive silence of Pope John Paul, who prefers to minimize the problem by being uncertain of the veracity of the testimonies of sexual abuses. The Vatican's inclination is to believe that all this is more motivated by the speculation of money, and that it is largely only an American problem. All together, the Vatican prefers to promote the policy of secrecy by silence the same way as during World War II, Pope Pius XII's failure to speak out forcefully against the holocaust. In the same way, the Vatican has never taken any serious action against Friar G., even I have written three long letters with my complaints.

Being alone and not having yet any help from outside, since the people still don't want to admit the power of possession, particularly if is hiding itself by the name of God, I decided to fight the abuse of

Friar G. alone. I convinced myself that whatever is negative, we have to turn it into a positive energy with our willpower. For example, when he is arousing me sexually, I send that energy to my brain by breathing, and by doing so, I stimulate and reinforce the power of my will and creativity. And when he causes me anxiety and fear, I have to convert it with my will power into a peaceful and positive energy. I have to learn to command my brain as to what thoughts I should accept and what I should reject. I should subdue his power over me and by focusing and concentrating on fighting his invasions, I should make my will power stronger and stronger to the point that I will be able to overpower him. This opposition to his brainwashing me and subjecting my neurons to his will should empower me so much that the will of my ego would be under my control to resist vulnerable impulses of my ego.

The same can be done with my biological system to direct and redirect his approaches by my will. It would actually be a process of our self-healing. By living that way, the negative aspect of life will disappear since the negativity would become positive and useful energy, and with the reciprocal love of our neighbors all over the world, we could live in peace without weapons, using just one weapon, our will power, which would educate our ego to eliminate greed. After years of being overpowered, I already feel much stronger by putting up a defense. The weakened, by constantly fighting the oppressor, tends to become much stronger than the oppressor himself, like the theory of the Big Bang at the last moment of life, regenerating itself into new energy.

Let's not forget that it is our mind that is God! We are God. Discoveries in technology and science prove the incredible intellectual power of humankind. We have an active conscience and an analytical brain that guides our choices, making us solely responsible for them, and even the natural selection of all cosmic population was created by our needs. God had nothing to do with it or any of the natural phenomena of the world.

After a long history of leaders fighting and killing people in the name of God and Jesus, we entered into a new age of enlightenment. Karl Marx, a philosopher rather than a leader, was the first to not appropriate God's name He actually transformed himself into a sort of God. What Marx succeeded in doing was transforming the transcendental God into an immanent one.

Marx came from a Jewish family, though his father converted to Lutheranism. The Marx family lived in Germany, where Lutheranism was connected to the government as the official denomination. He utilized Hegel's philosophical system that understood church and State as parallel manifestations of Absolute Spirit. And he incorporated Feuerbach's humanizing methodology that the ego, or I, only came to self-knowledge through encounter with others, who viewed community interaction to be a vital source of knowledge.

Feuerbach also believed that an isolated individual lacked awareness of himself and lacking this, tended to respond more by feeling than by reason. He noted that the vehicle through which humans expressed their feelings to transcend their limitations was the imagination. When imagination points to an object being imagined, it objectifies itself in the form of religious ideas as the concept of infinity and perfection to express God. Therefore, in lifting God up as a being, it pushed humans down. "To enrich God, man must become poor; so that God may be all, man must be nothing," Feuerbach said.

Marx agreed with Feuerbach, and also saw no value in this objectification in God. For him, "religion offered false hopes and turned people's attention away from the real sources of their problems—societal injustice and its material conditions. Consequently, religion becomes "the sigh of the oppressed creature; it is the opium of the people; it encourages alienation by viewing nature and history as of little importance." In this way, religion serves the larger political and economic structures of alienation.

Religion negates the idea of self-determination. Marx understood that the theological idea of God is isolating, and discourages the proper social development of humanity. It, therefore, suppresses the love humans could have for one another as self-conscious social beings.

Religion has to be attacked, so that humanity can be appreciated. It is the enemy of human advancement. This enemy has to be abolished for the sake of humanity. The philosopher wrote that "religion is only the illusory sun which revolves around man as long as he does not revolve around himself."

How right he is! His theory is exactly the same as my experience has taught me. Yet again, it confirms that there is only one truth, which is the love of wisdom that consists in the knowledge of truth. The truth can't be hidden, however, we arrive to it. It is not relevant from what point of view we approach it, whether from the anthropology of Feuerbach... or whether from the psychoanalysis of Nietzsche and Freud that hold that religious belief is a result of social or psychological conditions, not the rotten fruit of religion's faulty reasoning... or whether from Freudian criticism that believes that God is a projection of our own intense, unconscious desires, and that God is a wish-fulfillment derived from childish needs for protection and security... Or whether from Socrates' law, which gave us a method of questioning the rules of others by cross examination... or whether from scientific research on cosmology... the truth will always be one in the same which is that no one can prove in a rational way the existence of God. If we really want to face the truth and stop fooling ourselves, the conclusion will lead us to the inevitable truth that we have created God, thereby making Him the most powerfully political and economic alienator.

Marx understood this same truth that God did not exist, but that his name was used to take advantage of people. Marx also realized that the power of the Vatican was more political than religious and decided to copy the Catholic model to advance the cause of Communism. He adapted his theory of ideal society to the political and religious dogmas of the Vatican hierarchy, consequently obliging his society to dress alike, as the Catholic clergy. Everybody was equalized and alienated in the same way, solely for the purpose of working on God's behalf which in this case was to become the Kremlin

Just as Hitler copied the example of the Vatican's persecution of the Jews, in the same way Marx copied the history of Christianity. And just as a great number of people were killed to establish Christianity, so, to establish Communism in Russia required the elimination of intellectuals, aristocrats and the bourgeoisie. And just as the Church elevated Jesus above everything and proclaimed that only God was the source of knowledge, the Kremlin did the same in establishing its dogmas. It declared that it had a sole monopoly on the truth and was the sole authority. And how many millions of people would be killed in the name of God, as well as in the name of God-Kremlin in order to erase individualism and create a new Communist society in defiance of the lessons taught by centuries of evolution?

Marx declared religion to be the "opium of the masses" and that the only salvation lay in work. "Workers of the world unite, you have nothing to lose but your chains," he proclaimed in the 1848 *Communist Manifesto*. Taking their inspiration from Marx, the Bolsheviks shut down virtually all religious institutions upon assuming power in Russia in 1917. Churches, mosques and synagogues were closed and often demolished. Everyone had to swear fealty to the Communist regime. The only religion that counted was the state religion, which exalted the worker and glorified the scientist.

One day, the Communist state would wither away, that was the official line anyway, to be replaced by a worker's paradise. Given that kind of reasoning, why long for a heaven above when one can be established here on earth? I support the glorification of knowledge and science clearly demonstrated when the Soviets became the first nation to launch a satellite or put a man into orbit. But the way in which the system operated, turned it in the end to a most frightening, dictatorial regime, oppressive and authoritarian. When no different views are allowed, true knowledge cannot be obtained.

All ideologies, including Communism, Fascism and Nazism, have a religious dimension. Some, like the Communists under Stalin, tried to crush the religions, viewing them as competitors; other systems, like fascism, have tried to isolate them (as Mussolini did with the Vatican) or incorporate them into their dogmas. Hitler, for instance, believed in an Aryan empire, made up of perfect, blond, blue-eyed clones who would become the master race and dominate the world. Physically and racially imperfect people had to be exterminated in the name of this ideology. He based his ideology on Jesus, whose principal mission was to cleanse us from our imperfections. Even in some cases, political leaders will try to make use of supernatural powers to convert and control people. The late Haitian dictator, Doc Duvalier, kept his people terrorized for decades by exploiting their belief in Voodoo. Nor was he unique in his attempt to impose his beliefs.

Whenever any ideology begins to proclaim a utopian vision, it ends up in complete extremism, resulting in the perpetuation of terrible massacres. I hope humanity will eventually learn to put an end to killing others in the name of some God or ideology, making those ideologies more important than our actual, lived lives.

Though Marx was often misguided, being that his ideology resulted in famous cases of extremism, I still have to admit that in his thinking, he had many important things to say. And while I cannot condone the brutal methods the Communists used to suppress any sense of individuality, like all dictatorial regimes, I do believe that Marx might have been on the right track when he urged people to cast aside their faith in an illusory God, which negated the idea of self-determination by isolating and discouraging the proper social development of humanity.

My thoughts echo those of Marx—that love for an illusory God cancels the love that humans should feel for one another, instead developing a complete disrespect towards realistic rational approach to life by putting the illusion above rational thinking. He was absolutely right; religion has to be attacked so that humanity can be appreciated. It is an enemy to human advancement. This enemy has to be abolished for the sake of humanity.

But for a few rare exceptions, Communism, however, is dead while superstition, alas, is alive and well like never before, flourishing even in nations formerly part of the Soviet Union. With the wisdom accumulated over thousands of years, Christianity as well as all other religions, has been able to exploit the superstitious nature of people and encouraged them to believe in miracles. Because Christian henchmen knew how to exploit people's weakness, they enjoyed far more success in sustaining their power and winning and keeping converts, relying on a repertoire of clever magic tricks and miracles. Examples abound: portraits of the Madonna that weep or statues of Jesus that shed blood. Friar G. used my life to make such a spectacle, because the church gives more significance to these performances than it does to a person's life.

It is more important for the church to commercialize and sell Christianity, because wherever these visions of Jesus or the Madonna appear, thousands of worshippers descend, ready to spend money on any number of relics and votary objects. The church has many holy centers, where miracle cures are said to occur, the most famous being Lourdes. There you can find crutches that have been cast off by those who were crippled and who can now walk. Clothing that once belonged to children is scattered here and there, symbolic evidence that the children have been cured of whatever ailed them. It is heart-rending how the church takes advantage of people's faith and milks their money in the name of God and, what is even more despicable, the Pope, in the name of his imagined infallibility, supports such dishonest schemes and perpetrates what I consider to be the sin of sins.

The Madonna of Pompeii, the Madonna of Czestochowa and the Madonna of Guadalupe all represent the same phenomenon: Pilgrims will walk or crawl on their knees for miles and miles to reach these shrines, just hoping for a miracle. The commercial spirit of the church, which has often consisted in the selling of the so-called truth, reduces us to the state of beggars. Instead of taking responsibility with full conscience for our actions, we prefer to wait for the jackpot of miracles which can take for ever. Rather than teaching us the real truth by examining ourselves to understand the reason for our suffering, which in most cases, results from our own misunderstandings, wrong judgments, crass ignorance and inadequacies, we are forced to become mendicants, mortgaging our self-reliance and self-esteem.

Superstitions have survived, even Communism today in 2001. Witness the attacks on America of September 11. On November 21, The New York Times wrote that the attacks have invigorated the apocalyptic brand of theology embraced by many Christian fundamentalists, who view the collapse of the World Trade Center as the latest harbinger of the end of time. Biblical prophecy books are flying off the shelves, chock-full of commentary and interpretation on the meaning of September 11 attacks and their place in the prophetic timeline. The evangelist, John C. Hagee, writes about Biblical prophecy, quoting the Bible which says that there will be great sorrow before the end times and what happened on September 11 is just an example.

The leaders of the prophecy movement, beneficiaries of a multi-million-dollar industry, were always looking for cataclysmic events to validate their doomsday scenarios, which had previously failed. The prophecy leaders are finally happy that September 11 took place. After all, how many times could they be wrong?

The Biblical prophecies have linked the terrorist attacks to both complicated interpretations of scriptures and to a number of specific Biblical references from Isaiah 30:25 "In the day of great slaughter, when the towers fall" to revelation 18:10, "Thou mighty city Babylon! In one hour has thy judgment come."

Many pastors have taken to their pulpits to predict that the second coming is near. They make such frightening predictions to encourage their parishioners to get right with God. They believe that Jesus could return within two or three years; it literally could be any day. As usual, the frightening prophecies have always taken advantage of people for financial reasons or for herding them into congregations without hope of returning back.

Why don't we want to accept the truth—that after our death there is no other life and that Jesus can't come back within three years or at any time? We love to trap ourselves in dreams and illusions, just so as not to accept reality. Why don't we leave the dreams to children, and we adults, instead, try to live our life in a realistic and rational way while continuing to create history, since our history is not created by God but by us?

Most New Yorkers after September 11 identify themselves with religion. Even if they had not been religious, their patriotic acts seem to echo the religious fervor of rituals and hymns, composing slogans like, "This is a time to turn to your God. I've prayed to God to give us a sign that he is still here," while one pastor said, "I am settled on the fact that this happened for a reason; God was trying to get our attention."

I think that this God tries too often to get our attention, and when He does, it's always through tragedies and never through positive intervention. Why does this God never try to demonstrate to us His love, since He created the universe out of nothing in only six days by pronouncing one word. He created the earth, He commanded hydrogen atoms to fuse and become helium atoms, and in the process released energy in the form of light. Some of these fusion makers appear to be more than 6,005 light years from earth. God grouped them into collections and he called them galaxies, even though these appeared to be millions and even billions of light years from earth. He created Quasars, Pulsars, Novae and Supernovae and even Black Holes. He also caused subduction zones to build mountains and cause earthquakes.

Why then does God not eliminate such natural disasters, as earthquakes, hurricanes, tornadoes and floods, which cause many epidemic diseases, resulting in a high mortality rate? Even faced with logical truths, such as mathematics and fundamental rules of thought demonstrated during the last hundred years of scientific discovery and revelation, religion chooses to dishonor Galileo and dismiss evolution and the fact that the earth is billions of years old and was not created in six days.

How could superstition survive in an era in which scientific explanations for earthquakes and whole natural disasters are taken for granted? Why is superstition a better educator than the scientific world? I wish to know if anyone has ever seen the awards promised to us from eternal life! Since no one has ever come back from the after-life, these rewards remain a part of our illusions.

How many secular humanists and atheists have helped people without advertising themselves and without waiting for any reward, just out of respect for life and belief in people, rather than in God? Scientists and doctors are discovering considerable knowledge to cure diseases and make life better. And yet, it is an irony that they are often blamed most unreasonably and unjustifiably for many disasters. Doctors who clone are almost judged on par with the gays and lesbians in offending church values on reproduction.

The September 11 tragedy proved that religion does more harm than good, not only in America, but the world over. Most global ills and wars can be traced to ethical poverty and religious bigotry. Religion, since time immemorial, has sadly been the problem, not the solution. If we want real peace in the world, ethics and morals, not violence, should finally conquer religion, since their moral teachings are much more theory than practice. Otherwise, they wouldn't allow religion to divide humankind and cause havoc, as was done on that Black Tuesday.

Students need ethics more than prayer. They should be taught the consequences of lying, cheating, stealing, hate, violence, rape, religious intolerance—in short, of ignoring ethics. Ethics should be more precious than prayer, as it serves humanity in the act of donating time to the blind, the disabled, the retarded, or the desperate.

Another testimony to true prayer that gives meaning to eternal life would be the donation of one's own corpse to be used for research to benefit the living or as transplant organs for desperately sick people.

Just by teaching people to think how much the dead could do for the living by rejecting superstition, many lives could be saved. Instead, the growing business of extremely expensive funerals is doing more harm than good for poor people. Moreover, the New York Times has reported that some cemeteries in their vicious greed to make room for others are mixing body parts, even losing some of them, with those of different individuals and reburying them in other locations. Let's not forget the Georgia case in which hundreds of corpses that were meant to be cremated were hidden instead.

President Bush keeps brainwashing us by urging us to pray. But there is no mention of *God* in the Constitution. And when Thomas Jefferson mentioned God in the Declaration of Independence, he was referring to the God of deism, the rationalistic creator popular during the 18th-century Enlightenment. That God did not communicate with human beings or intervene in human affairs. Still for President Bush, the act of prayer, although no one is listening, is more important than compassion and love for human beings, of which the best expression is the support of scientific progress rather than empty words. This then is the real meaning of true love for humanity: the prevention of incurable sickness and the alleviation of pain.

Bush even encourages employers to give their employees time off during lunch hour to attend noontime services to pray for our land and to help sustain churches with donations, much the same way that Islam ordains Muslims to pray five times a day. Wouldn't it be better not to give time to a questionable God, but rather to encourage the staff during lunch hour to share time with their colleagues, and if possible, to give comfort and company to lonely persons? When Bush says, "God bless America" and Muslims invoke Allah to bless Muslims, they should be addressing one and the same God. Each believes to be blessed by his own God, but each, alas, considers the other to be evil. WHAT GOD? WHOSE GOD ARE WE CALLING ON TO *"BLESS AMERICA"?*

The recent tragedy of September 11 shows how religions can be divisive. The present war with Afghanistan accentuates adversity. Muslims threaten to destroy America and to fight against Christians. And in America, Christians are persecuting Muslims. One 76-year-old man tried to run down a Pakistani woman with his car, then chased her on foot outside a mall, screaming, "I'll kill you, I am defending my country!" Some Arabic children are beaten and cab drivers assaulted by rock-throwing, and many other vandalisms of hate have been manifested.

I would like to quote the Senate Chaplain's opening prayer, "God, you alone know who can change human hearts." But since we have the Muslim Allah, the Christian God, the Judaic God and the Hindu God, how can a change of heart come about if there are so many Gods, each hating one more than the other?

Politicians seeking to be elected try to court as many religious groups as they can, but, unfortunately, they cannot please all religious congregations at the same time. They know that a majority of Americans would not vote for a candidate, who doesn't believe in God, even though America was established as a secular and not as a religious nation. The Constitution wasn't created by God. Until the religious prejudices and the irrationality that stem from them end, our hearts will not change because religions, as practiced, create animosity, which prevents people from loving and respecting one another.

Shouldn't faith be rebutted since it can't be proved? All legal systems and scientific discoveries are working on the basis that nothing will be accepted without conclusive proof. Yet, 81% of the people in the world believe in an eternal life without logic or facts to support their belief. Science has come up with no evidence of an afterlife. Has anyone seen a person come back from death? During Egyptian history which goes back to 3000 BC, all kinds of magicians tried to make the pharaohs return from the dead. Could the prophets from the Old Testament with all their miracles resurrect Abraham and Moses from the dead?

Strangely enough, only the fanatical apostles have seen Jesus resurrected, but after that for another two thousand years, no one has seen anyone resurrected or reincarnated. Was Jesus more important than Abraham, Moses, Buddha and all other saints that he alone was resurrected? Have all who believe in miracles ever seen an amputated leg grow again, or seen someone who was resurrected or reincarnated? If so, please let me know; I would like to see them, too.

The pages of the Old and New Testament are full of miracles describing such impossible things. Why aren't such extraordinary miracles occurring today in the 20th century? An American author stated that a miracle "is an event described by those to whom it was told by a man who did not see it." In today's scientific world, no one can anymore claim violation of the laws of nature. Hopefully, we are growing scientifically literate and we cannot easily be fooled any more that faith has anything to do with reality.

Unfortunately, domination by religious institutions means respect for superstitions with belief in omens and malicious spirits, or in eternal life and in rewards after death. Therefore, superstitions still play a large role in the life of people all over the world. We keep rejecting the rational approach to life. I remember one day many years ago when I was in Singapore with my husband. I was trying to buy him some beautiful silk shirts.

My poor husband has always hated shopping and on this day he began stomping his feet like a two-year-old, screaming that he didn't want any shirts. One of the saleswomen in the shop, observing this scene, was surprised by his behavior. To reassure her, I jokingly said that my husband was a little crazy. Imagine my surprise when I saw her flee the shop and never come back. I asked the other saleswoman what had happened and she explained that in their country, sick people are believed to bring misfortune because they are possessed by evil spirits. Once again, we were facing the terrible consequence of superstitious beliefs that humiliate humanity!

And this reminds me of dolphins. Ever since ancient times these beautiful humans have revered mammals as being in possession of uniquely powerful knowledge. Some superstitious people have killed these mammals, not for food but because they are under the misguided impression that they can somehow acquire the wisdom that dolphins are supposed to have. It's an old story: Man acts cruelly and thoughtlessly in an attempt to obtain knowledge by making a talisman out of dolphins or elephants without any effort to go out and struggle to achieve it on his own.

Ancient peoples used to attribute unexplainable phenomena to the will of God. But we don't need to search so far back in history for the misuse of God's name. In our own day, people who want to legitimize their integrity claim to have God's blessing in order to become accepted and gain status. Politicians are no exceptions; they are constantly calling on God to justify their actions. Our placing God above us becomes a habit.

We think it is enough just to mention His name by making Him witness to our lives well-lived, as such as when we exclaim, "This was truly a great person, for how she loved God with all her heart!" And here begs the question: If she loved God with all her heart, what was then left for humanity? Some people prefer animals over humans, this I can believe. Animals never answer nor contradict us, just as God never answers nor contradicts any of our actions, good or bad. What a nice and easy way to love!

Let me return to the question I posed at the outset of this chapter: Who is then the real God? We are the only ones responsible for giving the right or wrong meaning to the universal energy, which cannot be changed by any other entity. If we do not recognize the existence of God, then He does not exist. There is no supernatural power, we are the only possible power. No exorcism, no voodoo rites or prayer will ever result in God's intervention; they have been tried frantically in vain. I challenge history or anyone to prove me wrong.

Each ideology, political or religious, seeks only to establish a church-state and to replace God. In the same way, the church has replaced humanity by placing God above us. And the pretender-saints, who also claim to be manifestations or proxies of God, are in reality striving for their own glory.

Only those human beings who do not hide behind God or search for supremacy by political domination or by declaring war in the name of God, will finally recognize that the perfect God of our dreams is EVOLVING IN US. THEREFORE, ONLY WE CAN BE THE ONE TRUE GOD. Our destiny rests in our hands alone and only we can help and show justice to each other. This is done not for the sake of reward, but simply for the sake of love

By doing good, the bad will eventually turn to good, because the whole universe is based on the generous intercourse between two elements resulting in procreation as the expression of donation. Therefore, the essence of human beings turns on the natural energy of love. Each person should be respected and loved. In doing so, we will finally accept humankind's inherent goodness and generosity, and thus, we will protect one another.

Let us create a new society founded on a humanism based on the search for truth by using science with its methods of critical investigation and logical reasoning. Humanism respects life and is concerned about happiness and freedom. The true secular humanist realistically accepts the idea without any illusions that our life begins and ends here, and thus wants to achieve the maximum out of life until he has reached fulfillment in knowledge. He loves life fully and enjoys each moment with awareness and perception, passion and compassion, work and play.

Humanism is the essence, the quintessence of philosophy which views life as finite, while recognizing that there is no time, no room, for tolerance of foolishness, ignorance, arrogance and superstition. The laws protecting human rights should protect the truth, since humanity has to grow and progress steadily, optimistically, truthfully. The truth will open the way for respecting and loving one another.

Epilogue

My mind, cleared of thoughts, allows me to concentrate only on one word and its meaning at a time. This gives me a metaphysical approach to the deepest understanding of the root of each word. All the possessed people I have mentioned in connection with Friar G. live in the same way, with an empty mind focusing on one word. As an example, let us take any one of the following words: hate, ambition, desire, obligation, and place it at the top of an imaginary triangle.

The Church

It has to love God

No room for two Gods—Man's power must be reduced

Man has to become enslaved—The symbol: Jesus on the cross

Humanity has to be humiliated

The existence of the Church is essential

Saints

Containers for God's love

Fanatics

Passionate

Violent—Reduced to no existence

Irritable—"I am because He is in me"

Highly developed mid-brain

Unconscious actions

Man

Evolving—animal

Idolatrous—Self-seeking

Superstitious—Searching for knowledge

Ignorant—Responsible/independent

Slave to the idea of God and ideology—Loving/reciprocating

Buddha

Enlightened Being

Independent Conscience—Love for Love

Free from Desires—Knowledge for Knowledge's sake

Free from the Idea of God—Total Realization in Freedom

I hope that the conclusions drawn from my ordeal may be helpful to my readers.

The first is the warning against believing in miracles and any outside intervention such as any supposed justice from God. Since everything is based on our biological system, it makes no sense to look for any accomplishment outside of ourselves. Rather we should try to better understand the functioning of our own physiology in order to resolve many of our problems. In order to set an example, I have fought Friar G.'s. insane transfer of the sickness of paralysis to me by stopping the symptoms through various medicines and my will power finally has discouraged and impeded Friar G. from continuing to vex me.

We should, we must, try earnestly, conscientiously to be independent of a possessive mindset and refuse to be possessed by various ideologies and refuse to blindly follow fanatical religious beliefs. Possessive attachment can be harmful because it prevents us from keeping distance and seeing ourselves clearly, objectively, while robbing us of new knowledge, blinding us to new frontiers of enlightenment. And in the end, this would estrange us from our one, true friend, knowledge, which without a hospitable, incisive intellect, we cannot acquire in a progressive exchange of thoughts and ideas.

Nothing should make us lose our balance, as life is too short and there is no time for petty concerns stemming from envy and jealousy. We have to develop the maximum power that is in us and try to achieve as much as we can from an intellectual and psychological point of view without seeking out sensations and unrealistic dreams, dreams that only make us deviate from the right path.

Our universe belongs to the repetitive unconscious life of the autonomic nerve system. All entities, as well as all past lives, if they remain in the universe, are acceptable only in the form of energy, automatically become a part of that unconscious repetitive system, Therefore, no one can answer and communicate with us or hear our prayers. Only we can help one another and do due justice to ourselves since only we belong to a constantly active and creative conscience. That is why we have to respect and love one another as we are the only true potential God. If we hurt someone, we would hurt a potential God who is actuated within us.

We have to die happy and be able to say, "Yes, I am ready. I have tried to accomplish the maximum in my life. Happiness is the only good. To be happy is to make others happy and to be happiest is to be truthful with ourselves. We have to live with joy and be proud without permitting anyone to possess us. It is difficult, but with discipline and hard work, we can achieve it because our firm will, directed by strict discipline, will never brook failure.

The love for truth and the love for the world will set us on the right path with regard to our friends as well as to all people. We wouldn't follow anyone out of blind love and overzealous admiration, but we would sift right from and wrong, and by self-respect and objectivity (no, not subjectivity), we would recognize what is in us and in others. We shouldn't mortgage our life to any purpose motivated by emotional or visceral feelings; we should love with love's pure energy and love for love's sake. And the love, the infinite love for truth will help us reach freedom, freedom even from ourselves.

With all my love and good wishes to all, Maria.

References

"The Life Times Of Grigorii Rasputin," Alex De Jonge

"Blessed Imposter," Mario Guarino. Kaos Publications

"The Merchants of The Vatican," Mario Guarini, Kaos Publications

"Secular humanism," web page

"Big Bang," Joseph Silk's

"First Light," Richard Preston

"Darwin," John and Mary Gribbin

"The Brain Pack," Ron Van Der Meer and Ad Dudink

"Emotional Intelligence," Daniel Goleman

"Gray's Anatomy," Gramercy

"Parapsychology," Trento Procaccianti Editori

Professor Adrian Dobbs, Nobel Prize winner for neurophysiology,

Prof J. Richard Gott III B. Brown, a neurophysiologist

"1001 Things Everyone Should Know About The Universe," William A. Gutsh, Jr.

"Tibetan Book of the Dead," (Oxford Press, 1957), edited by W. Y. Evans-Wentz.

"Buddhist Reflections," Lama Anagarika Govinda by Weiser

"I and Thou," Martin Buber

"Tantra For The West," Markus Allen

"Who Wrote The Bible," Richard Elliot Friedman

New York Times

U.S. News

Time

Daily News

CNN

NBC

About the Author

Maria Ferrara Pema, an accomplished film actress, was born in Poland during Hitler's invasion. The author is the daughter of a prominent aristocratic Tibetan doctor and a sophisticated Russian mother. At 16, she danced with the Warsaw Opera Ballet. Her participation in an international competition brought her to Italy, where she later launched an acting career. Ms. Pema has worked with noted directors Fellini, De Sica, Ferrari and others, casting her in many films.

The author plans to create a nonprofit organization whose mission is to protect innocent people, particularly children, from the dangers of religious cults by proposing to create new legislation. This would include protection for all of us if the freedom given to all religions goes so far as to manipulate young people to the extent of reducing them to an unconscious, suicidal state. These poor brainwashed are imposed with the mission of exterminating non-believers with their own lives; shouldn't then this freedom be opposed with new legislation to protect abuses in this area?

Pema, after having Polish and Italian citizenships, recently became American and currently resides in New York City.